A Pastoral Programme

Douglas Hamblin

Basil Blackwell

To Maggie Bradbury, who loved light, people and life.

© Douglas H. Hamblin 1986
First published 1986
Reprinted 1987

Published by Basil Blackwell Ltd
108 Cowley Road
Oxford OX4 1JF
England

British Library Cataloguing in Publication Data

Hamblin, Douglas H.
  A pastoral programme.
  1. Personnel service in secondary education
  ——Great Britain
  I. Title
  373.14′0941   LB1620.5
  ISBN 0 631 13635 5

Typeset by Freeman Graphic
in Helvetica and Plantin
Printed in Great Britain

Contents

Preface   iv

1 The background   1

2 Developing a pastoral programme   14

3 Content of a pastoral programme   28

4 Vocational development and the
   pastoral programme   61

5 Group interaction and peer counselling   100

6 The first year   116

7 The second year   142

8 The third year   166

9 The fourth year   186

10 The fifth year   210

Bibliography   226

Index   234

Preface

Pastoral care is a creative activity which aids the development of young people, reinforcing aspirations and maturity, consolidating positive mental health. It shows that teaching is a profession incorporating expertise used with integrity, and compassion, which encourages attainment of responsible autonomy in pupils. Pastoral care is not emotional first-aid or minor welfare activity: it is at the heart of teaching, helping the school reach its educational objectives. If well done, it is a source of job satisfaction for the teacher who has been deprived of both extrinsic and intrinsic rewards in recent years.

Many thanks are due to Patricia Ahier, James Askins, Colleen McLaughlin, Mary Mott, Ann Silcox and Mike Withers for producing and testing materials and activities for the outline programmes for each year. The final selection was made on the basis of simplicity and the avoidance of undue demands on already over-worked tutors. Freedom for year or house heads to develop topics in ways suited to their tutor team was also an important consideration: what is presented represents starting points to be developed, with the guidelines of earlier chapters giving direction. My special debt is to Dewi Williams who worked to bring coherence to the mass of material, and who gave support in many ways: my gratitude to him is great. Lindy Gummer also worked with zeal; not being off-put by my dreadful handwriting and frequent crossings out. I am grateful to her for a high standard of typing and presentation. Lastly, the faults – and there are many – are mine alone.

Swansea
January 1986

1 The Background

Beliefs and rationale

Most teachers are professionals with high commitment to the well-being of pupils. Pressures within initial training courses, the poverty of in-service provision, and financial economies affecting schools sometimes prevent them from expressing that concern effectively. But schools are also more powerful than the stressed and exhausted teacher realises. Himmelweit and Swift (1969) and Rutter *et al* (1979) argue persuasively that schools have an impact which is independent of family and neighbourhood. A balanced and relevant programme of pastoral work applied consistently over at least several years has a two-fold effect: it allows teachers to express concern and stimulate coping in ways which foster self-respect in pupils, while simultaneously supporting teachers in their arduous task. Involvement in a meaningful pastoral programme increases the job satisfaction of the teacher – a factor which has been sadly neglected in an era of contraction and uncertainty about the future.

A basic principle of pastoral work is that there is no single right way. Effectiveness comes from realistic adaptation to a particular school in which staff and pupils have a unique combination of attitudes, potential and skills. My concern is with the ethics, principles of development and possibilities of a pastoral programme, rather than with offering an over-precise prescription. I believe there is no final form of pastoral work. As the school advances so should the pastoral programme deepen.

The team which developed the ideas and activities presented here used the recipe analogy. *Ingredients* have to be selected, but they still vary in quality and quantity. *Mixing* varies: there are different ways of combining the ingredients, and also differences in the sequence of combination. *Cooking* is influenced by temperature, time, method of cooking and the efficiency of the oven or stove. Variations in *presentation* of the dish – garnish or size of portion – are also present. All these, and other factors, influence the completed food.

Mismatch between the quality of the ingredients, a different sequence in mixing, and other minor variations, have a cumulative impact which results in a very different dish. Let us also not forget that acceptance and response to the food depend upon the appetite and digestive powers of the eater.

This was a simple way of reminding ourselves of the principle of Gestalt: the perceived organised whole is more than the sum of its parts; it is an emergent product, the equivalent of a melody which exists apart from the separate notes which make it and apart also from singer or instrument. Kelly (1955) argues that events assume meaning through a process of interpretation, accompanied by prediction about the outcomes attached to them. To ignore this in developing a pastoral programme, by taking the perceptions of teachers and pupils for granted, may be to foredoom the programme to failure. Therefore we do not offer a recipe to be blindly followed, but material for inclusion in an open-ended dynamic programme which centres on developmental issues. We offer possibilities and encourage selection – not a closed programme which would be a prescription for sterility and lack of involvement.

Pastoral care is concerned with skills and feelings. It is about respect for the individual and the transmission of values as well as provision of skills. Transmitting values does not mean a process of indoctrination. It means the building of responsible autonomy and rational self-regulating principles of moral judgement, and not blind adherence to a code. It holds to belief in human integrity in an age when a crude utilitarianism is being foisted on schools. Watts (1983) traces the growth of the tendency to blame schools for inhibiting the production of wealth. We have to battle against the assumption that many aspects of secondary education actively hamper the profitability and growth of industry. Respect for creative activity, participation in the arts, and the possession of independent rational judgement which should be fostered by a pastoral programme, are not antagonistic towards entrepreneurial skills; indeed, they can reinforce enterprise.

Curle (1972) calls attention to a crucial distinction between identity through self-awareness and identity obtained by belonging. Sensitive understanding of the balance between these two forms of identity is important for constructive tutorial activity. When 'belonging' identity is predominant, then our identity is anchored more in what we belong to than what we are: we are what we belong to. The importance of this is obvious in the devaluation attached to unemployment. Peer groups, sporting allegiances and family are obvious sources of belonging identity. It is not impossible for pastoral activity to reinforce negative forms of belonging identity, e.g. 'He's one of the Browns', while claiming to be strengthening self-awareness. Belonging identity is not necessarily inferior or destructive; it tends to give stability and security in a period of rapid shift of perspectives and values. It may be a prerequisite for self-awareness, for we all need a safe base from which to explore. Put simply, we cannot be independent without experience of sound dependence.

Let us ask what kind of belonging identity is offered by the school. The forces of dissociation may outweigh those of affiliation. The first chapter of *Pastoral Care – a training manual* provides evidence that some staff and pupils view the tutor role and group indifferently, perhaps with hostility. Assemblies and ceremonial occasions introduce divisiveness, unwittingly supporting alienation rather than strengthening affiliation. Rapid social change strengthens the need for security rooted in a sense of positive belonging, yet the school appears to large groups of pupils to be irrelevant, if not actively rejecting.

Recognition of what to many appears to be a deep seated need must not blind us to the fact that identity by belonging may be embedded in the past. The drift of many writers, e.g. Large (1980), Stonier (1983), Toffler (1980) and Young (1972) is that there is a pressing need to obliterate traditional long-run social identities if society is to change constructively. A tension exists which is reflected by the dual camps of critics who complain that schools ignore the personality of the learner, seeing it as irrelevant and unhelpfully concentrating on instruction limited to the subject, or blame schools for excessive encouragement of individualism and neglect of social responsibilities. Perhaps the current state of affairs prompts the question, 'If society is sick or confused, what kind of identity can be derived from it?' On the one hand, the school must be a community which provides a basal identity by belonging, whilst on the other it systematically extends identity through self-awareness.

Let us be clear that building identity through self-awareness is not unthinking endorsement of complacement self-satisfaction. We are not erecting a delusory, self-protective screen. Identity through self-awareness is concerned with stringent evaluation of the significance of our powers and limitations. Perhaps it is best viewed as

4 A Pastoral Programme

building the capacity for rational self-vigilance. Discomfort is inevitable: but the capacity to tolerate it is essential for personal creativity. Therefore, those constructing a pastoral programme focus on the development of responsibility – perhaps prudent when demographic trends indicate a growing army of geriatrics to be supported by a relatively small working population! But pastoral activity can operate unwittingly to allocate deviant identities within the school, strengthening passivity or evasive tendencies in the pupils (Hamblin, 1984). Activities should contribute to the sense of control from within, breaking into the sense of helplessness, helping pupils to accept responsibility for themselves. Dweck (1975) indicates that learning to attribute poor performance to lack of personal motivation is better than learning to attribute it to lack of ability or events outside one's control. There seems to be growing emphasis on the need to liberate the individual from deterministic forms of dependency. Certainly, early closure on achievement and striving for success would be a questionable element in pastoral care.

This leads to the important fact that individual differences in the attribution of responsibility for success and reward, or failure and punishment to oneself or to others, are potent shapers of behaviour. The pastoral programme must explore with pupils the importance of intrinsic motivation or going beyond the performance demanded. Beliefs about the likelihood of success in different areas should be explored. My work in counselling suggests strongly that the tendency towards internal or external beliefs in control is not inevitably a global characteristic of personality. Individuals feel powerful in some areas and not in others. The reality of the attribution of responsibility to others or to the environment, with its consequent sense of helplessness, merits considered exploration in varied contexts. This is part of learning about learning and boosting autonomy by helping pupils understand the forces which impinge on them.

Responsibility takes other forms. A balance has to be achieved between a directive programme and the provision of vague suggestions. If teachers are merely given a set of books and activities, and instructed to carry them out, this would probably create conflict. Even if a programme could be made 'teacher proof', it would invite sterility and minimal performance. I have met many tutors who, despite goodwill, are unaware of the purpose of the activities, or their contribution to the teacher's mainstream task.

The companion volume to this one, *Pastoral Care – a training manual*, emphasises that schools should not be totally dependent upon an externally produced programme which sacrifices their autonomy – perhaps integrity – to an allegedly expert programme whose implicit values may be at variance with those of parents, teachers and pupils.

To undertake the development of a pastoral programme, without asking what parents, pupils and colleagues believe the school can teach legitimately, is risky. Conflict and distorted expectations of the intent of pastoral activity can only be reduced by examining all three perspectives closely and adapting to them in developing the pastoral programme.

Developing a sense of community

If a positive sense of belonging which acts as a foundation for responsible autonomy is to be developed, then we should consider the relationship of pastoral care to building a sense of community. Long ago, MacIver (1950) followed Durkheim in drawing attention to the significance of *anomy* which he described as the 'retreat of the individual into his own ego, the sceptical rejection of all social bonds'. He argued that such individuals have lost their moral roots, and no longer have any sense of continuity and social obligation. *Anomy* is the enemy of democracy. Such questions may seem remote to the head of year or house; certainly they have little connection with the trivial activities which sometimes constitute tutorial work. Yet the pastoral programme is concerned with building supportive but flexible bonds with society which prepare pupils for an unstable and intimidating future. Development of a meaningful pastoral programme depends on rigorous debate of the questions below. The danger that pastoral work will be a palliative or tension-reducing activity, maintaining the *status quo*, is now a commonplace. The limited perceptions of the role of the teacher reported over the years by many researchers, e.g. Morton-Williams and Finch (1968) and the current under-evaluation of the profession by the public create rigidity and limit our strategies. This is compounded by the fact that pressures on schools are unlikely to diminish. I hazard the guess that the answers to these questions will be found to be as important for teachers' job satisfaction as for pupils' development. Therefore they should be explored by the pastoral team.

1 *How is the school going to benefit from having each individual as a member of it?*

This applies to staff as much as pupils. The assumption underlying the question is that everyone has the capacity, desire and opportunity to contribute to the school as a community. This is not so, but we can examine the reasons for this and seek to overcome them. Some pupil sub-populations are hostile to the values of education; we seem unable to deal with this. Measor and Woods (1984) comment on the way orientation towards school is confirmed in the year of transfer through friendship groups which highlight conformity or deviance. Those constructing a pastoral programme have to evaluate honestly the impact of school organisation on pupils' behaviour. Profiles may attempt to assess initiative, but this is pointless if the organisation stifles or gives little opportunity for it. There is little likelihood of effectiveness if the pastoral programme has not been constructed with these issues in mind.

Heroism seems to be needed in some schools to survive the probationary year in teaching. The reversal of attitudes induced by initial training is well documented, e.g. Oliver and Butcher (1968) and Morrison and McIntyre (1969). Hargreaves' (1967) view, that for some teachers and many pupils school life was a necessary evil to be tolerated, still applies. Participation in pastoral programmes without training or support will limit the benefit from a new entrant to the school. Justice, however, demands positive comment on the high quality of probationers in the last three years. Commitment is needed to enter a contracting industry.

2 *What is the nature of the impact made by the individual on the school?*

A pastoral programme might take it for granted that the climate of the school is one which facilitates positive impact. This is not always so. We showed (Hamblin, 1984) that pupils had expectations of teachers which were not always met, and that this contributed to dissociation from school. Many teachers feel they are not listened to with respect, while young teachers may retreat to superficial performances because they feel that they are denied a voice in the management of the school, or that the alleged consultation does not lead to participation. They see it merely as the equivalent of a placebo – a treatment given to humour rather than cure the patient. Pastoral heads may unfairly blame personality, when organisational factors constrain individuals, creating the resistances about which the heads complain. Teachers resort to blaming the senior management, while that senior management criticises the inertia of the classroom teacher. Blame-pinning merely ensures that individuals occupy defensive positions, contributing little that is significant to the development of the school. One evaluator recently remarked of a school that 'senior management's aspirations were class teachers' fears'.

3 *What changes will the pastoral programme make to the school?*

It certainly will not provide instant change, nor can it correct defects in organisation. But is the school prepared to allow change? The joke that innovation is welcome as long as it does not change the way we do anything, is one the head of year/house should keep in mind. Resistance can be subtly expressed, cloaked in doubts about the validity of the pastoral enterprise which are never given expression in a way which submits them to rational scrutiny. Destructive processes exist. The work of Hargreaves *et al* (1975) suggests that teachers who provoke confrontations cast the responsibility for change solely on pupils. A sense of belonging is not going to be developed by a pastoral programme alone where such rigidities remain unmodified. Sometimes they are justified by the need for consistency, but rigidity is not consistency. It often turns out to be reliance upon inappropriate and habitual unthinking reactions.

Heads of year or house need to build on the strengths of those who will co-operate, attain credibility, and then initiate debate on the issues raised here. Realism implies neither passivity nor revolution, but evolving strategies. Change, within limits dependent on the ethos of the school, can be facilitated by raising the status, significance and power of tutors, allowing them to escape from the somewhat distasteful position of checking on the misdeeds of the form. A sound pastoral programme which involves pupils in their own guidance, accepting that pupils feel tutors should understand their tastes and viewpoints, not only respecting the individual, but acting as positive spokesmen for the form, can be an agent for development in an appropriate context (Hamblin, 1984).

4 *How does the individual have to adapt to the school community? What are the costs?*

Here the assumption is that adaptation by the individual is a necessary, proper and positive response to the school's function as a socialising agency. Adaptation, however, can be passive reaction, unwilling compliance, or the product of rational discussion leading to voluntary affiliation. It can be primarily to people or situations. Teacher attitudes compound the challenges from situations. Tutors and heads of year or house may vary confusingly in their demands or approaches, while peer pressures limit the adaptation that can be made without loss of status. Current coping capacity, susceptibility to stress, and unquestioned beliefs about what works, push teachers and pupils into costly or ineffective modes of behaving.

Legitimacy of the pastoral programme

In the tradition of Weber (1947) and Lipset (1960), legitimacy can be seen as the subjective perception of the extent to which an institution or activity is valued for itself, and also judged right and proper. Collins and Raven (1969), in discussing legitimate power, argue that legitimacy is a dimension of evaluation incorporating broad norms about the beliefs, behaviour and attitudes which are proper for actors in specific social situations. Legitimacy can be established in many ways: by tradition, current expectations of those in authority, expert or referent power and informational influence. The tenor of research and discussion is that legitimacy gradually occurs; therefore a process of education, explanation and negotiation has to be initiated through which the parameters of pastoral activity will eventually be established. This is an essential part of the task. We forget that legitimacy has to be acquired and is not inherent in the activity.

Enthusiastic teachers, concerned with the broader aspects of development rather than confining themselves to the mechanics of instruction, are worried that family and neighbourhood deny certain pupils the satisfaction of basic needs for nurture, security and recognition. This admirable, involved viewpoint, however, carries the danger of intensifying the idea that pastoral activity is designed for a small group of pupils seen as disadvantaged. The tenor of communication, the mode of interaction and the methods used, should be meaningful for all pupils. Intense feelings of inferiority, failure or of being unacceptable can be found in the able – they are not the prerogative of the deprived. Muddles will occur even when a pastoral programme is developed rather than imposed, unless the questions below are debated vigorously. As with the previous questions, I have no precise answers. Successive approximations, emerging from professional debate within the school, are the best for which we can hope.

1 *What are the needs we should, and can, legitimately meet through a pastoral programme?*

This forces inquiry about the source of definition of the alleged needs. Teachers' assessments of pupil needs differ markedly from those of parents, whilst pupils' conceptions of what they want may underline the distinction between needs and wants. Prescriptions of pupil needs imposed on the school by administrators carry no guarantee of validity. Their origins may lie in expediency or the need – sometimes unrecognised – to find a scapegoat. Current definitions of pupil needs, particularly the vocational, may be based on a questionable utilitarianism, actually containing long-term implications which restrict the individual and hamper his powers of adaptation to new lifestyles based on technological change. A salutary reminder is given by the inadequacy of guidance when US national interests urged counsellors to encourage, perhaps foist, scientific career orientations on American students after the 'sputnik scare'.

Planners must look at the various definitions of needs, and perhaps disentangle them from wants, for the desired is not necessarily desirable. They need to carefully evaluate the significance of discrepancies and convergences between interested parties. Long-term discussion is involved and the temptation to close early and impose instant meaning is to be resisted strenuously. The process takes place over years, requiring constant monitoring and modification.

2 *To whom are those building a pastoral programme accountable?*

This problem is eased if fellow teachers, pupils and parents are involved in the pastoral programme. Our frame of reference may see the pupil as the passive recipient of guidance. Role play and decision-making activities often operate in practice to suggest the right way. Parents may misunderstand or object to the values of teachers. It is crucial to debate whose demands are legitimate and to what degree? This question implies that legitimacy of demands could be seen as a hierarchy, and that the order of importance varies with the area of guidance. Nothing is inexorably fixed, but subject to informed negotiation. Our professional responsibilities and judgement cannot be jettisoned, but it is improper to use them as an excuse for denying the validity of the criticisms of pupils, parents and others.

3 *What methods should be employed?*

Accountability extends to the skills employed. Novel methods are neither intrinsically superior nor inferior, but should be assessed for their likely impact on pupils and teachers. Premature or ill-prepared sorties into role play activate doubt and insecurity in teacher and pupil alike. Activities which were an integral part of 'encounter groups' of the 1960s, which worked in the social context provided by middle-class, able and articulate adults whose sub-culture endorsed the desirability of self-exploration, may not be appropriate in the British school, particularly when those using them may not have understood their intent. Pupils are unlikely to be harmed. They will see the activities as pointless or puerile; at best showing tolerance of them. Teachers lose credibility as a result. We should not forget that school is seen as having serious purposes, and is taken earnestly by many pupils who question the validity of some approaches to pastoral work.

4 *What rewards stem from the pastoral programme for pupils and teachers?*

Pastoral Care – a training manual explores the growth of positive discipline in which meaningful rewards play a large part. Hopefully, the rewards for pupils are a continuity of concern, the growth of a sense of mastery and escape from stagnation. Teachers' rewards stem from the satisfaction brought by a more professional level of communication and interaction with pupils, plus the recognition that the programme wrestles with the forces which alienate pupils and create stress for the teacher.

5 *When is pastoral activity not legitimate?*

This is a question to which answers are manifold. From the point of view of those concerned in developing materials, pastoral care is illegitimate when it violates pupils' desire for privacy and encourages unthinking self-revelations. It is illegitimate if it evades reality by ignoring the situational and organisational contributions to behaviour, e.g. disruptive behaviour or under-functioning. It is possible to misuse pastoral activity as a device for 'letting off steam', i.e. as a tension reduction mechanism. Some creative teachers dismiss it as 'papering over the cracks' when it is confined to disciplinary or 'emotional first-aid' functions; others focus on the danger of diverting blame from the organisation to the individual.

Curious emotions focus on the pastoral programme. Some see it as an invasion of privacy or an overriding of parental rights; others attribute to it an unrealistic power as a cure-all for the ills of the school. The ethics under-girding a pastoral programme must be scrutinised and self-deception recognised as an ever-present possibility. In a multicultural society, are we sufficiently alert to unintentional violation of values? Lack of respect clothed in the language of caring is no better than that expressed more blatantly. Indeed, it may be more destructive. Self-deception has to be taken seriously. Is our experience and advice as relevant as we assume? Micro-technology, unemployment and beliefs about the nature of authority are major components of pupils' frames of reference to which we may not be orientated. Further complications arise through self-defeating tendencies. Do we tell young people that schools are about academic success, and then inform them by our actions that they are no good academically? Do we feed them the idea that school is not for them, while bewailing their lack of motivation?

Facing such questions is intimidating and it is tempting to ignore them as impractical. But evasion may mean we perpetuate ineffective practices. Approaching the pastoral programme in this enquiring way stimulates imaginative action. Is it inevitable or desirable that the tutor be tied to his form all the time? If there is a team working coherently together, the special strengths of individuals can be fully used. Tutors could undertake activities at which they are particularly good with other forms maximising the level of performance. This also seems to strengthen their relationships with their own forms. Problems of reciprocity may appear, but they are manageable.

Negotiation

The pastoral curriculum is, as Marland (1980) suggests, wider than the pastoral programme. Senior management will find it profitable and illuminating to look for overlap between the pastoral programme and subjects. Coincidence of topics occurs haphazardly, creating irritation. The pastoral programme, when negotiated properly, can prepare pupils for certain topics, develop certain aspects, or stress the relevance and application of what has been learned. Consultation with, and involvement of, heads of academic departments are necessary for success. Why court rejection by failing to explicate the links between the pastoral and the curricular?

In selecting topics we may give undue weight to the belief that the tutor has credibility with his form. Certain topics, e.g. sexuality, may be best covered in subject areas where pupils accept them as legitimate. The context in which a topic is introduced influences the interpretation of its significance. Pupils hold rigid ideas of what a 'proper lesson' is, and bring evasive techniques into tutor periods. Group work affords the opportunity for pupils to change the task weakening the distinction between illicit talk and behaviour and task-focused activity. Denscombe (1980) shows this exploitation at work in humanities lessons. There is also the danger that tutor periods could become outlets for tension, allowing the causes of the frustration to go unmodified. The topics and their treatment could be seen, and treated, as trivial, unless we work determinedly to prevent this.

What, then, is best covered in tutor time? Are the relationship of the tutor and form and the tutor's credibility key factors? In many schools the relationship is sterile, and credibility low. In constructing a pastoral programme is the tutor's relationship with the form a neglected variable, or taken for granted, when it is actually problematical? No easy or universal answers exist.

Our problem involves helping pupils change their definition of tutorial activity, while improving the competence of the tutor in using group activity. It also extends to the education and involvement of parents and school governors. A pastoral programme to which parents have minimal access will gain little support. Indeed, it may attract criticism due to misunderstanding. Negotiation with pupils, leading to their active involvement, is essential. We gave some evidence that relations with teachers were at the forefront of fifth-year pupils' conceptions of their needs (Hamblin, 1984). But this was not uncompromisingly negative: potentially productive tensions existed between rejection of school as irrelevant, open criticism of teachers, and desire for more personal and equal interaction with them. The task is to allow parents and pupils active rather than passive access to the pastoral programme.

Contributions of parents

Parents can be helped to

1 Interpret and reinforce the aims of a pastoral programme to their own children and other parents.
2 Provide information and materials which facilitate understanding of the links between subject choice and future career.
3 Provide ideas for decision-making activities relevant to the intended occupations of fifth- and sixth-form pupils.
4 Give considered information about the frustrations and anxieties which impinge on their children.
5 Offer up-to-date information about the topics which are salient in family affairs, e.g. drug-taking, neighbourhood problems or unemployment.

Contributions of pupils

Pupils can be helped to

1 Give considered feedback about the activities.
2 Construct materials, e.g. cartoons and tapes for the first-year induction course, or participate in subject choice sessions by explaining the nature of a subject from the learner's viewpoint.
3 Occasionally organise tutor periods themselves.
4 Develop self-help groups and undertake peer counselling.

2 Developing a pastoral programme

A caution

Pastoral programmes have been ineffective where tutors were asked to use published materials without preliminary training. In evaluating one scheme Bolam and Medlock (1985) found that lack of confidence, difficulty in explaining the approach to colleagues, antagonism to the methods and, less frequently, the resistance of pupils (especially in the fourth and fifth years) demanded attention from the innovators.

Continuous discussion and provision for immediate feedback from tutors to the head of year or house are essential if insights into methods and philosophy are to move from the latent level to that of active informed use. In earlier books I have described pastoral care as, among other things, an attack on inert and passive forms of learning. It is not too difficult to find tutor work, carried out conscientiously, which could be justly described as inert, contributing little to pupils' development because it lacks the cutting edge of intellect. Pupils are not being forced to reason and their imaginations remain untouched. In the old term, the pastoral programme must *stretch* pupils.

If the pastoral and the curricular are to be integrated, the programme must be related carefully to the issues of identity and positive discipline raised in *Pastoral Care – a training manual*. Pressures, including the need to justify ourselves, induce us to see a pastoral programme as an event to be introduced in a once-for-all way. In fact, it is a process to be fostered and monitored over a period of years.

Methods

Tutors tend to implement activities gathered from other sources rather than producing their own, unless the head of year or house gives leadership which encourages and supports those willing to innovate. Continuity is stressed by incorporating tutorial activities into a long-term programme, possibly in an attempt to overcome pupil resistance and anxieties by making tutor periods 'proper lessons'. Ambivalence exists amongst tutors and pupils about this phrase – certainly, there is little justification for tutorial activity if learning does not occur, but the form and nature of that learning should be open to negotiation within the school.

A pastoral programme cannot be separated from its context. Pupils are acute observers, quickly learning what is expected of them, therefore, it is pertinent to ask what models of social and working relationships, organisation, co-operation and authority we present. Counsellors know that pupils are well aware of tensions between staff and evaluate staff relationships accurately. Pastoral activities cannot be separated from our wider behaviour. It is useless talking about the pupils' involvement without first asking what principles of selection we use when we send someone on a message or allocate responsibility for collection of registers or books. The messages about pupils and ourselves, the justice and judgements inherent in such selection probably outweigh the overt messages of the tutor period activities. To provide tutorial work without assessing the realism and ethics of our choices is to engage in doubtful enterprise. What pupils learn about *who* is chosen for *what*, and *why* they are chosen is more salient than the message of the activities.

More is being demanded of teachers, even as criticisms increase, and resources diminish. Teachers need their confidence boosted; therefore, a full year is needed as a period of initial orientation in which the middle and senior management encourage experimentation and negotiation – providing skills and reinforcing individual strengths. Even in an established system this idea of a developmental year with one age level as the focus for experimentation can be a prelude to subsequent more extensive improvement.

Advocation of a preliminary evaluative year is neither evasive nor weak. The year is a period of education and attitude change, incorporating small-scale feasibility studies aimed at reinforcing the credibility of the pastoral programme through reasoned exposition. Middle management and others involved will not only educate and train, but also dispel extravagant or unjustified irrational expectations as they emerge. The tentative climate of the exploratory year allows explanation without the confrontation which polarizes attitudes in the staffroom. The aim is to create a core self-sustaining team of pastoral workers who can give support because they are credible sources of information. The members of this core team will not feel the need to attack or derogate doubters, although they will accept realistically that the occasional sub-standard teacher will be defensive in his reactions to proposed change, and the teams' influence and offers of support. Time has to be allowed for coping with crises of self-doubt.

The process parallels that described by Katz and Kahn (1966) of interpolation of structure – filling out incomplete areas of existing structure through creative improvisation and experiment. The futility of foisting a ready-made programme on schools is becoming clearer. When the tendency of institutions is to despatch the individual revelatory prophet or innovator to an appropriate doom, the case for an experimental year and a team approach becomes stronger.

Variations between schools make wholesale adoption of published programmes problematical. These include:

1 *Formal structure* – 11–16; 11–18; middle schools; junior and senior comprehensive schools;

2 *Neighbourhood* – rural or urban; traditional or rapidly changing industrially;

3 *Social class and pupil composition* – multi-cultural; co-educational or single sex; primarily disadvantaged or middle-class;

4 *Incidence of teacher stress* – falling rolls; amalgamation and redeployment; split sites;

5 *Attitudes* – experience and interest in pastoral care; the history of innovations in that school;

6 *Training opportunities* – availability of help locally; degree of support from the LEA;

7 *Organisation* – factors impinging on methods and use of pastoral time, e.g. vertical or horizontal tutor groups; tutors and/or heads of year or house moving up with age groups; money allocated for materials.

The main thrust of a developmental year is indicated below. This is only an illustration: it is not intended to be exhaustive, neither is it implied that developers should work through the areas sequentially. They will probably return to each area on several occasions as insights accrue. The weight given to wider sources of influence is noteworthy.

Identification of needs and possibilities in the exploratory year

1 Consumer research on attitudes and needs of   { Pupils / Parents / Staff }

2 Estimation of the impact of the mass media and significance of political reaction to major educational issues.

3 Critical appraisal of the curriculum offered in the school, particularly its presentation to different sub-populations and its relevance to a post-industrial society.

4 Searching for ways of incorporating into the pastoral programme the opportunities offered by day-to-day events, e.g. an avoidable accident, an incident of discourtesy or achievement; failure to cope in response to some stress.

A pastoral programme inaugurated without consideration of these factors could be trivial. We are concerned with the individual in a social setting and his transactions with a changing environment.

Clarifying the content of the pastoral programme

1 Sharpening the social and learning skills to be developed. It is easy to talk in global terms, but specification and concreteness are more productive. To talk of listening is inadequate – it may be listening to detect the salient, distinguishing it from the peripheral; to separate fact from speculation; or to detect the steps in a spoken argument.

2 Evaluation of the developmental tasks of the individual, ensuring the programme incorporates them. Issues of autonomy, moral judgement and relationships are obvious examples.

3 Assessment of pressures faced by adolescents, avoiding loose assumptions about the trauma of adolescence, without discounting the problems.

4 Relating the demands of school to developmental issues, e.g. the choice of subjects at a time when there may be confusion about personal matters due to physical development.

A pastoral programme can leave pupils with the impression that they are not being respected if activities are imposed on them without explanation and their involvement in the construction of materials is not sought. This failure in communication then reinforces the suspicions of older pupils that pastoral work is an impertinent encroachment on individuality. A good pastoral programme interprets what is happening in school and analyses the learning process, helping pupils make the most of the knowledge and experiences offered by the school. A good pastoral programme realistically enhances the sense of mastery of the current environment and allows positive anticipation of future demands. Above all, it reinforces the image of the teacher as someone whose overriding concern is the best interests of those for whom he is responsible.

Marshalling ideas for monitoring the programme

1 Collection of ideas from colleagues and pupils as to how the programme should be assessed. Arrangements for early feedback from both sources seem critical for success.
2 Detection of sources of frustration and irrelevance.

It has been argued that if one sends food to a developing country, temporary alleviation occurs, but if one teaches the people to fish and grow crops, then they are permanently secure. Similarly, the basic task of a pastoral programme is not providing immediate support, but inducing the skills of constructive coping. Efficient pursuit of this goal requires:

1 Themes which are extended and deepened each year in ways which avoid the complaint, 'But we've done this before!'.
2 Opportunity for flexibility and innovation by the tutor, without loss of purpose.
3 Incorporation of problems and topics meaningful to all concerned, including parents. Explanation and justification is necessary if the pastoral programme is not to be condemned as 'a bad case of loose concepts'.
4 An intellectual component which challenges and 'stretches' pupils.
5 Activities which encourage analysis and clarification of values and examination of the functions of attitudes held by pupils, while still respecting individuals' inhibitions and sensitivities.
6 Emphasis on mastery learning and striving for success without blunting concern for others, i.e. self-management without selfishness.
7 Encouragement of thoughtful altruism.

Skills

Pragmatism impels us to get on with the construction of materials, but premature forays into this without the buttressing derived from an adequate rationale may activate resistance. It is questionable whether pupils and their parents want growth in the way that some existing pastoral programmes see as desirable and unproblematical. A pastoral programme must take into account the possibility of a divide between what society (admittedly a vague term, but for most of us it has meaning) sees as the purpose of schools, and what we as teachers assume as our professional stance.

Welford (1968) points out the wide nature of the term 'skills'. A pastoral programme should see skills as closely linked to information processing. Versatile ways of handling information, allowing pupils to draw inferences and behave more flexibly, instead of being tied to unthinking repetition of past behaviour, are germane to achievement and discipline. Kelly (1955) stressed the capacity of the individual both to represent reality, and to make new constructions of it as pathways into the future. We have failed to achieve this in pastoral programmes, perhaps preferring to stay on apparently safer ground. Yet in my own teaching I found that allegedly less able pupils coming from disadvantaged backgrounds were able to engage in this imaginative, but not unrealistic, endeavour.

Marland (1980) properly calls attention to the fact that the curriculum is not restricted to the cognitive. The reverse also obtains, for the pastoral programme is not confined to feelings and attitudes. Precision in reasoning, recognition of the complexity of situations and widening one's range of knowledge are as important as expression of feelings. The simple 'What would you do if . . .?' approach often used in pastoral activities is inadequate for promoting the learning essential for fulfilment in our changing society. Reasoning is a safeguard against stimulating omnipotent and paranoid fantasies in adolescents. Blind blame-pinning has been the disagreeable outcome of some well-intentioned pastoral activities. Any fool can take the lid off and reveal seething resentments, but replacing it is more difficult. Letting off steam can be destructive. Some years ago, I had to cope with a class who had been subjected to a pastoral session which resulted in scapegoating of the school and teachers. I met almost implacable hostility because of the teacher's unintended stimulation of aggression in pupils. They were locked together into a false definition of the reality of their school.

The incident was dealt with, and pupils' sense of responsibility and balance restored. But such incidents can easily occur, especially if the tutor is compensating for insecurity or has a tendency to identify with his form against authority.

Pastoral care is misused when it labels pupils and diverts justified blame away from the school organisation and methods, but it is equally reprehensible where it creates states of powerful egocentric arousal in pupils. De-tensing, through a carefully structured ending, is an essential skill even when the emotional states are positive. Colleagues faced by pupils in states of emotional arousal are at a loss. They rightly object because they do not understand it; the disjunctions inherent in current teaching methods limit their ability to adapt to the moods of a class. Poorly-designed activities can arouse crude dogmatism of the 'nothing but' type, e.g. 'He's nothing but a teacher, Pakistani, thief or deviant.' The teacher then has to battle against the tensions provoked by the crystallisation of these feelings. We can, however, use identity through belonging and self-awareness to develop positive developmental activities.

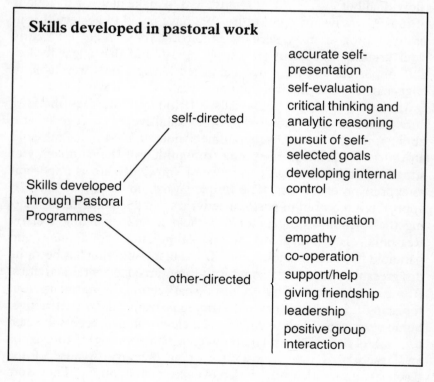

Skills developed in pastoral work

Skills developed through Pastoral Programmes

self-directed
- accurate self-presentation
- self-evaluation
- critical thinking and analytic reasoning
- pursuit of self-selected goals
- developing internal control

other-directed
- communication
- empathy
- co-operation
- support/help
- giving friendship
- leadership
- positive group interaction

This is not exhaustive, but it suggests the lines on which those developing a pastoral programme should work. The involvement of pupils in determining content is essential.

Tutor skills are crucial. It is tempting to focus on the use of questionnaires, tapes, role play, etc, but some basics need careful consideration.

1 *Adapting to the physical environment*　Classroom seating may be formal, hence the tutor has to adapt. There is no point in lengthy, noisy and disorderly rearrangement of desks, tables and chairs. Acceptance of environmental constraints, and adaptation of activities, is better than agonised attempts at modifying the environment – which lead eventually to abandonment of effort.

2 *Realistic use of the time available*　Over-elaborate activities reduce the amount of reflection and detract from application. Topics may have to be spread over several sessions if adequate discussion and processing is to occur. Decisions about the length of small group activity or discussion; when to use partner work rather than small groups; how to select small groups, e.g. same sex or both sexes, teacher or pupil selected; when to change them, are all associated with the use of time.

3 *Ensuring pupil activity is task related rather than evasive*　Ways of intervening when 'clowning' or devaluation of the topic occur, and exploration of the discrepancies between pupils' objectives of 'enjoying themselves' and the tutors' demands for effort and seriousness, are ignored all too often. Continuity of method, incorporating increasing demands, has to be given expression in the programme. It would be ill-judged to introduce new methods of simulation or role play in the fourth or fifth-years unless such active ways of learning have been established and accepted earlier.

Tutors need the confidence to bring these issues out in the open with pupils. Perpetuating the mechanisms which erode the sense of purpose of pastoral activity merely frustrates or exhausts tutors, putting them into collusion with ineffectiveness. Straightforward analysis and explanation without giving the impression of carping reinforce self-respect on both sides.

Encouragement of experiential learning which *pupils* subsequently evaluate is no easy task when the work on study skills suggests that teachers' classroom questioning often requires a 'right' answer – even where none exists. Experiential learning does not mean using half-an-hour to allow pupils to discover something which they could be told in 20 seconds, then *not* going on to explore its implications, nor does it imply vagueness or a lack of guidance.

We are striving to provide learning experiences which will enable young people to go beyond the levels of competence, creativity, honesty, love and compassion reached by the previous generation. Are we to lag behind in the affective aspects of education? Those concerned with micro-technology explain that they are currently creating the groundwork for careers they did not visualise ten to 20 years ago. They are intuitively aware that occupations are developing of which they merely get occasional glimpses. There is a danger of growing imbalance between technology and education of the emotions. Whether we acknowledge it openly or not, the thrust of pastoral effort has been towards reinforcement of the *status quo*; attainment of an overtly tension-free state of equilibrium between staff, pupils and parents; and the equation of personal guidance with a delusory contentment. Pupils' needs for affiliation, approval and reward are basic; they form part of essential identity by belonging. But this is merely the platform for creative striving and responsible identity. Klein's (1960) and Jahoda's (1958) ideas of positive mental health stress active attempts to master one's environment; comparison with the current emphasis on emotional first aid in pastoral care is enlightening.

The middle management team will need to develop a justifiable taxonomy of skills. The work of Bloom *et al* (1956), and especially Krathwohl (1964), provides useful material, but heads of year or house should, *as a group*, work out their own list and order of priority. Why? Such a list embodies values. We have returned to the position of Allport (1961) who remarked that failure by schools to teach values has the effect of denying them. Consistent, but positive attack on the dilution of values strengthens both types of identity. This alone is justification for the pastoral programme. The emphasis must be on reasons, i.e. justifications undertaken in an open-minded way. Indoctrination is not pastoral care. McPhail (1982) should be required reading for the pastoral team. Pastoral workers must ensure that activities do not strengthen existing stereotypes nor encourage unthinking approval or disapproval, rejection or acceptance. Instead, activities should encourage rational evaluation of the consequences of holding specific attitudes and values, not only for the holder but for significant others in his or her life space.

This leads to questioning of our own behaviour. Have we been remiss, paying scant attention to the pupil's, 'Why should I?'. Or have we responded arbitrarily, missing an opportunity for stimulating growth? Have we taken for granted that because certain practices prevail in our school, these are necessarily right? Consultation with pupils would illuminate the fallacy and bring new vitality into the pastoral programme.

The team developing the illustrative materials focused on the skills below, although a specific hierarchy is not present:

Skills to be reinforced, extended or developed through pastoral activity

1 *Skills related to the social self:*
   – co-operation, even within overtly competitive situations;
   – using peer supports constructively;
   – presentation of self, learning to relate flexibly to different situations without suffering a loss of integrity;
   – dealing with comparisons and predictions, favourable or unfavourable;
   – self-management, including rational use of energy and time;
   – coping with social anxieties;
   – taking the standpoints of others.

2 *Skills related to the self as a learner:*
   – study skills, including reading, note-taking, revision and listening;
   – oral skills, e.g. the ability to describe accurately and coherently;
   – applying the motive to achieve in co-operative, competitive and challenging situations;
   – analysing and developing one's own learning style;
   – coping with frustrations and managing tensions associated with learning;
   – planning and target setting;
   – understanding the influence of predictions and self-fulfilling prophecies;
   – developing the capacity for inferential thinking.

---

3 *Skills related to the development of values and mature judgement:*
   - decision-making;
   - tolerance and overcoming prejudice;
   - understanding sources of influence;
   - evaluating risks;
   - examining the nature of, and reactions to, sources of threat and when necessary, modifying them;
   - developing the capacity for concern, and the ability to translate it into practical help;
   - understanding, evaluating and controlling the attribution of intent and motive to others.

There is overlap in this taxonomy between the headings, which reflects reality. Once again, it is merely indicative rather than complete. But it does make clear the serious purpose of the pastoral programme and the thought required in planning it. Leading a team of tutors requires heads of year or house to initiate debate *as a team* on the skills they believe should be developed, moving to negotiation with tutors as a second stage. Clarification and modification will be time consuming, but the effort is worthwhile. The idea of a long-term process also reminds us that there will be continuous change – there is no final form of pastoral care.

Development

Once a working agreement has been achieved, decisions have to be made about the structure of the pastoral programme:

1 Is it to be a linear programme, lasting for either a term or academic year?
2 Is it to be a series of short units focused on a theme?
3 Are the same themes to be repeated each year with extended content?

These questions cannot be separated from the basic organisation of the pastoral system. A good tutor gets rewards for his investment of energy if he is given at least a second year with his tutor group.

Certain pupils find the continuity of relationship very supportive. But how far can this properly be taken? An obvious danger is that of lumbering some groups with inadequate tutors. The interchange of tutors mentioned earlier does alleviate this a little, but strategies for coping with such circumstances need to be spelt out. The ideal situation is for tutors and heads of year to remain with their groups from years one to five, but certain precautions and provisos are necessary:

1 There must be real communication and support at middle management level to alleviate the increased demands on the head of year or house. Sharing of materials and ideas is an obvious example.

2 Arrangements must allow pupils to transfer from a tutor group without creating blame or a sense of inadequacy in either tutor or pupil.

3 The head of year or house must provide supportive training for tutors.

This structure is likely to ameliorate the decline in pastoral activity in the fourth and fifth years, described by Bolam and Medlock (1985). The use of short units allows tutors freedom to change the order of presentation and modify content in a responsible way. I have reported the desire for treatment as equals and for signals of respect found in fifth-year pupils (Hamblin, 1984). Pupils seemed to be indicating that school was failing them, yet they also had high expectations of teachers. A pastoral programme which evolves through teamwork can take these issues on board in a fruitful way.

Evaluation of activities

The pastoral management must develop a framework for evaluating tutor activities which is then made available to tutors, who should have the power to reject and replace a particular activity. Tutors are often seen as of low status, significance and power, unable to initiate action or innovate, and therefore having little to which they are committed. Clearly, the outline overleaf will need modification. It is best seen as a point of departure.

Key questions in evaluating a pastoral activity

1   Are the objectives clearly laid out for tutors *and* pupils?
2   Do you feel the objectives will be meaningful to pupils?
3   Will other teachers endorse the activity as legitimate, and likely to foster a responsible attitude in the pupil?
4   Are the instructions simple and clear?
5   Is the activity directly related to the heart of the problem or issue?
6   Is it easy to set up, not demanding undue preparation from busy tutors?
7   Does it include direct help with application and follow-up activity?
8   Is there a productive balance between tutor input and pupil activity?
9   Do you feel there is a realistic approach to time? Can it be fitted into a tutor period with sufficient attention being given to application? Is a separate period going to be needed for follow-up?
10   Does it impinge on personal privacy in a distasteful way or invite misperception of the motives of the tutor?
11   What, if any, are the latent messages about the pupils? Does it convey positive expectations of responsible, thoughtful behaviour?
12   If you judge the activity as appealing or potentially successful, on what is the judgement based? Is humour, excitement, significance, or some other factor the basis of your judgement? Is the validity of your assessment unquestionable?
13   Do you think the intended learning is likely to occur?

Taking this evaluatory approach endorses the pastoral programme as a series of experiences designed to function within a specific school rather than a body of immutable knowledge. Evaluation of the activity prevents tutors reinforcing pupils' sense of inadequacy by asking questions which are incomprehensible to them, or blocking pupils from formulating their own questions. At best, attention is drawn to the latent learning in tutorial work which, I suspect, accounts for the resistance appearing in the later years. Pupils may feel that teachers have not met their expectations as I have discussed (Hamblin, 1984), but this alone does not account for their rejection of tutorial activities. We often fail to comprehend the factors which erode dignity and make positive identity problematical. Pupils react to these pressures by insulating themselves against demands through behaviour which ensures their acceptance by peers. They strive to build identities which defend them, on the one hand, against the danger of being written off as stupid, and on the other, of becoming a 'high flier', labelled as a snob. It is remarkable how much energy is invested in the secondary school in pursuit of mediocrity. Pastoral programmes have to challenge such forms of identity by belonging if we are not to be in collusion with them.

3 Content of a pastoral programme

A note on feelings and basic elements

The neglect of the learner's self-picture has become a commonplace in pastoral discussions, but this is merely a symptom of the conspiracy of silence to which pupils' emotional lives have been subjected as Kubie (1958) critically comments. Little has been done to break this conspiracy, despite the urgency which stems from dramatic changes in career prospects and lifestyle after school. Anxiety about unemployment or fear of coping with threatening styles of living and associated stress, can preclude learning. Balanced management and acceptance of emotions are an essential requisite for responsible personal freedom. Good discipline, i.e. self-discipline, is strengthened when feelings are appreciated and become part of the substance of a constructive dialogue between tutors and pupils. De Charms (1968) suggests that to feel oneself a pawn erodes effort and responsibility and, more damagingly, leaves a profound dissatisfaction with self and others. If pastoral care is about responsible affiliation and positive mental health, why have we neglected these issues?

Inadequate analysis may have left us uncertain whether the socially endorsed attribute of autonomy which appears so often in statements of pastoral intent is a set of skills, a personality quality or a right accompanied by obligations. As I see it, the autonomous person has a high, although not inhibiting, measure of control over his emotions and actions; a wide range of choices, together with an accurate knowledge of the probable outcomes of different actions and expressions of feeling; and his own criteria for evaluating what is desirable and of worth.

The prospect of open discussion of emotions threatens some tutors, perhaps because teaching itself is deeply permeated by the tensions inherent in a task which asks us to occupy a quasi-parental role while avoiding improper emotional involvement. Others see such discussion as distasteful intrusion into the life of the pupil, or feel that it leads to questionable judgements of personality. A few may see it as a self-indulgent evasion of their basic instructional task. But no loose permissiveness on the part of the tutor is implied by a focus on feelings, nor is it an encouragement of laxity in demanding the best from pupils. Pastoral work accepts that experience of frustration is an almost inevitable part of growth, and that the important thing is to learn to cope with it constructively. Neither is anxiety *per se* condemned or seen as inevitably destructive. A concerned analysis of the antecedents and consequences of both positive and negative emotions, coupled with assessment of individual responses to stressful situations, offers safeguards against defensive and unrealistic ways of coping which create problems for adolescent and adult alike.

We exhaust ourselves battling with apathy, passivity and indirect forms of aggression to little avail. Such self-defeating forays are better abandoned in favour of measures which alert pupils to the processes which either trap them into reliance on short-term efforts to stave off trouble – pupils investing energy in maintaining fragile balance between the demands of peers and those of adults – or cause them to adopt a pugnacity or bravado which alienates them from their fellows. Pupils often complain, 'Why do things go sour on me?', or 'I don't want it to happen, but somehow it always does!'. The following topics are grounded in feelings which are crucial for the adolescent's adjustment:

1 Loss of face and how to contend successfully with the humiliation and sense of vulnerability it brings.

2 Working through frustration without resort to aggression, apathetic withdrawal or depression.

3 Dealing with emotional blackmail of varying degrees of subtlety without impairing relationships or abdicating their desired standards.

4 Accepting just blame, criticism or praise. The word 'just' has a number of implications which should enter the activity and discussion. The issue of why we are ashamed of being praised seems to have a particular poignancy for the mid-adolescent.

5 Overcoming fear of the consequences of deviation from peer definitions of desired behaviour.

6 Dealing with feelings of inadequacy or helplessness in particular situations, e.g. examinations, answering questions orally, going to a party . . .

7 Understanding, and then controlling, behaviour in situations where aggressive responses escalate into severe trouble.

8 Tackling self-devaluation arising from comparisons with others, whether the comparisons are self-initiated or come from others. (Emotive elements will be strong when bodily attributes or oral skills form the foci of the comparisons.)

This is probably sufficient to illustrate the range of highly emotive situations which operate in schools. Almost unnoticed by tutors, these situations teach a pupil who she or he is, in relation to others. Comparisons and predictions focused on social interaction and emotional control are at the forefront of adolescent concerns, in spite of appearances to the contrary. Current trends towards criterion-referenced learning higher up the secondary school may help to alleviate the potentially debilitating effects of such concerns, but all too often pastoral activity simply manages to gloss over the fact that they exist.

A pastoral programme obviously attempts to deal with the personal disjunctions caused by transition from primary to secondary school. It tries to resolve or balance the tensions created by differences between social, emotional, physical and intellectual puberty and consequent discrepancies between the individual's ability to cope and the legitimate demands of home, peer group and school. Allied to this are the less obvious system related functions of providing continuity and anticipating later educational developments.

A pastoral programme builds on, and extends, the activity-based learning of the primary school, with its emphasis on group work and what for the moment can be called discovery or experiential learning. When these methods are implemented well, they produce learning marked by vitality and initiative. But such approaches can degenerate into purposelessness or become a sham. Neither is discovery learning necessarily more effective or commendable than that derived from sound teacher exposition. Bearing these warnings in mind, it is still likely that real benefits come from using active methods. In 1971, in an unpublished conference paper, I argued that there is more in common between the primary school using these methods and the university than between the university and the type of learning that dominates the first five years of some secondary schools. The pastoral programme is just one way in which learning demanding initiative and involvement can be extended in the secondary school. It may offer special opportunities for pupils to experience and benefit from the integration or co-ordination discussed by Heathcote *et all* (1982).

It is obvious from the evidence of Bolam and Medlock (1985) and Hamblin (1983; 1984) that pastoral care is becoming increasingly problematical. Courses such as TVEI, CPVE, BTEC or CGLI stress integration, negotiation and formative assessment. We should benefit from ROSLA experiences, where well-designed and relevant courses floundered, largely because they demanded skills and attitudes which, if possessed by pupils, only existed in embryonic form. Pupils and teachers alike tended to devalue the experiential learning involved. Although welcome evidence exists that students react enthusiastically to today's courses, e.g. TVEI Insight (No. 1, 1984; No. 2, 1985), it is still essential to ensure that students are equipped with the skills which give them a headstart at entry. Self-evaluation; building their own learning and interactional profiles; problem-solving; constructive verbalisation of their own point of view while retaining the ability to appreciate the standpoints of others, are skills which should play an important part in pastoral work.

In our battle against apathy, profiles incorporating formative assessments along with other elements of the new courses can be sources of motivation. This must not be jeopardised simply because the individual is bereft of self-evaluatory and communication skills. Problems have to be overcome if guidance and counselling are to be integrated into these worthwhile innovations. The corollary is concordance between the methods employed in the pastoral programme and the objectives of vocationally-based curricula. Paradoxically, it seems that if the pastoral programme is successful in fostering the skills mentioned above, it creates the conditions which will eventually destroy it. A paradox at first sight: but a creative one. It can be fully integrated into the 14–19 curriculum with profit to all.

It is now appropriate to discuss some aspects of method in greater depth, recalling that the pastoral programme involves both content and method. The two are equally important: neglect of either can lead to failure or unwanted outcomes. The latter can never be taken for granted. On one occasion when using material which appeared to be constructively concerned with attitudes and perceptions, I obtained unexpected results. With middle-class pupils understanding was boosted and sympathy enlisted, but pupils from disadvantaged backgrounds had their prejudices reinforced and clung more strongly to their original conceptions. The outcomes were different, although both content and process were identical. Initial orientations in both groups were strengthened and given greater credibility. We should be alert to self-defeating elements; our intentions of increasing self-respect or inculcating self-evaluation may result in the former becoming complacency, and the latter becoming unhelpful self-detraction.

Most of us would agree that a pastoral programme should build consistently positive expectations of success in problem solving and a less pessimistic approach to prospects of learning. But this has to be achieved through guided reflection on the experiences provided. Is it enough to present adolescents with a cartoon or verbal description of a problem, and without more ado pose the question, 'What would you do?' It is almost inevitable that some pupils will have rigid perceptions, or may lack the capacity to discriminate, either between situations or between aspects of a situation such as intent, setting and action. Consequently, the discussion in response to this question may reinforce or give added justification to existing limited patterns of behaviour. Tutors have realistically to take into account the possibility that what a pupil sees in a situation is biased or limited. The pupil's view can be illogically determined by past experiences, rigid beliefs about what ought to be, or myths – induced by family or neighbourhood – about the reasons for behaviour.

Those responsible for a pastoral programme should submit it to the same critical scrutiny given to any major curricular development. Statements of intent, couched in laudable terms, may hide a reality in which ill-conceived content and poor methodology interact to produce very questionable outcomes. This danger may take many forms. We claim we wish to eliminate distorted conceptions of gender and reduce their effects, but we ignore the fact that the overall bias in the programme is in favour of males. We may avoid discussion of equality of opportunity which gets to the heart of the problem, e.g. 'Why does a woman have to be so much better than male applicants to get a top job?' or 'Should men be as ready to move to foster the wife's career as the woman has been to help her husband?'

Feelings and the education of the emotions are endorsed as important parts of many pastoral programmes, but, in fact, affective goals such as self-control under stress or managing social anxiety remain at a level of imprecise specification compared with more academic goals. Even academic learning is not exempt from unintended destructiveness; although we may wish to stimulate open-ended or exploratory learning, and actually provide experiences which stimulate it, we then destroy what has been achieved by constrictive questioning which implicitly devalues both pupils' learning and their original ideas. Discussion is essential. Expositional teaching is not to be condemned as inescapably authoritarian, for it can highlight alternative points of view or hammer home the message that there is no final answer. In any case, experiential learning can be trivial or misleading. Pastoral workers sometimes go beyond experiential learning to invoke discovery learning as the sole desirable form, i.e. learning in which the principal content or skills must be found by the learner without teacher intervention; significance then being allocated by the pupil. Too great an emphasis on discovery *per se* is obscurant. What is important is the activity of the learner, if Bruner (1966) is to be believed when he says that knowledge is a process rather than solely a product. Perhaps the relevant question is: whether a particular approach to learning is efficient, motivating, or both? The two elements are obviously connected, but not identical.

If we take efficiency first, then we have to admit that there seems to be no firm evidence that at any stage of learning it is necessary for the learner to discover principles independently in order to understand them or use them meaningfully. Is discovery learning itself self-contained? Gagné (1977) suggests that in practice it depends upon previous learning. This implies that the main thrust of our effort should go towards fostering questioning attitudes; encouraging and teaching pupils to recognise and challenge assumptions; developing the skills of distinguishing between assertions, hypotheses and facts; and above all, helping pupils question the inferences which operate in areas of living all-too-easily ignored by the school.

Motivation is an old source of concern for teachers, which has been intensified by the feeling that traditional incentives have lost their attractiveness. Intrinsic motivation, which by definition is independent of external rewards, looms larger in our considerations. Bloom (1968; 1976) implies, in discussing mastery learning, that formative evaluation has a potentially motivating effect on the learner. The combination of autonomy and involvement which seems to be at the heart of formative evaluation is part of the active learning inherent in problem solving and it should have a similarly energising effect.

Ausubel (1968) suggests that no particular method of learning is superior, therefore recipes are inappropriate, and the onus is on the tutor to select what seems best for her or his group. What creates confidence in the tutor will, if the tutor is a person of integrity, be good for the group. Whatever method is employed, surely the aim will be inducement of questioning of unthinking perceptions of life, and an end to the closure or dismissal of information which stifle personal change. Bruner (1973) provides further illumination when he sees man as an information processor, thinker and creator. He emphasises rationality and dignity as characteristics of man on which learning should focus.

Problem solving should therefore figure prominently in the pastoral programme. Echoes of Bruner's approach can be found in the work of Natale (1972) who shows that training in critical thinking is an effective way of promoting insights and empathy. In an appendix, he cites the work of Raths (1966) and others, from which four areas of teacher skill which seem necessary for fostering positive critical thought are identified:

1 Creating the climate which facilitates valuing and thinking.
2 Using techniques which evoke evaluation and inviting pupils to think within a climate of safety, i.e. acceptance.
3 To be sensitive to such thinking and valuing as does occur.
4 Helping to clarify thought by asking questions which encourage exploration without any implication that the teacher has a right or desired answer in mind for which the pupil should search.

Problem solving is fostered when teachers take this stance, encouraging pupils to talk thoroughly about every stage in the process and developing awareness of key skills. Almost inevitably, discussions of problem-solving rely on Dewey's (1910) analysis. I can find no better framework for elaboration of problem-solving as part of pastoral care, and offer no apology for using it.

In daily life a problem may only be recognised slowly. It emerges out of vague doubts, perplexity, frustration and an elusive aware-ness of difficulty; gradually its relation to one's purposes is seen, and possibly its significance as a challenge to cherished aspects of self. This aspect is obvious in the situations listed on pages 23–24 and 29–30 as a focus for tutorial work. The skills outlined by Natale should be employed at each stage.

In the first stage, critical thinking is focused on raising questions about the nature and accuracy of definition of the problem. (Counselling techniques stress that the client's perception of the problem may be clouded by emotions and unquestioned assumptions.) Pupils have to acquire the habit of asking if the problem is *really* that which was originally defined. Attention given to apprehension of the dimensions of the problem, ventilation of misgivings, or questioning of assumptions, is rarely wasted time, for we have an unhelpful tendency to concentrate on our immediate frustrations.

Next comes concentration on the problem as revealed and the development of hypotheses about its resolution. The latter is seldom as straightforward as we would wish. Other people's expectations about how we ought to react can acquire a compulsive character, interacting unhelpfully with our own impulses to create tension. Pressures creating vulnerability or feelings of inferiority make us grasp at the first apparently practicable solution, and this leads to later disillusionment. Insecurity and frustration can lead to animism, i.e. endowing inanimate objects with will and other attributes associated with sentient beings, e.g. 'the damned door won't open'; they also encourage reliance upon false assumptions. We must be alert to the possibility that initial hypotheses can be determined illogically by past experience, personality, or culturally derived beliefs about what the nature of the problem ought to be. Application of critical thinking skills stimulates a process of step-by-step clarification in which the formulation, testing and rejection of hypotheses leads to an eventual proposal for a realistic solution. The skill of the tutor is crucial: she or he must be sensitive to the possibility that some pupils have been conditioned by home and school into a rigid belief that only one right answer exists; others will need reassurance that they can properly harbour, consider and value highly subjective ideas.

Ausubel (1968) argues that the ability to verbalise a solution refines insights, and probably allows greater transferability to other situations. It is crucial that pupils' proposed solutions are followed by their own critical activity in which they discuss where a particular type of solution is likely to work and where not. Tutors have to instigate this guided discussion if activities are not to be reduced to a mechanical level. The tutor's task is to support a more active and vigorous search for a solution to the problems produced by pupils as well as those given as part of the programme; to encourage questioning of feelings and assumptions; to induce attitudes towards reasoning that are positive and not contaminated by fatalism, and to boost realistic self-confidence in the pupil's ability as a problem solver.

What does all this mean for the pastoral programme? The emphasis on activity and experience clearly does not do away with the importance of substantive knowledge – this can never be eliminated. Next, the majority of writers, e.g. Ausubel (1968), Gagné (1977), Galloway (1976), Laycock and Munro (1972) and Mueller (1975) more or less explicitly argue caution in assuming that automatic or global transfer of training is possible. But an alertness to possibilities and a questioning attitude can be fostered. The active use of knowledge provided by the tutor, plus the guided discovery produced by problem solving experience, will link the pastoral programme to the curricular development of later years. Feedback from tutors is vital, but it should not be a deadening imposition of the tutors' views. Instead, it should be the type of questioning that invokes examination and justification, as Natale suggests. The stages of recognition of the problem, search for hypotheses and formulation of potential solutions, should all be subjected to this analytical and verificatory process.

Experiential approaches have the merit of incorporating the expectation that all pupils are able to learn and to achieve success on concrete tasks. They also help us change the interaction within a class or between classes. One way, particularly appropriate to the pastoral system, is that of putting pupils into helping roles with one another. Some versions of mastery learning incorporate the use of a proctor: a student who has completed the task and who then tutors those finding difficulty. Vertical tutor groups offer obvious opportunities for this, but in year-based systems we could sometimes use pupils from the year above as helpers or coaches. Fifth-year pupils are often aware of the deficiencies in subject choice – a regrettable state of affairs, but one which would allow them to be effective helpers with the third-year programme. Over 12 years ago I witnessed with pleasure fifth-year girls explaining in an honest, positive way, the less obvious facts about commerce as a subject, including the function of an economics project which was a bone of contention for some girls.

The pastoral programme should not only deliberately elicit helping behaviour, it should also take aboard the developmental facts of impaired or retarded decision-making and problem-solving skills. Different rates of development are highly visible in physical matters, but they can escape our vigilance in cognitive and emotional areas. Personality maladjustment and emotional problems push certain individuals towards making unrealistic or self-punitive decisions or attempts to 'solve' problems hopefully, on the basis of wish fulfilment. Those whose rate of development is slower cling to factors such as the desire to outwit or evade authority when the majority of their peers have realised that this is futile. If there is a uniform programme, does this mean we attempt to push all pupils through it in the same way, and at a standard rate of progress? I believe there can be a place for pastoral programmes in which some version of the old Dalton Plan is used: perhaps a set of tasks forming a 'month's work' which is negotiated with a small group, and which they tackle in their own way, evaluating their degree of competency before proceeding further. Such adjustment in the nature of tasks, the time available and the element of responsibility alleviates the stress (perhaps stigma) for some pupils of feeling they could not cope, and for others the boredom of marking time. A resource bank of activities is necessary, requiring a high degree of practical management by head of year or house, but the significance of the tutor is increased.

Most of our experiential learning will be indirect – films, games, simulation and role play – in the earlier years of the pastoral programme. Role play causes concern to many tutors, although it is a powerful and motivating form of learning. The drama specialist in particular, and the English department more generally, should be involved in monitoring the use of role play. For those interested, the most useful and interesting guide I have found is provided by Ments (1983). Role play can be daunting for both tutor and pupils: therefore sensitivity and support are crucial. As described by Ments it fits well into a problem-solving methodology, and allows one to take an objective approach. Precision in specifying objectives is necessary because the technique has so many potential uses: it can be used to apply or examine facts; to create awareness of the parameters of a topic; to apply the skills of discrimination, standpoint-taking or problem-solving; to examine the likely consequences of a course of action; or to reveal ambiguities. Tutors can use role play as a way of introducing a theme, as a way of highlighting an investigation or small project, e.g. a third-year project on work in the neighbourhood, or as a follow-up. The point at which it is used, the purpose, and the amount, can only be decided by those on the spot. No prescriptions are possible.

Some facts do emerge from those experienced in the use of the technique. Watkins (1981) stresses the need to stimulate ideas by 'warming up' activities and carefully devised post-play reflection. A graduated introduction with built-in signposts for action for the role players will be probably necessary, e.g. a tape presents a problem situation which ends with suggestions about lines of action, their likely costs and advantages. Such material need not be dull, it can be presented in a compelling, thought-provoking way. Small groups should evaluate the possibilities for themselves, only trying out the roles after anticipatory discussion. Graduation will also be concerned with time and complexity. The time initially allowed should be brief, gradually increasing as pupils gain in confidence. The number of players is important: initial emphasis could sensibly be on partner work, before small group exploration of the topic is attempted. This helps ensure that pupils have developed their ideas and can contribute to the role play. The old principle of moving from the familiar to the less well known should also be employed. Such techniques as Life Space Plays (Hamblin, 1974) can be employed. The structure is supportive, but there is room for imagination, while the experience of co-operative planning is as valuable as the play. Strategies exist for coping with situations where the role play may be judged risky or threatening. The players may distance themselves from the topic by interviewing each other in turn about it, or by partner discussion.

Let us return to helping relationships. Observers could be appointed who are charged with helpfully evaluating what happened in the role play, thereby deepening the cohesion of the group. If it is a decision-making role play then observers could assess the realism, likely costs, level of risk or sources of influence, discussing this helpfully with the small group. The contrasts between the observer's perceptions and the participants' beliefs about what they were doing can be intellectually stimulating and raise questions for whole group discussion. Another device is initial 'brainstorming' by the tutor group, where information and ideas are collected without comment. The small groups submit these ideas to critical scrutiny using what they consider relevant in their role play.

Little things matter! Good activities in role play can be marred by two things. First, the names allocated to characters often have a facetious quality which invites caricature, or they are described pejoratively or moralistically, in a way that reflects the writer's evaluations rather than describing the behaviour of the character. Second, great care should be exercised in allocating roles as cowards, sneaks or bullies; this initiates reverberations which help no one.

Overt intent and apparently precise positive statements of learning objectives may conceal unrecognised and less reputable processes. Glandon (1978), cited in Ments, pinpoints three areas of unintentional learning which are sometimes present in simulations: those where the authority of the teacher is strengthened without this being made explicit; the incorporation, into what are apparently objective role descriptions, of widespread evaluatory attitudes towards role behaviour, i.e. an endorsement of unthinking social desirability; and finally, approval, reward and reinforcement of manipulative behaviour based on 'playing the system'.

Stress and insecurity insidiously encourage us to resort to somewhat devious strategies. Hargreaves (1979) analyses such processes at work in the classroom control of pupils or in bolstering the position of the teacher. But do we see the possibility that the use of role play could be contaminated similarly? Ments points out that allocation of roles can be a subtle form of stereotyping. I have noticed curious discrepancies, in the past, between concern and action. Pupils have been described as 'feminine' with clear implications of undesirability in all-boys schools, but they were very likely to be allocated the female parts in the school play! Bias and stereotyping in role description and allocation can only be prevented by constant vigilance. Pupils must be alerted to the likelihood that they themselves manifest bias. Initial discussion can sensitise them to this, and post-play evaluation will draw out the consequences. Another useful ploy is the occasional application of a questionnaire or simple attitude scale. Both can crystallise illformed opinions or create them, therefore vigilance is demanded of the tutor, but the intent is to induce examination of gender prejudice or to undermine complacent assumptions about roles, especially within the family or at work! The basic technique of role reversal is sometimes under-used. Particularly in pairs situations, pupils should immediately play the opposing or other role, so that they can appreciate both view points.

I have stressed (Hamblin 1983; 1984) the desirability of involving pupils as peer judges of activities and decisions. Pupils attached to the small activities groups can be charged with describing the feelings and attitudes they believe they have detected in the role players. A gradual introduction is necessary, and tutor support essential, for the observer can feel threatened by or alienated from those he observes. Where schools have built on primary school methods there is less difficulty. Again, it is stimulating to sometimes bring in observers from the year above, remembering that although we wish to develop the cohesion of the tutor group, strengthening its identity positively, there is a need to initiate and develop stimulating transactions between it and other groups.

Ments' discussion properly stresses that debriefing or post-play discussion is an indispensable element. Why? Reflection can be brought to bear on the experience: beliefs can be modified by new insights; the contribution of feelings and investment in established positions understood; and connections made between what pupils know about the situation and what they actually need to know if they are to make balanced judgements. Insufficient time for discussion reduces the value of role play as surely as lack of structure. Both go together in practice, for shortage of time pushes the tutor into a doctrinaire position which makes the earlier experience less significant than it could be. Application and the final sharpening of learning are also lost. It may be best to avoid tutor activities requiring role play in these conditions.

The content of the pastoral programme

Interaction between the developmental stages of the adolescent and the legitimate demands of peers, home and school provides a framework for development of a pastoral programme. Topics focusing on adolescent development include those associated with physical and social puberty, e.g. physical growth and its psychological correlate, body image. It is all too easy to forget the profound dissatisfaction that many young people feel about their bodies, although we recognise extreme cases such as the grossly obese or those suffering from anorexia nervosa. Peer pressures and the struggle to maintain a sense of individuality, or over-reliance upon social approval are among the 'legitimate demands' which should be considered.

Current tendencies in curriculum development in the later years of the secondary school are reflected in the use of modules. Rather than a complete programme, short modules may be more appropriate. They offer the tutor greater opportunity for exercising his judgements about the selection of materials; give greater opportunity for feedback and subsequent modification; and, perhaps most valuably, allow tutor involvement because they provide a point of departure on which the tutor can build. There are many headings under which modules can be developed. The following is just one illustration.

Modules for a pastoral programme

1 The self as a learner.
2 Self-management and self-appraisal.
3 Moral development, social responsibility and identity through self-awareness.
4 Vocational development and industrial change in an age of economic uncertainty.

The self as a learner

Why is this major element in the output of the secondary school so neglected in guidance? The concept of the self as a learner goes beyond what is sometimes offered in study skills programmes. Marton *et al* (1984) highlighted the way students adapt to demands, showing how in higher education they transform the task into something superficial in order to meet the demands for answers to factual questions. They found that some students focus on the content of the text or passage as what has to be learned, whilst others treat it as a means through which they attempt to comprehend the underlying meaning so that they emerge with an enlarged or new conception of the topic. Thus in the tradition of construct theory (Kelly, 1955), learning in the deeper sense is a matter of allowing the topic to assume personal significance through a process of interpretation. Learning then involves the attempt to validate and extend these personal meanings by communicating them to others; hence my emphasis (Hamblin, 1981) on the style of learning and processing methods, especially for the sixth-form student.

Some approaches to study skills incorporated into pastoral programmes avoid the dynamic factors associated with motivation. Pupils are left unaware of the way in which their self-subverting beliefs about the nature of ability and undue vulnerability to pressures contribute to failure or underfunctioning – and thus they are not helped. I have sometimes felt that there are tutors who believe they are teaching study skills by giving advice or telling pupils how to learn. Yet a skill surely is a *practised* ability or facility in doing something. Thus, by definition, controlled practices are required which are then transferred, knowingly and with motivation, to a particular context.

More attention could be paid to Marland's (1981) contention that more is needed than learning in context alone: the didactic and contextual are both necessary. Practice should be followed by discussion structured to encourage wider application and aimed also at stimulating constructive awareness of learning strategies as part of building a unique learning style which is productive for each pupil.

Assumptions based on gender have to be debated: for example, beliefs about the probability of success in certain subjects for males/females, or about the advisability (even propriety) of male and female involvement in certain areas, i.e. midwifery for men or dirty and heavy occupations for women. Discussion could then move to less extreme examples of work and learning. Proper indignation at the imposition of constraining and trivialised identities on women may hide the fact that males are equally likely to be victims of such processes. Harding (1983) suggests girls are likely to reject science automatically whilst boys equally unthinkingly accept it. Prejudiced thinkers of both sexes avoid doubt and ambiguity by closing on problems immediately, refusing to admit further evidence into their considerations. Such foreclosure is not confined to theoretical problems: it is at work in vital life decisions. Pastoral programmes incorporate stereotyped assumptions about the sexes – a relatively easy matter to correct. More penetratingly, tutors must ask themselves if, despite open-minded contention in pastoral activities, they continue to communicate rigid expectations of both sexes through their behaviour. Marland (1983) cites Stanworth (1983) who remarked on the many pervasive and elusive ways in which classroom interaction activates and reinforces sex stereotyping. Quite so, but it is as strong in the alleged caring process we call pastoral care. The medium *is* the message all too often in pastoral work: as shown in Chapter 1 we need to question our actions, for they contradict our statements.

Even in the fourth year when important examinations should be close enough to create a sense of urgency, pupils still display apathy or exhibit attitudes which allow them to cope with tension in the short run but which have costly long-term consequences. Energy is invested in maintaining their position defensively, although when gently questioned in an accepting, safe atmosphere they admit they are engaged in the old occupation of cutting off their noses to spite their faces and they are partially aware of the folly of evading challenge. To such pupils, learning is amorphous. It is categorised as something you either can do or cannot do: while the capacity to analyse their learning skills seems almost totally absent.

If profiles and records of personal achievement are to facilitate mastery learning and build confidence in one's competence, the skills of responsibly assessing academic or practical work and building one's own learning profile will have to be inculcated early in the secondary school. Conscientious marking by teachers is valued by the majority of pupils, but formative assessment, later to be important as a motivating force, is at least as important. A pastoral programme should help pupils evaluate their achievements as honestly as possible. It should encourage them to make realistic proposals for improvement based on a step-by-step analysis, incorporating support from friends. An important resource is lost if we do not stimulate peer support and help in resolving learning difficulties. Failure to consider this possibility could be tantamount to accepting the inevitability of 'us against them'.

Learning about learning encourages responsible attitudes when it includes discussion of pupils' beliefs about the relative contributions luck, effort, ability and difficulty make to success in various areas of the curriculum. Encouragement and imperatives leave distorted perceptions and crippling beliefs untouched. Pupils want to do well, but their beliefs make success unpredictable, if not a mystery, whilst failure is coped with defensively.

It is beyond the scope of this book to offer an appraisal of current work in achievement motivation. Indeed, that could be unhelpful, for much uncertainty and apparent contradiction can be found. A delusory certainty would be unethical, and I am uneasily aware of the ever-present danger of falling prey to mechanistic conceptions of achievement derived from over-simplifications of the models formulated by researchers. While the challenge of ambiguity may be stimulating, there is no doubt that humility is wise; work reported by O'Connor *et al* in Atkinson and Feather (1966) suggested that students with a strong drive for achievement benefit from the competition provided by a homogeneous ability group, whilst those low in such motivation may be more likely to thrive in heterogeneous ability groups. This is a healthy reminder that we are far from controlling the variables associated with learning. Difficulties in generalising, across cultures, sub-cultures and time show that it is fallacious to attempt to transform experimental results directly into dicta for classroom practice. But we can acquire a sensitivity to what is happening in school by pondering on the implications of research.

Achievement motivation is disconcertingly subjective as Atkinson and Feather (1966) and Weiner (1972) demonstrate. The former work directs attention to the incentive value of pupils' perceptions of the probability of success. The latter (1971; 1972) applies attribution theory, arguing, for example, that ascribing failure to lack of effort rather than to lack of ability contributes to perseverance in striving for success. A pastoral programme can usefully help pupils understand how their judgements of the chance of success in different subjects are formed; how they assess what the consequences of success or failure will be; and what all this means to them in developing a direction in life – for stagnation is repugnant to the majority of adolescents. There are disturbing indications that able girls not only doubt their capacity to achieve as well as boys in certain fields, but often passively accept this as inevitable.

It is important that we look at the topic candidly, although discussion of gender stereotypes and achievement trigger emotive reactions and a sense of threat in many of us. A number of theories, not always easily demarcated when applied to the problem, should be taken into account by those who regard the teacher as truly professional, e.g.:

1 Learned helplessness (Garber and Seligman, 1980).
2 Locus of causality and the relative balance of external or internal control (Rotter *et al*, 1972; Phares, 1976).
3 Predictions, expectations and comparisons (Kelly, 1955; Rosenthal and Jacobson, 1968; Brophy and Good, 1974; Pidgeon, 1970).

Heads of year or house should realise that adherence to one theoretical formulation is cramping. From a position rooted in awareness of sound theories they can assist tutors to debate these issues with their forms, creating a propositional climate in which pupils are encouraged to explore the different facets of achievement, failure and learning. Rejection of what the school offers is irrationally or impulsively adopted by the pupil; discussion in a climate of warmth and acceptance may help some pupils perceive the erroneous hit or miss nature of their reactions. It is a good educational principle to insist that if pupils *do* reject school they should do so on rational grounds! But it is better still to help them affiliate.

Pastoral programmes are fundamentally interested in identity and the processes through which it is constructed and, sometimes, manipulated. Left to themselves, some pupils invest energy in strengthening identities which incorporate rejection of school values and activities. Measor and Woods (1985) show how quickly such tendencies are activated after the initial honeymoon period which occurs at transfer to the secondary school. It may be too simple to dismiss such pupils as unmotivated. Motives are seen as providing energy for behaviour, but they also set directions. A fairly large group of pupils are motivated to avoid the extreme positions of the 'thickie' or 'swot'. They then find themselves balancing the demands of their peers and adults. They become adept in the tactics of staving off trouble in the short run: taking the line of least resistance; indulging in 'tit for tat' behaviour; and running their lives on the basis of expediency. They emerge from school with this minimal survival kit, but its value in a technological and rapidly changing era is questionable.

Such shallow forms of behaviour embody indirect and passive aggression. They are part of the hidden curriculum we neglect; yet they should be challenged vigorously. This is no vindication for the teacher's use of authority in a capricious or politic way; it is a plea for helping pupils comprehend the forces which impinge on them and critically assess their pretexts for behaving in the ways just described. Undoubtedly, one would have to work through the unsettling effects of bringing such issues out into the open, but a competent tutor should know how to calm his group, ensuring that the next teacher does not meet a class which has to be quelled. It is, however, just as likely that they will be more receptive and co-operative, meeting the teacher at least halfway.

Economic uncertainty and technological development of an unprecedented pace generate the feeling that one is a hapless victim of a veritable maelstrom of events. In discussion with the young unemployed, I find that this defencelessness emerges as a major problem, leaving the helper feeling inadequate! A very human reaction to change is to place heavier reliance upon chance. Responsibility is shifted, independently of objective consideration, to forces outside one's own control. Experience of what seems to be a threatening world accentuates susceptibility to irrational and simplistic explanations often incorporating elements of fatalism or near superstition. There are difficulties for those who want a pastoral programme to be significant; thinking about self-eroding experiences realistically and recognising the complexity of causation is initimidating and offers no immediate recompense. Much can be learned by adolescents if they examine the behaviour of adults under stress. They will see how many people resort to ready-made formulae to explain events, or retreat to unthinking commitment to a course of action.

At this point a *caveat* is essential. The need for consumer research must be emphasised. Nothing must be taken for granted. Pupils' reliance upon luck to explain their life events will vary enormously and may be partially dependent upon what has been inculcated at home. In practice, pupils also refer to ability, effort and motivation in a socially desirable way, which brings the approval of the teacher. Why, then, should we be concerned? The pastoral programme is developmentally orientated, and luck appears frequently and strongly in discussion of future success and predictions about life. In adolescence each of us develops a personal fable – or, more grandly, a *theory* which provides a chart for our progress in life. Through this, objective and subjective reality are put into a complex and intimate relationship with one another. We must not assume that luck will inevitably play an important part in an individual's achievement beliefs, but those beliefs do need to be examined.

Deputy heads and pastoral heads should think deeply about such issues, which underlie all pastoral effort, and particularly the development of a pastoral programme which reflects the commitment of teachers as professionals to the well-being of their charges. Let us relate the discussion of luck to responsibility in a way which hints at the demands made on those who operate a pastoral programme. Initially, the pseudo-explanation of bad luck can reduce self-blame, but time often reveals a hidden cost, in that pupils' fatalism has been bolstered unhelpfully. (I should also say that the bad luck explanation can be valid.)

As teachers we need to ask if uncertainty about the future will promote credulity or irrational fear of the unknown and occult, thus reinforcing alleged explanations of destiny to which vulnerable pupils become prey. There could be a malignant undergrowth accompanying these tendencies. Rubenowitz (1963) in his factor analysis of a Swedish version of the Californian Fascism Scale indicates the linkage of luck based statements with repressive beliefs. A pastoral programme requires sensitivity in those who construct and operate it to counter such repressive tendencies. The Protestant Ethic in its extreme or 'hard' form perniciously calls out contempt of, destructive pity for, or even suspicion of, those who fail. At the other end of the scale, dependence upon chance as a basis for interpreting and predicting the meaning of life could permanently infantilise. Fortunately, these extreme positions are rarely met, but the tendencies are responsible for much that is negative in life.

A pastoral team should begin by taking seriously enhancement of insights about these matters. Open-mindedness will allow them to see that rationality does not exclude feeling; that belief in luck does not always preclude effort; and that rejection of materialism need not entail denial of benefits flowing from new technology. The aim should be that of creating an accepting climate in which tutors and pupils battle with these vital issues, without fighting each other.

Dionysian man may be today's child, according to Musgrove (1974), who cites Bennet Berger's argument that Dionysian social roles are available in 'bohemian businesses', entertainment and small scale individual enterprises. Elements of Dionysian values may be more relevant than the educational socialisation of earlier generations would allow: to admit the possibility may cause unease and a sense of guilt. Yet there is a danger that, instead of vitality, creativity and determined use of initiative, pastoral programmes may encourage pupils to develop belief systems which stifle enterprise and dynamism, supporting the norm of low level conventional satisfactions which currently dominate the lifestyle of the unemployed in a self-eroding way. A pastoral programme which is truly educative recognises that adolescents can be trapped in the tensions between internal phantasies of omnipotence and external reminders of helplessness. Through identity through self-awareness they can break free from the traps of what Huxley (1974) called 'herd intoxication', or unthinking identity by opposition, without becoming prisoners of convention.

Gender stereotypes and equality of opportunity should be debated vigorously. Currently, and accurately, females are seen as the chief victims of such stereotyping, but males can be equally handicapped. We are beginning to give greater legitimacy to overt female expression of aggression, but is there equal acceptance of the male's manifestation of the expressive and sensitive aspects of personality? Pressures towards early crystallisation of career choice, along with familial and sub-cultural influences lead some boys to falsely define themselves as primarily practical, mechanical and scientific, when it would be better to keep their options open. For both sexes, the pastoral programme stimulates the capacity to take the standpoints of others. Girls often seem to have a greater facility for this, but there can be heavy costs. Kramer (1982) comments on the way unemployed girls strive to maintain their male peers in positions of unwarranted dominance. Both sexes have limited repertoires of perceiving and evaluating sex role behaviour or situations, although it seems that boys hold more limited and derogatory views of women than girls of men.

Marland *et al* (1983) helpfully call attention to the pervasiveness of the processes at work. The FEU (1985) comments in discussion of recent developments that gender stereotyping will not go away easily. An apparent move towards equality of opportunity may conceal biased course content and material. Taking mixed groups in the crafts does not automatically redress the balance as regards the deprivation of experience that girls bring into these courses. There will be little point in confining exploration of the topic to the pastoral programme: courses may still encourage girls to take up passive roles and expect boys to be initiators; while there may be a paucity of same-sex models for girls in science and technical subjects within the school. Some schools have used an employment coach to help pupils understand life at work but we may have ignored the need to use pupils who have successfully overcome sexual stereotypes as mentors for others. Social Europe (1985) argues that new problems of identity, mobility and social uncertainty are being ignored in training schemes. The need for men to share traditional tasks with women, or take them over altogether, so freeing women for work, is a challenge a pastoral programme cannot ignore.

Sexual biases permeate interaction within the school: not only are they difficult to detect, but those maintaining them are unaware of what they are doing. Women are as guilty as men, although the sexually biased assumptions held by men are more deeply entrenched and harder to uproot. Marland (1983) critically looks at the traditional association of women with pastoral care in the school. But this is a more acceptable version of derogatory assumptions which have to be tackled in a pastoral programme. Can we justify the statement that motherhood represents the fulfilment of women? Is fatherhood then the crown of masculinity? Is there inevitable tension between a career and caring for children? Some women are competent and creative in their work roles and as mothers. Many permutations exist, but they are a product of personality, situations and cultural expectations. Women have escaped from compulsive domesticity. A mother pushed back into it may be bored and frustrated, with disturbing consequences for her children. Men still cling to the assumption that women are passive sexually but also wish to attract men, despite the evidence against this. This is one detestable example of the way in which male exaggeration of their status is maintained, but an unnecessary dependency and delusory inferiority in females is frequently reinforced in encounters within the school.

Girls and boys with high needs for affiliation, who are consequently sensitive to disapproval, suffer if sexual stereotypes are applied unthinkingly by peers and adults. Boys feel they have to adopt a 'macho' stance, finding themselves devalued if they cannot maintain the standard stiff upper lip. Tears are not permissible, therefore a façade of toughness or emotional flatness is established. Yet as many sixth-formers have pointed out to me, the fear of this front being breached is never far away.

Boys receive more attention in class, largely because they pose more potential control problems. Classroom interaction, teaching methods and materials are biased towards boys, therefore they feel more important. Other factors strengthen the differences, e.g. examinations test performance and not potential, yet as Harding (1983) argues, this distinction is ignored when girls do badly in science examinations. The upshot is that girls are more likely to learn that the causes of failure are beyond their control, which encourages them to predict that change is impossible. This opting out is facilitated by the failure of illustrations and texts to reflect the concerns of girls and validate their place in the sciences, crafts and other male dominated fields.

A pastoral programme attacks these tendencies, beginning with entry to the school. Beliefs about the kind of person who succeeds in a subject; the ethics of science; questioning of beliefs about gender-related competencies; understanding classroom climates and looking at alleged helplessness should all be part of the induction programme. To ignore the attitudinal and emotional aspects of learning is to put oneself into collusion with incipient underfunctioning. In the second year, help should be given with feelings of frustration attached to sex role expectations, before these feelings affect motivation in other areas. Modification of peer group interaction is crucial if there is to be improvement.

Attention should be drawn to unthinking acceptance of signals about deviation from peer group definitions of masculinity and femininity: Has the group the right to impose an identity on one member? How can pressures be dealt with and labels refuted? We fail to protect pupils against moral and emotional blackmail which imposes a false identity when we ignore such issues. Third-year subject choice offers an opportunity – often neglected – for intensive education on the topic. Discussion could focus on false beliefs about the nature of subjects; the demands they make; and critical examination of the links, pupils (*and* those on whom they model themselves) see as existing between gender and competence. The TES (9.8.85) gives a brief account of fourth-year sexism in which the most acceptable description of a woman is 'an object of ridicule'. If the looking glass held up by boys to girls reflects such distorted images, it is imperative that we resolutely deal with this gross prejudice which must influence girls' self-perceptions. We must question the immaturity and defensiveness of such expressions by boys, recognising the possibility that the outer expression may not be the whole reality. But even a thorough attempt at attitude change flounders if teachers' classroom behaviour unwittingly supports discrimination.

Perceptions of women as necessarily poor decision-makers hide the reality that in many families the mother makes all the important decisions. Frequently the males abdicate responsibility, although the father may have a ceremonial function of endorsing the intended action. Tacit collusion between the sexes was seen in the tendency of some 15-year-old girls with whom I worked to see women negatively in work roles. They saw men as the breadwinners but the women's work role as subordinate to their home interests. They automatically assumed that women's attendance at work would be erratic because of home commitments, and rejected the possibility of the man staying at home whilst the woman went out to work, as vehemently as the boys. Girls occasionally cited instances where this was happening, but made it clear that they saw it as an unfortunate aberration. Similar results were found in a study of a sample of 250 students in nine comprehensive schools, undertaken by the writer and his students. Part of this study is reported in

Hamblin (1981). Sixth-form pupils were ready to take more flexible approaches to the balance between male and female career aspirations.

Self-management in a social context

Over-simplified notions of stress and storm as inevitably character-istic of adolescence have been discarded by counsellors. Realistic recognition that adolescence is a time for pleasure in the body, and often a period of unparalled grace, at least as much as it is occupied with anguished wrestling with feelings of bodily inadequacy has restored the balance. In pastoral care many heads of year or house are alert to the possibility that theories can be reduced to common-places which give a distorted picture of the reality. Erikson's (1968) concept of identity crisis has sometimes being misused in this way: it is reprehensible to ignore the danger of pupils deriving identity from opposition because we do not support them, but it is even worse to gloss over the possibility of constructive change, or even suppress it, by not providing the tools for effective self-management.

Self-management in a social context has to be the object of deliberation and consumer research. There will be a special combination of needs in each school or catchment area. As illustration (without suggesting that this is the total reality) it is possible to postulate that pupils from the stockbroker belt, whose parents are socially adept and hold high aspirations for their children, meet demands for social competence and are pressured towards a pseudo-maturity. Those coming from allegedly disadvantaged areas, where physical aggression is valued and the need is to function success-fully in a climate of 'trouble', have a different set of needs. The illustration is superficial, but it is sufficient to underline the need for assessment rather than the blind imposition of allegedly realistic content. It provides a healthy reminder that it is the responsibility of the mature to adapt to the needs of the immature.

Escalation of demands and the need to meet them in unfamiliar contexts, however, mean that frustration, embarrassment and loss of face are ever present risks. Kline and Cooper (1985) argue that, on the basis of generally acceptable tests, rigid thinking is not related to rigid personality. They also state that this means flexible and creative thinking can be fostered in all pupils independently of personality: a state of affairs which should be welcomed by pastoral heads.

The first step is to highlight factors which impinge on pupils to constrain and limit their responses to tension and their methods of self-management. There is the pupil's tendency to compare himself or herself with others, including close friends and family members, coupled with strong reactions when someone else compares him or her unfavourably. The former seems to be an attempt at validation; the latter is sometimes interpreted as denial of individuality or erosion of confidence, reminding us that the same processes are allocated very different meanings on the basis of the intent imputed to those who use them. Keeping face has obvious links with sensitivity to praise or blame; the possession of strategies for coping constructively with a social gaffe; and, vitally, examination of the attitudes and values of the group which provides models for emulation, and from whom deviation is threatening. Judgements of others bring questions about immediate responses to differences in social background, race or age, and the way these initial assessments influence our predictions about other people's behaviour. Fourth- and fifth-year pupils confess that they are aware of their tendency to pre-categorise groups such as the police, old age pensioners and businessmen negatively and without real evidence, yet they feel unable to change this tendency, although many want to.

Conflict, competition and co-operation preoccupy some; for some a major growth point may be recognition that ubiquitous 'putting down' of others is due to insecurity. Compulsion to compete may assume more salience than the achievement, sadly turning the pupils' life space into an emotional desert. Striving for success is praiseworthy, but if it is achieved almost solely through the humiliation of others, or by pleasure in their discomfiture, then intervention through the pastoral programme is necessary. Co-operation and competition, when relieved of their emotional trappings, seem to be ethically neutral. It is the use to which the activities are put which is developmentally important. The pastoral programme, however, explores the negative possibility, that competition creates a view of a hostile world which diminishes zest for life. Tensions between parental, school and peer demands and standards are of prime importance to self-management and responsible autonomy. Individuals may see conflict between the demands of school and peers which is not there in reality. Indeed, some pupils manipulate such unnecessary stresses for their own purposes. It is possible to be successful in one's peer group *and* at schoolwork;

enjoyment may stem from both areas, often in mutually reinforcing ways.

Self-management implies understanding and overcoming the threats to individuality inherent in the questions:

1 Does the group have the right to impose an identity on me?
2 Because I find a group attractive, do I have to do everything its members do?
3 What are the limits to membership of a group? When do other commitments become more important?

Understanding why one is rejected, seen as deviant or given a leadership role, is a protection against the blind trust or education for obedience which Milgram's (1974) work describes.

The objectives of the self-management element of the pastoral programme can be condensed to:

1 Suspension of immediate reactions and judgements.
2 Insertion of thought between the impulse to react and the behaviour.
3 Development of the desire and ability to see a situation from the other person's viewpoint.

Self-appraisal and self-management are facilitated by giving pupils opportunity for discussion of group dynamics. Pupils should look at their behaviour in different groups. It may be erroneous to conclude that they behave similarly in all the groups to which they belong; the old statement, 'a devil at home and an angel in school', or the reverse, illustrates the point that people assume different roles, and attract different expectations in the various groups to which they belong.

The initial step could be that of identifying what they gain from a group. Does membership provide status, security or reinforce a particular self-image? A logical move is then to examine how they get what they want from the group. This leads to discussion of bargaining; acquisition and loss of leadership positions; methods of marshalling support for oneself; and the rewards offered by the individual to others. Preferences for certain roles and the unwilling occupation of others merit evaluation. Pupils may wryly comment on the discovery that they seem to have the capacity for pouring oil on troubled waters, but if they try to initiate action, then they are ignored. They may have to face the fact that they are in danger of occupying a scapegoat role, or realise that others are beginning to expect them to be the resident cynic who devalues the aspirations and actions of others. Analysis of beliefs about the ideal member also invites exploration of the models emulated by the pupil and the needs they satisfy. This provides a deeper understanding of the nature of interpersonal attraction.

The question, 'Can I change the group?' evokes consideration of persuasive communication and the nature and balance of power in leader-follower roles. The possibility of a trading relationship between leaders and followers may have been excluded because of unthinking acceptance of leadership being a matter of personality. Closely associated are the issues of decision-making within the group, including the ways in which credibility is gained or lost; and the pattern of communication, e.g. assessing and establishing the significance of who tends to initiate topics, who is supported by whom, and for what ends, whose opinions are listened to, and then acted on, and whose contributions are habitually disregarded. Questions can be asked about the relationship of the group to the context in which it is set; the interaction between members of the group and others; and who seems to control the links! Profitable insights can arise from a close examination of the reactions of a new entrant, and of the characteristics which shape their acceptability or rejection. Study of the deviant from a particular group illuminates the values of members.

Our concern should be with helping pupils understand what is happening within the groups to which they belong, learn from this, and apply the understanding to new situations. Caution is essential: no outsider can make judgements about how, when, and if this should be done. I certainly do not wish to collude in any form of pastoral activity which could become psychological striptease or psychological rape! McLeish *et al* (1973) provide a clear overview of group processes, whilst Babington Smith and Farrell (1979) give helpful accounts of small group training from which many ideas can be derived for the pastoral programme and staff development.

The relationship of authority to the pastoral programme

Self-management leads us to the problem of authority in relation to a post-industrial society and the impact of long-term structural unemployment. The Victorians were sustained by evolutionary beliefs, which after assimilation into contemporary values, gave the comfortable assurance that involuntary progress was the human lot. These beliefs allowed them to nurse the illusion that what currently existed was the best there could be at that time, and that the future, equally certainly, would be better. For them, protected by trust in an irresistible benevolent movement towards a better future, there was no alternative. A caricature indeed; but caricatures contain the salient elements of a situation or person. Regression was almost incomprehensible as they contemplated society, but we have met the impact of primitive urges and seen the power of group movements which erase identity and personal responsibility. We have painfully learned to tolerate uncertainty. Religious beliefs gave a sense of purpose, providing a bulwark against anxiety that could overwhelm, and protecting people against the creeping apprehension of a potential void. Traditional guidelines have now vanished or are seen as highly questionable, making the signposts to the future difficult to decipher. Where then lies authority and who possesses the credentials to tell us what is a good life?

I meet many young people who are uneasily aware of unpredictability. Some, of course, attempt to evade anxiety by a single-minded pursuit of qualifications; the validity of the statement by Adorno *et al* (1950) that understanding of the world is an artefact of self-knowledge becomes apparent! It also has a special bite for us as teachers in relation to our ambivalent attitudes to authority. Anxiety about the assessment of competence, lack of promotion and professional rewards; fear of being found deficient in classroom control when faced by disruptive pupils; and the experience of compulsive expectations coming from colleagues and parents, may diminish our desire, or even our capacity, to tackle this topic open-mindedly. Submerged conflicts from our own adolescence may still be at work, although we quell them by applying simple-minded formulae to situations or denying them conscious consideration. These conflicts are given indirect expression in attitudes and behaviour that create barriers between us and pupils and prevent the growth of mutual respect. Perhaps the situation is worsened by our own hidden curriculum which inhibits critical examination of our reactions to authority. Congruence between what we feel and see, and what we require of pupils, is crucial if positive acceptance of authority by pupils is to occur.

Incongruence stimulates blamepinning and the creation of scape-goats; family background, headteachers and administrators all take their turn as the focus for irrational feelings about authority. Versions of 'us against them' are not the prerogative of the disadvantaged: they appear in various guises in education, e.g. resort to 'policing' forms of discipline; perceptions of pupils as possessing violent or aggressive tendencies which are unjustified when rationally examined; or allocating pupils a façade identity to which we respond, despite lack of evidence. There is an ever-present danger that some of us who find certain disciplinary and educational practices distasteful may succumb to the temptation to identify with the disadvantaged in ways more to do with our own need for self-bolstering and inner life than with sensitive appreciation of the reality of their position.

Perception of oneself as a caring person brings the temptation of denying the creative nature of authority in caring relationships. A healthy reminder comes from an unpublished study by a group of youth leaders under my direction which suggested that young people, many of whom were unemployed, had a more favourable attitude towards authority vested in the police and teachers than the investigators and their colleagues anticipated. Interestingly, a deep ambivalence manifested itself about parental exercise of authority, although there were no dramatic overtones of rebellion. The hard fact may be that our beliefs about adolescent reactions to authority may be coloured more by our pasts than by current reality. It is imperative that a pastoral programme affords many opportunities for pupils to become aware of, and explore openmindedly the complexities and contradictions inherent in the exercise of authority, rather than unintentionally allowing pupils to impose instant meaning, and ascribe intent automatically to the actions of those in authority. Once pupils adopt the latter stance, modification of their viewpoint is interpreted as a loss of face.

Difficulties about the content and operation of a pastoral pro-gramme need to be related to the larger context of the school as a social system, and to teaching as a profession which makes heavy emotional, as well as intellectual, demands on its members. Wilson (1962), in an important theoretical analysis, drew attention to the role conflict experienced by the teacher. He or she is often required to use personal warmth and establish a relationship in order to induce the desire for, or urge the child towards, achievement which can be objectively measured or compared. Contradictions exist between the socialising functions which seem to require some equivalent of a wider nurturant role and the more specialised technical role of instruction. Wilson indicates that prestige is increasingly attached to the specialised and technical: a statement which mirrors what some teachers have felt about pastoral care.

Dilemmas are inherent in the expectation that we will produce innovators to meet the needs of society, stimulating critical thought and initiative in pupils, while also inducing respect for tradition and currently accepted values. Postman and Weingarten (1971) are disposed to believe, however, that the bias of the climate in many schools is towards trusting and appreciating authority somewhat blindly rather than stimulating independent judgement. They argue that effective learners know what is relevant to their survival and resent being told what is good for them because they prefer to rely on their own judgement. I would suspect that many pastoral systems are teaching, despite counter claims, that the source of the message is more significant than the content. Teachers can facilitate responsible questioning to face the challenge of change.

New tensions are appearing as the rate of social change accelerates, whilst the palliative changes imposed on schools may not reflect the fundamental nature of economic upheaval. Arbitrary changes could create a schism between school and social reality. As a result the teacher loses authority based on consent; and is pushed towards exaggerated, yet essentially weak, forms of positional control – 'I'm your teacher.' But what is authority? Surely it is not a synonym for power, for we can claim sensibly that a person has authority, but lacks power. (This statement has made a good introduction to the theme in the fourth and fifth years.) The importance of this difference comes into focus in helping drug takers and solvent abusers. An essential step is to free them from reliance on the authority of the peer group. We help them appraise the nature of power within the peer group by encouraging questioning of the legitimacy of pressures against deviation from the peer group. They then see that the group permits only one definition of the situation to exist. Pupils usually begin to see that the authority of the peer group is no more than pressure to conform to the behaviour endorsed by the majority. The developmental aspect, which could be given appropriate shape for each year level, is whether it is necessarily more mature to prefer peers to adults as a source of authority.

There is urgent need for justifiable authority and a better understanding of it. It is naïve for people to assume that acceptance of authority necessarily connotes suppression of critical judgement.

Indeed, acceptance should be based on examination of the reasons for the existence of that authority, and careful checking of its credentials. What then causes one to believe in, or accept, a particular authority? Friedrich (1964) argues that authority is a form of hidden reasoning: one which entails evaluation of the authority as justifiable and justified and as beneficial to those subject to it, in the long run if not immediately. Authority is interpreted, therefore, as a latent rationale which connects the imposed rules and dictates to overriding values and beliefs. The underlying assumption is that compliance is rooted in acceptance of those values which provide legitimacy for the authority. But is this merely a convenient myth? Inertia could make people accept the rightness of things as they are without such considerations ever entering their heads.

As soon as we ask how clearly the predominant values are articulated in a pluralistic society, the need to debate the topic and relate it to the school as community is obvious. What is found in the larger society is also present in a school. At best, there may be a torpid acquiescence, maintained as the least line of resistance. But commitment is absent. Vague consensus offers pupils little guidance for accepting or rejecting particular forms of authority and those who claim to be authorities.

If it is a fact that a pastoral programme is an important part of the endeavour of educating open-minded, compassionate people then we have to help pupils shed their attachment to authority based on coercion – no matter whether it be reward or threat – and move towards Kohlberg's (1969) self-referring principles of conscience. This cannot exist unless some measure of self-awareness has been achieved.

Toughmindedness and courage are needed: if a pastoral programme is not to be used as a tool for encouraging unthinking obedience, searching questions about authority have to be incorporated into its content. They are as relevant for us as for our pupils. The failure to look at authority may have contributed to the perpetuation of abortive punishment in schools. It can be taken further in relation to the authority of the specialist or expert. Musgrove (1971) claimed that heads who wished to extend their power over fellow professionals could do this by abolishing the specialisms and integrating the curriculum. The authority/power distinction is clear in his argument that the authority vested in the specialist acts as a check on the power of autocratic heads. Interdisciplinary integration could bring equivalent dangers, despite valuable benefits.

'Obeying orders' has been used as a reason for inhumane actions all too frequently. The question is: Under what circumstances will people abdicate their responsibility for judging the goodness or badness of what they are told to do? Milgram's (1974) work on obedience to authority is frightening: the differences between what people believe and say they will do and what they *actually* do, under pressure from authority, are appalling. Why? Excessive reliance on the expert or legitimate authority allows one to cast the responsibility for harm on them. Ideological justifications abound which can be manipulated to allow orders to be obeyed with a good conscience. They encourage identification with the authority, negating personal accountability. Analysis of situations can be undertaken in which the twin processes of blind trust in the expert, and bolstering by specious explanation, are starkly revealed as harmful. Pastoral heads could begin by using the situations in Kohlberg (1976).

The explosion of technical knowledge could encourage unthinking trust in the expert. A pastoral programme should inculcate the skill of asking responsible, critical questions which require the expert to justify his position as an authority and his right to make decisions about the conduct of others. This is not advocation of blind distrust of experts. Not only are they inevitable features of a technological society, but we may also need them as a safeguard against prejudiced or Machiavellian expressions of power. Fault will probably lie not with the expert but with those who, by their actions and attitudes, preserve young people's infantile dependence on limited or negative forms of authority. Handy (1984), discussing the future of work, argues that we must develop the skills, capacity for self-management and ability to seize opportunities that for too long have been the privilege of the middle-classes. I believe that part of this package is the skill of asking searching questions about the validity of authority. In 1974 I remarked that while the middle-class lifestyle has little, if any, intrinsic superiority, it has instrumental superiority as a more effective lifestyle leading to greater success and satisfaction. Balanced attitudes to authority and the capacity for mature moral judgements are ends to be pursued in a pastoral programme.

Curriculum developments now stress the negotiation of content, but are we aware that relationships must be similarly negotiated? The need is urgent: fifth-year pupils express concern about the way teacher–pupil tensions are resolved in some schools; they also feel that their maturity is denied. A pastoral programme must accord with the development of formative assessment which encourages tutor–pupil partnership and increases motivation and self-responsibility for learning. In TVEI modular learning is occurring where different age groups work together. In community schools which are implementing the concept thoroughly this includes the middle-aged and elderly. The other side of the coin is shown by Reynold's (1976) claim that many pupils see teachers as exercising illegitimate power and intervening in the lives of pupils in question-able ways. This gnaws away already marginal commitment to school. Schools must be places where authority relationships are debated or refined: this does not imply any loose permissiveness. It certainly does not support an extension of the strategy of using moral justifications to legitimate teachers' behaviour, as described by Hargreaves (1979) who concludes that this leads to control passing for teaching.

Adolescents have needs for approval, recognition, direction and structure within which they can display initiative and independence with regular opportunities for evaluating and explaining their behaviour. Pastoral workers should keep an alert eye on the possibility that the insecurity of unemployment and the threat of the unknown cause the timid or anxious to identify blindly with authority as an illusory form of security. Others take up exaggerated forms of identity by opposition, which accentuate similarities with peers who feel alienated and simultaneously inflate differences between them and adults they perceive mainly in terms of authority. They then judge such people automatically as autocratic or irrelevant. Crude assertions of power on both sides may be provoked by demands for submission. I ponder on the old saying: freedom for the cheetah is death for the gazelle; but who is the cheetah?

4 Vocational development and the pastoral programme

When the pastoral programme involves pupils over a period of time in tasks which require them to be problem-solvers and decision-makers, relationships are established between tutors and pupils and, crucially, between pupils and pupils, which strengthen their sense of belonging to a worthwhile community. Integrated into this long-term process, often eluding our consideration, is the search for meaning which is at the heart of Kelly's (1955) work. Put simply: the events each of us will face tomorrow can be given as many meanings as our wits will allow. It is to these self-created meanings that we respond, rather than to the objective facts. But some interpretations are more positive and rewarding than others. Potentially threatening occurrences such as interviews, tests, surgical operations . . . may be entirely transformed when we construe them differently. Apparently immutable circumstances may be subject to alternative constructions which change their significance. This viewpoint strikes at simplistic teaching which assumes a single meaning for an event, or emphasises the 'right' answer or response. To deny the possibilities of growth imminent in this perspective is to cut ourselves off from a source of strength as we face the unpredictability of the post-industrial society.

Responsibility can never be evaded by the individual, because it is he who interprets events. In doing this he holds the key to his future; therefore only he should dictate the meaning of those facts. Denial of this responsibility by allowing others to impose their meanings on the individual creates an uneasy sense of falsity or malaise resulting in difficulties of vocational direction and ambivalence in relationships. It is tempting to dismiss this approach as fanciful or self-indulgent; but it is down-to-earth and almost alarmingly practical. Interpretations embody predictions about the consequences associated with an event which determine the way we respond to it. In social encounters our interpretations of the intent of others, the gains or benefits for us, and the evaluations of those who witness the event, cause us to react and thus call out constructive or destructive responses from others. Far from being hapless pawns, we shape our destinies through the meaning we give to events. We fail as educators if we omit analysis of these processes from a pastoral programme. We unwittingly stifle or underestimate pupils' capacities for creative interpretations of life events. Or, equally regrettably, we fail to see, as Armstrong *et al* (1981) illustrate, the way in which the struggle against persecutory anxieties travels with the person into work, permeating his relationships with others, making him suspicious and provocative.

A limited interpretation of the nature of the move towards a post-industrial society could encourage us to jettison the work of Ginzberg (1951; 1971), Super (1953; 1957), Tyler (1969) and other researchers into vocational development. Anxious focus on 'Getting a job is what matters!' could distract attention from pupils' personalities and individual differences, including different rates of maturation, in a way which undoes the good we wish to do. Roberts (1984) points out that unemployment does not mean that work is finite; similarly Handy (1984) argues that work is essential to full humanity, but that does not mean it has to be set within the context of a traditional job. Work is separable from traditional employment, in which it is a commodity sold for the best possible price. I claim that the pastoral programme should draw on vocational development, which can be applied validly to any work which gives a sense of direction and purpose to the individual, reinforces his values and lifestyle, and maintains self-respect through voluntary exchange relationships with society. Alienation cannot flourish where responsible inter-dependence is the norm. More than this, vocational development motivates individuals to develop self-reliance and flexible entrepreneurial skills; it promotes their capacity for scanning their life spaces positively and interpreting challenges more creatively.

Change cannot be denied. A job no longer suffices as the main measure of status, identity or purpose in life. But tensions abound: if, as Watts (1983) argues, unemployment is repudiated by pupils, are we in danger of attempting to condition them into acquiescing with a negative identity? Hamblin (1983) refers to the fact that fifth-form pupils feel that unemployment brings experience of devaluation and becoming objects of blame; it means lack of credible identity which impedes social interaction. No easy solution can be found in providing extended education for, as Watts argues, many pupils would not welcome it.

A pastoral team has to adopt the attitudes of TVEI and CPVE where careers education is interpreted widely. We should welcome the fact that we are, as Roberts (1984) argues, moving away from providing qualifications which employers can use as a screening tool, but which give no direct evidence of their holder's competence as a worker. We should be clear, however, that the types and nature of working roles will be subject to constant change. It is equally clear that a retreat to preparation for leisure is just that: a retreat from reality; for technology does not obviate the need for work. But there can be no assumption that increased production necessarily implies more jobs within that firm or industry. In common with other writers, Handy (1984) anticipates enlargement of the service industries, which tend not to be capital intensive, but personal, moderately skilled and open to both sexes. The challenge for the pastoral team lies in equipping pupils to cope with the move from the life-long security preferred by some professions and large organisations, to relative insecurity and lack of protection. Some might say that the less able or disadvantaged do this already, but my rejoinder would be, 'At what costs to themselves?' Their adaptations may be unnecessarily constraining, defensive and self-defeating. Speculation is rife, but it may be helpful to consider the possibilities below:

1 A shorter working life, involving later entry and earlier retirement. The former may be easier to achieve financially, but the latter presents grave developmental and social problems.

2 More fixed-term and flexible time contracts, accompanied by portable pension schemes.

3 The development of a number of forms of job-sharing; i.e. the growth of part-time jobs.

4 A growth of current versions of local enterprise trusts which offer advice and possibly finance, while encouraging individuals to enter national, as well as local, markets.

5 A greater use of the home as workplace, utilising improved communication technology. This will reflect a growth of information services.

6 Extension of distance learning which is undertaken at home or in small local groups. Schools and colleges could then be freed

to develop learning packages which stimulate problem-solving and initiative.

7 Fees replacing salaries and the growth of sub-contracting as a consequence of the dispersal of the organisation. Handy (1984), in his helpful analysis, highlights the issues when he talks of the choice between trains and terminals, i.e. between computers and locations outside cities and traditional concentration of the organisation in the city.

For us, the question is whether we can free ourselves from our pasts and fixed beliefs about the nature of work and employment. Our dependence upon organisations and traditional work structures may block us from providing pupils with the modes of perception and thought which will ensure, not merely their survival, but that they experience success in a world where frames of reference are no longer provided by the past. The dispersed organisations mentioned above bring new problems of communication. Failure to develop the necessary skills of analysis and reporting will cause confusions to spiral into profound misunderstandings. Federal organisations may be commonplace in which the component units surrender significant rights to the centre to benefit from economies of scale. Managers of such developments, and those with subsidiary posts, will require high levels of skill in negotiation and planning. Part of the foundation for this should be within a pastoral programme where there is genuine debate between tutors and pupils leading to understanding of the processes mentioned here and in the preceding chapter.

Roberts (1984) wisely draws attention to the danger of encouraging pupils to take *any* job. Personal standards and self-esteem can be eroded by taking a job at variance with the young person's fundamental beliefs about herself or himself. Contradictions in our reactions reveal themselves to the keen eye: intellectually, we subscribe to the idea that a limited opportunity structure is fundamental to the problem; in practice, when dealing with a young person, anxiety or the desire to be of help push us towards behaving in ways which suggest that personal shortcomings are inevitably responsible for his or her dilemma.

Discrepancies abound: Ginzberg (1979) claims that an inappropriately and insufficiently educated labour force is at the heart of Great Britain's problems; but Roberts comments on the fact that pupils are currently offered financial incentives to terminate education. Emphasis on training and alleged generic vocational skills ignores the fact that people have to be motivated to attempt to transfer skills as well as be aware of their nature. The relevance of low level skills of manual dexterity, computation and speech should not be dismissed, but the future seems to demand higher levels of technical and intellectual achievement. Current training opportunities may be tied more to beliefs about the industrial past, than to the reality. Values and attitudes relevant to the last century now reinforce disadvantage and inadequacy because their possessors are incapable of interpreting the changes that surround them. At best, such courses are an annexe to reality, offering a brief respite from the task of adapting to new demands. Such backward-looking guidance and training offers deceptive comfort when the real need is for the tensions associated with initiative, independence and determined pursuit of knowledge.

Vocational development

Careers education, when interpreted strictly, is an ambiguous and misleading term. Rational planning, considered investment in qualifications and expectations of step-by-step advancement on a ladder known to the careerist, accompanied by intrinsic satisfaction derived from the job, are phenomena relevant to middle-class or able pupils. The idea that jobs hold meaningful satisfaction is laughable to many pupils who know that like their parent, they will find their jobs boring, if not degrading. Fathers socialise their children into seeing employment as involving frustration and exploitation, which is countered by evasive and outwitting tactics. Their tolerance in the face of careers education which contravenes their knowledge of reality is amazing.

The idea of work as separable from a job is not new. For many people their most vital and significant work is undertaken outside their job. Good careers teachers and officers have always recognised that the context and peripheral elements of a job could be crucial, stimulating – through the search for a satisfying lifestyle – pupils' ability to formulate searching questions, activating them to find their own answers rather than being the passive recipients of our non-wisdom.

The task remains unaltered: our prime concern is the growth of personal competence rather than automatic adaptation to the needs of the labour market. A one-sided impression could be received by the reader. In practice, the danger highlighted by Ginzberg (1971) of the futility of adding to the pupil's self-awareness without helping him probe and assess the realities of the world of work was usually recognised, and the balance maintained. Informed choice could then occur, when choice was possible. Careers education helped young people define their goals in life, rather than merely inventory their capacities.

Vocational development is one facet of adolescent development which is described in Hamblin (1984). The marked feature is the growth of new perceptions of self coupled with evaluation of others: the result sometimes being excessive and painful comparisons; but there is also the conflicting thrust for independence. Riesman (1951) outlines three major types of adjustment found in social roles, which should be debated as part of vocational development. First, there are those who are *tradition-directed*, whose transactions with life are produced by attitudes, behaviours and thought uncritically derived from parents or older people; a ready-made identity is adopted, resulting in unquestioning emulation. Second, there are the *inner-directed*, who present a picture of apparent greater autonomy: but their course is set by an internal gyroscope of values inculcated during socialisation within the family. These values become ends in themselves and behaviour concordant with them yields feelings of rightness and safety. Yet the inner-directed are captives of parental images, admittedly reflecting the parents as they have interpreted and experienced them, rather than the objective reality. It seems that the inner-directed are not only launched on their life journey in a particular direction through family socialisation, but they habitually clarify events by reference to the internalised figures. Third, and perhaps encouraged in recent years, are the *other-directed* – often over-sensitive to the evaluations and reactions of real and imagined others. Strong needs for approval of valued people and groups wear away their individuality, resulting in a labile personality or one whose stability derives from rigid adherence to group norms.

Obviously, these extreme types are unlikely to exist in reality, but they embody aspects of socialisation which impinge on individuals, and illustrate trends in adjustment. To use his talents to the full, a pupil must be helped to understand the impact that all three forces have on him.

Our task is to create the conditions in which the pupils can knowingly retain what is valuable for them, and reject, without becoming trapped into unthinking opposition, what they find distasteful; gradually sharpening the outlines of meaningful identity. Conflicts are inevitable: traditional values are challenged by changes in the economy and a bewildering kaleidoscope of values calls into question old certainties. In no area of guidance is this stronger than in the vocational.

The pastoral programme recognises that the concept of self is largely a product of social learning. Examination of this learning and its consequences facilitates vocational maturity. Adolescence brings the urge for comparisons with others as a way of validating identity. When this is coupled with the need for social support the results can be damaging: misery seeks out misery; failure reinforces failure; and the arrogant combine to devalue others. Peer interaction then consolidates destructive attitudes and maintains self-constraining behaviours. Pastoral workers have to support and not condemn; but they have to guard vigilantly against sentimentality, the tendency to trivialise adolescent realities or the urge to run away from challenge.

Our task is to provide good experience; but that good experience can be intimidating. Creating false confidence, or encouraging premature closure on vocational questions to allay anxiety are antithetic to development, which should entail experience of doubt and involve keeping an open door to possibilities. Doubt provokes tensions which tempt pupils to retreat to apparent certainties which are delusory. Yet when it is well-handled, doubt spurs students to growth, clarification of values, and eventually, balanced affirmation of self. The pastoral programme does not deny the existence of doubt and anxiety, instead it encourages adolescents to face and use them creatively. Misgiving has to be experienced before a responsible, personal commitment to a particular lifestyle is achieved. Traditional values and the quest for security meet head-on the vulnerabilities and tensions coming from the unpredictability of industrial and economic change. Denial of doubt and threat beget primitive forms of coping in which the denier attains a delusory security through rigidly splitting his world into what is good or bad, right or wrong, true or false, weak or strong, thus ignoring the complexity of change. The pastoral programme cannot collude with that retrogression.

A pastoral programme concerned with vocational development is not a substitute for the work undertaken by careers teachers and officers. Although different from careers education and guidance, it complements them by increasing identity through self-awareness.

Negotiation and co-operation are necessary if a fruitful interaction is to come into being. It is an organic development within the school: it cannot be achieved successfully by imposition from outside – either by mandate, or, indirectly, through strict adherence to a published scheme of work. This section therefore is not a description of careers guidance, but touches on a long-term developmental process which is a facet of self-realisation.

Careers education itself is a process, as Hayes and Hopson (1971) and Herr (1974) demonstrate. Failure to see it as stretching over the years, could reduce it to advice given at the critical point of choice, where the urge to abdicate responsibility may be compelling. Pastoral care and careers education share the aim of enhancing responsible autonomy. They take a developmental approach, with all the implications that has. Foremost is the need to reject dependence upon normative approaches incorporated in tests: the key word being dependence. Kelly (1955) objected to the 'statistical-dragnet' approach to personality where surveys or mass testings show what is most typical of a population. He argues that it perpetuates the erroneous assumption that the 'greatest volume defines the greatest truth.' We may unthinkingly behave as if the average is necessarily desirable or incorporates a healthy state. Developmental perspectives imply individuals in a state of becoming which resists clear definition. Norms can be used as traits which suggest that a man is a static thing, capable of being described completely. Used badly, they foster a reductionist approach to our fellows. Description cannot be avoided in pastoral work, but it must occur in ways which reflect the principles of formative assessment. There is a constant danger that tests, whatever form they take, perpetuate the *status quo*: people who are like current or past holders of occupational or academic roles could be encouraged to unthinkingly enter areas of rapid change.

This developmental emphasis does not allow us to discard caution: pupils still have to make decisions within limits, but the limits may be very different from what parents, peers or sub-culture have led them to believe. Balance has to be achieved between self-exploration and the realities of life; but the world cannot be used to full advantage until reasonable self-knowledge has been acquired. Validity of information carries no guarantees that pupils will not misuse it.

Key areas and elements of vocational development include:

1 Creating awareness of the fields of human activity to which the pupil is attracted through his or her personality, background and aptitudes. Current reactions to unemployment stress selection *of* the person, rather than selection *by* the person. The latter leads to commitment and involvement rather than superficial adaptation. Opportunities now appear unduly restricted, yet I still find lack of knowledge of existing alternatives. Self-generated constraints come from submerged or unacknowledged needs and motives such as dependence upon the family, or the inability to escape from crude, yet compelling rationalisation, based on the theme of 'I'm not going to get a job, so why should I try?'

2 Sharpening the concept of a satisfying lifestyle, even if unemployment is likely to be a reality at sometime in later life.

3 Comparing the pupil's lifestyle as currently defined with the interpreted demands of a particular occupation or field of work.

4 Boosting decision-making skills.

Developmental approaches are not alone in questioning the equation of the desired with the desirable. Is what the pupil *claims* he desires really that? If he had more knowledge, would he change his goals? May his desires not reflect immaturity or pathology? These are proper questions for us to raise and discuss with pupils. If we proceed to make our own judgements about the answers, then it is imperative that we are alert to the possibility that such conclusions can be a product of our concept of a superior career pattern, which unacknowledgely, we tend to foist on others. Even if such a career pattern is socially and morally valuable we can still question the propriety of the attempted imposition.

Retarded or impaired vocational development invite highly subjective definitions. But they are phenomena with which, in practice, we have to contend. They mean that recognition of the need to make a decision is not present when it should be, for this is a product of maturity. Changing the content of vocational decisions does not decrease their importance for the individual. The fact that the choice may now be between taking a place on a YTS course and being paid, or staying on in the sixth-form for a one-year course; rather than between taking a job and staying on at school, does not diminish the need to estimate risks and probable outcomes, neither does it make understanding of underlying values less crucial.

Pastoral activities and personnel still have to stimulate awareness of, and foster independence from, authoritarian and emotive influences on decisions. Well-meaning, but seductive or coercive suggestions from friends and relatives; tensions aroused by real or imagined contrasts between the lifestyle seen as inherent in the job and the values of admired peers, are just two examples of the problems fifth- and sixth-year pupils wish to explore.

Lack of confidence in their ability to express themselves clearly, or fear of being laughed at, may inhibit pupils. These problems reveal themselves in group work. I have seen the conflicts aroused when a job involves activities which are threatening (e.g. being the only young person in a group of much older workers, or having to act as a buffer between the public and the other workers) but the student feels he or she should take it. Counselling skills will be required to create the safe climate in which feelings can be aired, while the tutor resists the temptation to gloss over the difficulties or provide superficially plausible answers. Realism is essential.

The elderly have sometimes attributed unrealistic powers of sexuality and violence to adolescents which bear little relation to our experience of them as their teachers. Yet adolescence brings, to some, unrealistic fantasies of omnipotence and achievement. Without forcing the issues, for this would be counter-productive, a pastoral programme should encourage detection of unhelpful fantasy elements in vocational thinking. Powerful fantasies incorporating a need for adulation and success can be strong motivators, but if they hamper preparation for the future or take the pupil along dangerous paths then the tutor must intervene.

Retarded and impaired vocational development cannot be ignored. The former consists of vocational thinking, behaviour and choices reflecting factors usually typical of early adolescence, e.g. parental injunctions or glamour. The latter involves personality maladjustments which prevent decisions being made, or have created a rigidity which inhibits any admission of error, poor planning or lack of aptitude. As one would expect irrational factors are strong in those showing impaired vocational development. Denial of change, accompanied by reality-blindness, marks pupils I meet who are still unthinkingly maintaining the same relatively orderly sequence of career preparation as their parents did. This tradition-directed process blots out patently changed circumstances; rendering them vulnerable to unanticipated disappointment without the protection of planned alternatives.

Two groups worry me at entry to sixth form. Members of the larger group have chosen A-level subjects or sixth-form courses without a clear career direction in mind; presumably they hope light will come in the sixth form. In fact, they are in danger of wasting two precious years. Any gains that ensue will be haphazard or difficult to utilise, and their sixth-form experience has little impact on their future. A smaller group have unrealistic levels of aspiration, but resist the tutor's attempts to discuss this. They may be acting out parental aspirations; sometimes being conscious of the false identity that has been allocated to them, but unable to find an escape route.

Problem-solving exercises set in conflict situations may help pupils understand what is happening. Fourth- and fifth-year pupils benefit from problem-solving activities using the typology and ideas of Miller (1951; 1964). He postulates three important types of conflict:

1 *Approach – avoid*

The situation might be that of making one's own job or starting a very small business: the approach tendency is motivated by the need to avoid unemployment, gain independence and avoid devaluation by others; avoidance stems from the strong risk element which is reinforced by self-doubt.

2 *Avoid – avoid*

Unemployment brings deprivation of consumer power and impulsive reactions can be strong. For example, pressure is being put on a young person to take part in shoplifting by others in a group of unemployed. But he or she is trapped between the need to avoid rejection and ridicule by peers and the anxiety about being caught and the subsequent shame, or guilt.

3 *Approach – approach*

In such conflicts, dissonance is experienced because something has to be given up. The more equal the attraction of the alternatives; the stronger the discomfort is likely to be, e.g. the student simultaneously wishes to go into the sixth form, pursuing subjects he enjoys, and at which he probably will be very successful; but also wishes to accept a well-paid job which promises security.

A useful way of thinking about vocational development is to see it as the linkage and comparison of two domains of meaning, the occupational and the psychological. Starishevsky and Matlin (1968) argue that statements about an occupational field or job can be translated into statements about the self-picture of an individual. A process can be launched in which appraisal and matching occur between the characteristics of the individual and the occupation. Greater self-awareness and more accurate powers of discrimination emerge from this dual process of matching and comparison which can begin in either domain. A *caveat*, however: just as pupils hold distorted stereotypes about the kind of person who is good at certain subjects, so they possess occupational stereotypes based on prejudice, unquestioned assumptions and hearsay. The long-term evaluation of both areas advocated as part of a pastoral programme can interrupt this. But we should not assume that contact, indeed familiarity, with a job prevents stereotypes being held. It seems from some of the preliminary work on the Schools Council Careers Education and Guidance Project (1978) that pupils are likely to have partial and distorted conceptions of the teacher's job, despite daily contact.

The pastoral programme is not blind preparation for unemployment, nor is it education for leisure. It takes a questioning, but positive approach to change. Reconsideration of the nature of employment is stimulated: the focus being on the question whether it can offer identity in the same way as it did in the past. Encouragement of the stable pursuit of a single occupation contains too high a level of risk. Change and retraining seem the commonplaces of the future. Unemployment – the major concern of fifth- and sixth-year students – in conjunction with the advent of training courses means that students are now captives of a protracted marginal position in society. To cope, positive identity needs to be strengthened and values sharpened; for social anthropologists point out that values determine the ways people mobilise resources to cope with their environment, or more hopefully, to master it.

Simple techniques can be employed to facilitate vocational development. Some are given below, but the list is far from exhaustive.

1 Individuals, partners or small groups can sort occupational titles into three groups:
- those I would do
- those I would not do

– those about which I am unsure

It is often helpful to begin with discussion of the exclusions first because adolescents have sharper ideas about them (reflecting their tendency to gain identity by opposition).

2 Situations with vocational and identity implications can be presented as pictures or written statements, e.g. working at a lathe, answering a telephone or using a computer terminal. The tutor stimulates small group discussion on how the pupils feel about these situations. Pupils relate them to their own preferences and abilities. Discussion of the skills involved and the importance of such activities in certain jobs could lead to small scale projects on local firms.

3 Sketches or pictures of workers wearing overalls, a donkey jacket, white coat, lounge suit or dress and uniform allow discussion of body image and the picture of self that pupils would prefer to present at work. Gender stereotypes often appear in the discussion and challenge of them is vital.

4 Listing of the personality qualities and skills involved in certain occupations is undertaken, and then compared with pupils' self-assessment. Essays on the self as a worker; written as if the pupil were someone else, but someone who knew them better than even their best friend could; form the basis for self-assessment.

5 The construction of profiles assessing learning skills, but also including statements about relevant behaviour such as punctuality, leads to valuable discussion, acting as a preparation for formative assessment.

6 Friends assess one another's potential as workers. This could be general potential or related to particular fields, e.g. computational, practical, mechanical, literary, clerical, social service, etc. The checklist would have been developed by the form. Follow-up would question the validity and objectivity of such assessments.

7 Simple published checklists and questionnaires have a place, e.g. *The Job I Would Like* Hamblin (1974), or Hopson and Scally's (1979) *What I Like About Myself*.

8 Values can be examined through such simple techniques as this: A ladder is drawn on the blackboard; pupils start to rank qualities such as responsibility and initiative in order of

importance. After the tutor has ensured they have grasped the idea, pupils build their own ladder of important values. It is stressed that there are no right answers, but pupils have to justify their rankings through small group discussion followed by class discussion.

9 Parents can be encouraged to contribute materials drawn from their jobs as the basis for decision-making exercises. Pupils should be asked to:
- think deeply about what *should* be done;
- decide what they would be *likely* to do themselves;
- evaluate the level of risk in their suggestions. (The tutor gives this more precise form related to the nature of the situation);
- decide *who* might have to be kept in mind.

10 With the help of parents, pupils can be encouraged to draw up sketches of a competent worker in local industries. Checks can be made with personnel officers and their feedback used in discussion.

11 Sources of stress or critical incidents could be presented as short dramatic tapes or narratives, e.g. a nurse on her/his first night duty, or a teacher with a missing pupil on a school trip. Pupils draw out, and then evaluate, possible actions.

12 In the later years, pupils can be encouraged to plan ahead in imagination, looking at what they hope to achieve in 5 years, 10 years, 20 years and by retirement. Discussion focuses on the discrepancy between desire and expectations, examining positive ways in which the gap can be reduced.

Before deepening the discussion of content, it is helpful to see that vocational development is an area where parents can give much. When allowed access to the pastoral programme, parents and pupils have much to offer. We do not have to 'go it alone'.

Jenkins (1983) reminds us of the long tradition of pessimism in disadvantaged groups. Carter (1966) perceptively described the background which inculcated negative attitudes in 'roughs' and which then permeated their attitudes to employment. Willis (1978) demonstrated the way deprived adolescents socialise themselves realistically for what awaits them after school. As I see it, *some* members of such groups resort to satisfactions derived from a search for thrills and excitement, they seek pleasures coming from minor outwittings of authority, or displays of bravado. But many do not, and to me the latter seem to be truly unfortunate, because they acquiesce to circumstances which should not be tolerated. Genuine idealism is one thing: false romanticism is another. In pastoral work we need to be realistically aware that employment offers few intrinsic rewards for many people, but we must also heed Jenkins' warning that lack of positive occupational goals encourages some pupils to drift into unskilled employment by default.

At the heart of vocational development should be problem-solving and decision-making activities which allow partial reconciliation of the individuals' beliefs about themselves with their view of the environment. Real discrepanies have to be accepted, and their implications faced as part of the constructive honesty of pastoral care. It is necessary to break into stubborn refusals of those who are too rigid to admit that viable alternatives exist. With other students it is important to create awareness of the possibility that earnest consideration does not mean that one can guard against every eventuality. Judicious balance between prudential thinking, the assessment of risk and the willingness to adventure can combat pessimism and passivity. Spur-of-the-moment decisions have to be avoided, but we should beware of unintentionally reinforcing some pupils' inclinations to surrender the power of decision-making to those whom they see as experts.

Planning the work on vocational development

There is a need to see that the pastoral programme itself is, like vocational development, a process and not a static entity. This has its costs: energy and time have to be invested in negotiation and planning. The illustrative discussion below reflects the approaches I have taken in courses and with schools over the years. There is no ideal programme or approach to vocational development. The characteristics of pupils and staff; the peculiarities of local conditions, especially in levels of employment; and the provision for careers education and guidance within the school all have to be recognised as providing parameters for effective strategies. Equally, the existence and quality of CPVE and pupils' attitudes to YTS and other training courses, cannot be excluded from planning. Behind debate and negotiation, albeit unacknowledged, may be some equivalent or form of Turner's (1961; 1964) views, and Wilson's (1967) findings that peer group influences operate strongly on educational aspiration and performance within the school. Therefore in planning we need to ask specifically how learning which goes on in peer groups at school mitigates against the development of vocational maturity.

Turner also claims that individuals from disadvantaged sectors of society can be orientated towards future success without learning crucial skills: they value academic success, but lack the skills to attain it. They are restricted to the superficial appearances and activities of the lifestyles to which they aspire, but have no access to the attitudes, 'working values' and skills which make them productive. Despite the development of profiling, this can be underplayed as part of guidance. Study skills programmes omit self-management and motivational elements as specific areas for development, but vocational development activities should not compound this weakness. Jenkins helpfully comments that although the question, 'What do I want to be?' is a middle-class one, the desire *to be* something is held by many working-class pupils. Vocational work incorporated into a pastoral programme may help turn desire into reality by clarifying pupils' ideas about *how* they can attain their aims.

It is tempting, in current conditions, to begin by producing an impressive list of objectives. But most pastoral heads are wise enough to avoid that trap! A first step is for them to debate the goals among themselves as a prelude to wider consultation. Once broad agreement is present, further refinement is possible. Objectives should be submitted to further specification, examination and justification. Critical scrutiny must be applied to claimed benefits of self-assessment rather than taking them for granted. The types and content of useful occupational knowledge must be specified. The case for decision-making and problem-solving skills has to be presented persuasively to tutors who question their necessity. Negotiation is not restricted to interaction with the careers or social education departments, but is also instituted between tutors and pastoral heads. Tutors can produce excellent ideas, but some pastoral heads ensure that they are still-born. A process implies ongoing activity and not neat conclusions: involvement of fifth- and sixth-year students extends the process, especially if they are organised into working parties which gather evidence and ideas from younger pupils as well as peers.

Certain questions merit more attention. In the field of *self-*

appraisal, topics to be investigated include the relation of what is known about oneself as a learner to vocational development; knowledge of interests, including the ability to discriminate between temporary and marginal concerns and the long-term interests which have vocational significance. Attitudes, aptitudes and beliefs about ability should be brought to the forefront at relevant points, e.g. in the preparatory work for subject choice.

Occupational and vocational development, because of its importance, is vulnerable to distortions from false assumptions learned at home or in the neighbourhood. Stereotypes and prejudices will emerge, the significance of which will be hidden unless one understands local gossip and perceptions, e.g. despite good prospects and pay, girls in an area beset by unemployment would not take jobs with a certain firm because local opinion firmly held that female workers there were 'no better than they ought to be'. Heads of year must discuss ways of coping with such sensitive aspects of what, at first sight, seems uncomplicated. Nothing can be taken for granted, pupils are often unaware of the need for training and qualifications in jobs where this seems to be prime. The nature of decision-making and problem solving is still not understood by some fourth- and fifth-year pupils who appear tied to specific contexts and are unable to extract the general principles: yet such understandings are prime for coping with future tasks.

The problem of providing adequate coverage of vocational topics and extending it each year without creating boredom or *deja vu*, has bedevilled many pastoral teams. It is usually better to bring such feelings out in the open with pupils, rather than stifle them. Linkage with other areas of pastoral activity is crucial. First-year pupils, for example, may relate their vocational unit to preceding activities on local leisure provision e.g. the skills of being a good youth club member – regular attendance, reliability as a member of a team, taking one's turn in a fair or accepted way, or sensibly coping with upsetting experiences such as not being chosen for an activity. Conscious and justifiable balance of the methods used in self-assessment is essential if minimal involvement is not to be the norm or 'keeping my tutor happy' regarded as the major pupil objective. Adjective checklists (Hamblin, 1974); actual/ideal self scales (Hamblin, 1974; 1978); questionnaires; self-reports; profile building and decision-making have to be introduced in a varied way.

Factors of work adjustment and establishment of a meaningful life style can be explored through industrial contacts and parental involvement. The careers officer can contribute uniquely, but thought has to be given to the best use of a valuable resource person with limited time. Yet some pastoral 'teams' give such matters no consideration. Equally, it is only sensible to enlist the help of the drama specialist to ensure productive introduction of role play and simulation; and, more crucially, if we are to avoid boring pupils, guidance in using these methods in more depth in the later years. Lorac and Weiss (1981) offer creative ideas which should be taken up by the pastoral team.

Lastly, a few topics for discussion:

1 What will be the appropriate balance between modules specifically directed towards vocational development and other units of guidance? Unnecessary overlap exists, but can we afford it when time is in short supply?

2 The problem of focus, i.e. making the units more specific in the later years, highlights the need for close co-operation with the careers department, but do we work to ensure this is productive?

3 Have we unquestioned assumptions and pre-conceptions of the appropriate age level for each type of activity? Is there a place for tutor group visits to industry in the first two years of the secondary school? If so: how do we select the experiences; what is the purpose; what preparation and follow-up are needed?

4 Do the vocational development activities prepare for, or move towards, work experience and CPVE etc in a planned way?

5 How do we prepare pupils to use their interviews with the careers officer constructively?

6 Do the vocational development units of the pastoral programme exist in isolation, or are they accompanied by a complementary plan in which tutors gradually garner information about pupils' spatial and visual ability, physical ability and health, aptitudes and attitudes?

Work experience, work adjustment and the prospect of unemployment

Here we are not concerned with traditional employment alone. I have already discussed these issues in Galton and Moon (1983), and a programme is set out in *Guidance: 16–19*. The task of the pastoral programme is, through promoting vocational development, to contribute to the school's endeavour to provide the skills, not merely for survival, but for joyful, self-extending living in a technological age. New forms of exchange relationships with society, which maintain self-respect and the sense of potency necessary for psychological and physical well-being, are goals that are worthy of vigorous investment of energy. The search is for the sense of status and significance, which is as important as money for self-respect. In the transitional years, these new exchange relationships will be necessary to insulate young people against the devaluation, blame and contradictory attitudes which leave them feeling – as do the handicapped – that they are less than complete adults.

Educators have to be alert to false appearances, and to be willing to go behind facades to get at the roots of a problem. Parsons and Bales (1956), in a searching and still relevant analysis of the family, argued that the male role is anchored primarily in the occupational world, while the adult female role is seen fundamentally in terms of 'within family' activities. Obviously this has been modified by economic trends which make us feel that both parents must go to work to maintain a decent standard of living, resulting in what Rosser and Harris (1965) described as the release of women from compulsive domesticity. Yet behind this exists a surprising tenacity of Bales and Parsons' view that a woman can usually only feel love sexually, in a deeply committed way, for a man who can take his place fully in the occupational world and accept economic responsibilty for the family. Again and again in work with 15- to 18-year-olds, I meet versions of the statement, 'It is the man's job to support the family.' In spite of changes in family networks and role changes incorporating greater sharing of duties, this old viewpoint remains entrenched, contributing to young people's tensions when unemployed. It contributes to the situation reported by Kramer (1982) where unemployed girls went to great effort to support their unemployed boyfriends in positions of apparent dominance. Tutors should encourage debate of the justifiability and costs of such behaviour for both sexes. It is worth bearing in mind that Edwards and Morris (1981) and Kramer (1982) are only two of the sources which suggest unemployment has a greater impact on females than males.

The skills of seizing initiatives and considered risk-taking are towards the forefront of those needed for coping with current unemployment problems. CPVE and TVEI are promoting these competencies with the pastoral effort hopefully consolidating the essential attitudes. This is no easy task when scarcity of employment makes it appear that getting a job is more a matter of luck than of hard work or enterprise. Furthermore, complications related to the mythologies of family roles and responsibilities underlie the FEU's (1985) proper concern with the failure of TVEI to fulfil in reality its obligation to create equality of opportunity. The roots of the problem are left untouched; we have the equivalent of treating symptoms and ignoring causes. Family interaction and relationships give rise to a view of the world which shapes the reactions to life of those socialised within it. Pupils interpret their life chances through this world view. Despite ability they remain prisoners of the original formulation. A pastoral programme, embodying respect and caring, challenges these taken-for-granted perceptions.

Adjustment to work involves the pupil in adaptation to a different set of values from those operating within the school. Respect for individuality (or the reverse) and tolerance of deviation from prescribed behaviour take different forms, and are subject to different sanctions from those met at school. Adjustment to employment is hampered if young people have not been helped to cope with norms of working groups which challenge their ambitions and honesty. Work experience is not necessarily totally artificial, but it can be sheltered: therefore the tutor should highlight potential value conflicts. The need to gain credibility with fellow workers and ways of achieving it should be discussed, but it should not stop there; ethical questions and the hidden costs of such adaptations are only evaded at the risk of failing our students.

Some young workers do not understand why they attract adverse reactions from established ones: they fail to see their contribution to the difficulties they experience because they are cocooned in egocentrism. In units on work adjustment I explore:

1 The assessment of signals sent to others which create the impression of arrogance, weakness or responsible maturity.

2 Ways of developing the ability to put one's viewpoint without seeming naive, brash or incoherent. This helps pupils look at how a person can extend what others have said, create a climate of support and acceptance, put statements hypothetically and/or tentatively without asking for the statement to be dismissed.

3 The importance of such things as dress or manner which are salient characteristics for the judgements of others. Another aspect may be that of gaining understanding of the process through which impressions are formed.

4 The need to learn, and adapt to, existing routine and method without rejecting it or attempting to modify it prematurely.

5 Discussing the reality and functions of the generation gap at work.

6 Coping in situations where both sides behave as if the other had no right to their own point of view.

7 The need to look at the way motives are attributed to oneself and others, understanding how this can make matters worse where conflict or dissatisfaction exists.

My technique has often been that of teaching pupils some of the skills of counselling: active listening; reflecting back; searching for underlying feelings; asking open questions; helping someone clarify their ideas about the nature of the problem, its causes, and the likely course of events. Even the ability to send signals of acceptance which show respect for others, although we differ, can significantly change interaction. Unrecognised barriers which prevent the use of pupils as resources in a pastoral programme also prevent us from seeing that counselling provides a set of tools which we can give to pupils. Decision-making is improved by clearer perceptions of self and reality: as is adjustment in the first job. Counselling skills as tools for pupils help overcome the problems associated with the advice proffered by adults who are perceived as manipulative, condemning or lacking understanding. The problem is real: many adults see themselves as sound sources of advice, indeed they may be accepted as such by young people, but in fact they are not equipped to offer advice because the experiences from which they draw it are now irrelevant. The difficulties worsen if being older – and consequently wiser – is a prized part of the adviser's identity. They may, in fact, be as insecure as the adolescents they advise, in the face of major changes in their own role. Indeed, they may be bolstering their own tenuous hold on reality by advice giving. Rather than giving advice based on insecure foundations it is better to create awareness of the vastly increased number of family and work roles that can, and do, function satisfactorily.

Work experience can be related to the pastoral programme provided that it incorporates analytical and evaluatory approaches that create healthy critical attitudes. Social Europe (1985) argues that, although training programmes are to be welcomed, they may pay insufficient attention to the fact that the demand for labour will fall. Small-scale entrepreneurial ventures will be helpfully developed in many such schemes; but job-sharing, a shorter working day, later entry to work and alternation between employment and unemployment are also prospects which should be taken into account. The cry, 'Generic vocational skills for what? Jobs which don't exist, or exist now, but won't in ten years?' is reasonable. It could also be, 'Work experience for what purposes? To perpetuate the present or past, or stimulate change?' It is a familiar story: one of new problems of identity, mobility and uncertainty stemming from social change; yet one that is ignored in some pastoral programmes.

Watts (1980) raises key questions about work experience. What is the effect and value of learning generated by a situation in which work tasks are experienced without the student assuming the total responsibilities of a worker? A superficial and temporary experience will not provide experience of the real pressures. Like teaching practice, work experience can be a misleadingly sheltered event. Some of my past students have commented on the distortions produced by work experience. Some pupils return with unrealistic expectations because a carefully-planned programme over-emphasised the positive and interesting; others have met monotony and near-exploitation due to employees shedding monotonous and boring tasks which were then undertaken by the pupils. Most of them put the experience into perspective, but some do not. All, however, need help in drawing out other less obvious learning. Some have recognised that supervisors are mines of misinformation and contradiction, happily unaware of the confusion and anxiety they cause. It is salutary for students to come to terms with the fact that such authorities are unable to admit mistakes, and, in fact require appeasement, even although this is undeserved. I have found it useful to help students look at:

1 Reactions to praise and blame in the particular work situation, comparing and evaluating what they observed.

2 The formal and informal sanctions and workers' measures for coping, evading or outwitting. Comparison of the disciplines of school and workplace can be illuminating.

3 Coping with loss of face, and the obverse, restoration of it. The tactics of dissembling, making secret fun of managers and automatic blaming coupled with rejection of the legitimacy of the supervisor's behaviour, can yield material for deep discussions. 'Walking a knife edge' between insubordination and staying within the framework of conventional relationships is a matter of comment surprisingly often.

4 Frustration, and the ways workers cope with it, usually needs attention. Students look at necessary (and unnecessary) frustrations, self- or system-produced, and how workers resort to indirect means of coping which inhibit group cohesiveness, and therefore lower productivity.

Jamieson (1983) raises salient questions in his discussion of work experience. He demonstrates the tensions: on the one hand, pupils cannot get meaningfully enmeshed in work relationships with adults; on the other, the visits of teachers undermine any attempt by students to assume more adult roles. Watts and Jamieson seem to question whether work experience as currently practised achieves its objectives – even if work experience is the best way of attaining them. Indeed, one suspects that the objectives are not always clearly held in mind by those who implement work experience. The *for* and *about* objectives are important. If it is *for* employment, then Watts' argument that there is little point in giving experience of a job into which the student is unlikely to go is prime; if it is *about* employment then the experience – albeit somewhat contrived and artificial – of the different life styles of other groups, provides useful data for vocational development.

Jamieson also refers to his 1981 research which found that work experience was unlikely to change long-established attitudes. Realism demands that we face the results of long-term operant conditioning, or shaping processes, in which parents and peers have been active over the years. If these negative or positive views have been assimilated, then work experience will, *by itself*, have only a temporary or marginal effect. It is salutary to ponder on the likely effect of work experience on a student whose family and neighbourhood have built up a predisposition to respond negatively to authority and work. He or she may then go into an unskilled or other area of employment where, as Jamieson suggests, the managerial view of the working world has scarcely permeated. I have found situations where transactions between supervisors and workers are based on distorted views of intent, suspicion and mutual blaming are strong, and every action – on both sides – is misinterpreted. Unless there is follow-up which seizes on these issues, work experience confirms pre-existing views. One is left asking open-mindedly whether work experience stimulates forward-looking and imaginative responses, or whether it perpetuates traditional and undesirable attitudes and behaviours, inhibiting enterprise.

Even simple follow-up to work experience can be useful. A group of pastoral periods might well explore, for example:

1 How well was the job explained to me? Did I understand the purpose of the firm or organisation, and how the job fitted in with others?

2 How well was the work explained to me? Was the explanation accurate? Did I understand what I had to do, and why it had to be done?

3 What skills were needed? In what ways do I need to improve my skill?

4 Which tasks did I find enjoyable? Why? What is the implication of this, if any, for my choice of a job?

5 What seemed important about the relationships between workers doing the same job, between different groups of workers, and between workers and managers?

6 What rewards were there for hard work and good performance?

7 What happened when somebody made a mistake or did not do very well?

8 How could the job be improved?

9 What information did I get about how well I was doing?

Although they are simplistic, I have found that these questions stimulate intense – often heated – discussion, increasing students' grasp of their experiences. This outcome partially depends on the tutor's skill at running discussions and adapting his structure to the needs of the group. He will need to move between organised exploration of precise questions he has set, small group or partner work based on students' ideas and interests, and informal discussion by the whole class. The skills of group counselling, (Hamblin, 1974; 1983) will be necessary. Difficult topics cannot be evaded and will sometimes lead to critical discussion of what happens in school. Interesting continuities between school and work are spotted by students. Pupils have learned that if you show you are good at a task, your 'reward' is being given more of that work. This also happens in employment. Similarly, difficult pupils get away with evasion and poor performance because the attempt to compel them creates unwanted tensions and so do difficult workers. Laziness and evasion therefore attract rewards in both spheres.

Feedback is endorsed as desirable: yet in reality it is often superficial, inaccurate, irrelevant or non-existent. In a study of problems of absenteeism and turnover of workers in what was a concerned, well-organised factory, I found that gross, but un-recognised anxiety was created through lack of feedback in train-ing. The personnel officer and supervisors were well aware of who were competent trainees, but the girls did not know. As one put it 'I feel I'm not doing well enough, and then I go home and worry about it.' The form of feedback is important: if the charge hand merely asks 'Why has your production gone down?', or the manageress tells the sales assistant, 'Your figures have dropped — why?', the reply will be, 'I don't know.' Perhaps, as with some of the trainees above, the result will be, 'I don't know, so I go home and worry about it, and then I don't want to come to work next day.'

Discussion of these processes is as important as helping pupils develop skills. Analysis of actual and likely differences in the interpretation of events is a valuable ploy. Likert (1961) showed how different the viewpoints of supervisors and workers can be, especially about giving praise for good performance or effort. Both groups felt unappreciated! How we see things determines what we do. To evade these issues in guidance is to send students into employment, courses, or unemployment handicapped because we have deprived them of understanding the actual processes of living. Stress and overwork may make us baulk at the task; we perhaps feel it is impossible, but concern and commonsense are the major tools, and these are part of the armoury of every effective teacher.

The problem falls into perspective when we realise that young people at work face dilemmas and interactional stresses that parallel those we help them cope with in school. Fifth- and sixth-year students who have been on work experience are able to locate threats to self-respect. Brainstorming or individual listing of diffi-culties produces more than enough material for discussion and problem-solving. Let me illustrate. Some have realised that when they feel they can't cope or feel frustrated, they start blaming others, especially older people. They shrewdly note that the individual who accuses others of aggression or laziness often possesses these characteristics but cannot admit it. They may then proceed to discuss the ways in which the inability to accept one is at fault poisons working relationships. They become aware of displaced aggression (the equivalent of 'kicking the cat') noting that some workers choose targets who cannot retaliate effectively. Critical responses to the evasive, superficially plausible excuses used by some workers to avoid doing their fair share appear, although this does not guarantee that pupils will not use such excuses if the occasion arises. Work experience, however, offers students opportunities to acquire insight into such behaviour without activating defensive reactions. Can we afford to ignore it?

Formative assessment and profiling:

The brief discussion of work experience above indicates that it is the *learning* from experience which matters, and not the experience as such. Work experience can be used in pastoral care to answer some vital questions about what happens to people in working groups; and to raise searching questions about the part played by intelligence, hard work, initiative, friendliness, conscientiousness and co-operation in employment. Formative assessment and profiling can be linked to work experience, facilitating insights and boosting performance in school or college. Formative assessment is theoretically and practically separable from profiling and work experience: the greatest returns, however, may come from their integration. The Clydebank Project (1984), for example, found that the work experience assessments of employers were taken more seriously than those of teachers.

What is formative assessment? It is an attack on inert and reactive learning. It incorporates recognition that the learner has to take responsibility for his learning, and the expectation that he is capable of successful learning. *It is concerned with changes of behaviour and perceptions through self-modification.* Formative assessment requires teachers to take a wider view of their role than simply that of instructors. It asks them to give constructive feedback, *and accept it as well.* Appraisal of student performance is, at least implicitly, evaluation of the success of the teaching methods employed; therefore willingness to consider adaptations to students' needs and modify methods is a key concommitant of formative assessment. Development of formative assessment without seeing this is the equivalent of living in cloud cuckoo land: there is the strong possibility of coming down to earth with a devastating crash!

Tutor and student work as partners in the matter of assessment. This partnership could well be based on a contractual relationship (see Krumboltz and Thoresen, 1969; Thomas, 1974; Nelson–Jones, 1982; 1983) which is negotiated, ensuring that the student is clear that the responsibility for progress rests with himself. Obligations are made explicit for both partners, and are only changed after considered renegotiation. An evaluatory and self-modificatory process should be launched which requires all concerned to take a problem-solving approach to learning, i.e. formulating hypotheses about the causes of difficulties and the way strengths can be extended, then constructing and testing out lines of action.

The diagnostic element of assessing individual strengths and weaknesses appears to provide motivation for pupils to improve their performance. IFAPLAN (1984) gives indications that pupils are more strongly motivated when asked to appraise, and not just record, their performance. Caution is necessary: despite rejection of benevolent paternalism and maternalism, these same pupils are strangely dependent on teachers – sometimes behaving as if they had a tame teacher to take into examinations to tell them the meaning of questions! Attitude change is difficult to stimulate, especially when pupils' peer groups support negative evaluation of school activities, and status is derived from dismissal of achievement. This makes it even more imperative to use assessment techniques which involve pupils, increase their motivation, and deepen their grasp of learning skills.

There is a plethora of potentially useful ideas and techniques which pastoral heads may have to drag from their original contexts, modify, and apply to new circumstances. One example is the valuable idea of training for skills ownership – despite its association with the doubtful concept of 'occupational families', thoroughly criticised by Johnson (1984). Training for skills ownership is a creative concept which could be at the heart of pastoral programmes, but what is it? It includes the ability to redeploy learned skills and knowledge in unfamiliar places and occasions; an awareness of the relationship between existing and required skills; and an appreciation of the relevance of the skills to be acquired to the attainment of success in the new situation: clearly, it is a complex activity.

Feedback and reflection are at the heart of the process, but how are they to be fostered? Again, the skills of counselling are crucial. Tutors must create accepting climates which allow expression and elaboration of feelings about failure or success, and clarification of problems such as self-defeating tactics of pretending that one doesn't care. Factors such as predictions, comparisons, judgements and early closure (where pupils refuse to consider other possibilities) will be at the heart of discussions. We may fail to see that one of the aims of counselling is to equip students with diagnostic skills which they apply to their life situations, so gaining versatility in coping. Counselling is a process where the subject and object of learning are identical; the learner is learning to diagnose his own feelings and reactions rather than remain a victim of amorphous forces.

Formative assessment has long been part of counselling, and is concerned with two broad areas. One consists of the motivational elements and personality factors, e.g. the tendency to react to difficulty by saying, 'I can't do it!', *agreed* by tutor and student as relevant. The other covers the competencies necessary to master specific learning tasks. I have, within the broad divisions, found it productive to engage with students in an examination of four skill areas:

1 The exploratory and descriptive;

2 The analytic and diagnostic;

3 Receiving and appraising suggestions for improvement;

4 Ways in which pupils modify and adopt the joint proposals for future work.

In practice, there are no sharp distinctions between these areas of enquiry, and one oscillates between them in the interaction, finding that unpredictable degrees of emphasis occur in sessions with the same student as he or she discards habitual defences or a new aspect of the problem is uncovered.

The disturbing outcome of the learning experiences of some pupils is that exploratory skills are often attenuated, absent or not seen as their responsibility. Home and school may have unconsciously conspired to reinforce reliance upon rote learning and production of *the* right answer. Pupils dominated by fear of appearing wrong and consequent loss of face have often learned to resist thinking about their learning, remaining tied to narrow definitions of learning as reproduction of the facts given in texts or lessons. They maintain this stance in the face of exciting curriculum development and teacher enthusiasm: such developments wash over them, leaving them untouched by the experiences. Exploration and description of performance are foreign to them. The tutor will need to take carefully judged steps to avoid reinforcing their tendency to dismiss formative responsibility because they rely on the teacher to tell them exactly what to do. Complaints of boredom are no guarantee that the activity of formative assessment will be welcomed! A pastoral programme incorporating formative assessment requires a supportive ethos, and planned, long-term inculcation of helpful skills (including the judgemental), beginning at entry to school.

A first step is to encourage development of the skill of finding out, and then describing, good performance in the particular field of learning. This is part of formative counselling; the tutor employing reflective questioning to assist the student to sharpen, and correct, if need be, perceptions of what is salient and what is marginal. Why? Often pupils unwittingly hamstring themselves by behaving as if everything were of equal value: a tendency not restricted to the content of learning, but more destructively incorporated into the process. Through devising simple diagrams or applying checklists, (see Hamblin, 1978; 1981) the student is encouraged to identify task requirements and match them to his own capacities. Tutors must be prepared to meet resistance or resentment; equally, they have to be flexible: the inability to specify good performance may be fundamental to the problem, therefore the tutor has to provide an example.

Self-observation is a cause of behaviour change as Watson and Tharp (1972) show, but many students have never observed their learning behaviour purposefully. Formative assessment can include brief observational projects where students set out to observe their learning behaviour for two or three days and then follow this by collecting comments from teachers and peers. The evaluations of peers are extremely useful, striking home without being destructive. Such exercises can lead to peers being put into the position of coaches to each other – a helpful extension of formative assessment, making students resources for one another. Reasons for good performance can be paralleled by discussion of beliefs about poor performance and the questioning of habitual explanations. Flexibility and experiment should be prime. I agree with Heathcote *et al* (1982) who, when discussing curriculum styles and strategies, remark that if teachers are asked to be innovative, then what I describe as the 'hard form' of the objectives approach is unsuitable because they have engaged themselves in something where the outcomes are uncertain, and possibly unknown.

The self as a learner has been neglected, although it is a major part of the output of the secondary school. Students should be encouraged to develop their own measures for evaluation, looking at reading skills (including speed and comprehension) planning skills and self-management. Above all, they should develop ways of using self-help groups for better revision. The aim is to encourage delineation of strengths and weaknesses, and thereby break into the global, undifferentiated perceptions of learning that handicap their holder. Balance sheets and techniques such as incomplete sentence instruments are useful, provided their use is dictated by the two principles of readiness and precision. Questionnaires and tests are often used at the behest of the teacher, but the rationale of a formative approach demands pupil involvement in the decision to use them. The tutor has to justify the selection of a particular test or questionnaire, but again this increases the willingness of the student to make good use of them once agreement occurs.

Readiness and precision are key concepts in formative assessment. The former implies that tutor and student both feel the student is able to take a step forward, or has acquired sufficient awareness of the existence and nature of learning problems to justify further exploration. Precision means that the scale, checklist, or whatever is acknowledged by the student to have, apparently, at least, relevance to the perceived problem: a cautious statement which acknowledges that the danger of self-deception is ubiquitous.

Formative assessment embodies a principle about testing which most counsellors would endorse, i.e. that although the evidence and forecasts provided by the test have to be taken seriously, it cannot be allowed to make the decision. Tester and testee combine forces to devise strategies for overcoming any negative predictions in the results. Formative assessment founders when tests are brought in without a problem to which both partners seek understanding, or when the test is allowed to initiate a negative self-fulfilling prophecy.

The exploratory and descriptive skills are concerned with clarifying learning problems, including attitudinal ones, and encouraging students to move from diagnosis to specification of the steps necessary for their resolution. Students are encouraged to break down the remedial objectives into steps, specifying the first step in detail. The tutor applies the counselling skills of anticipation and inoculation. To omit them runs the risk of allowing students to meet difficulties unprepared, and then retreat. Inoculation against self-doubt, frustration and peer derision, stems from anticipation of difficulties. The tutor is not engaged in vague encouragement; dealing with debilitating reactions to attempted improvement is fundamental to formative assessment. Tutors can doubt the necessity for this, yet even able sixth-formers taking subjects demanding intensive reading lack basic skills – often to a greater extent than their teachers suspect. They do not scan an assignment to gain an appreciation of its import, proceeding to break it into meaningful sections to which they apply their knowledge of study skills to extract, process, and attempt to extend the key facts and their implications where relevant. All pupils benefit from formative assessment.

Justification for a demanding and time-consuming process has to be incorporated into staff development. To implement it without creating awareness of the skills and difficulties is to invite superficial performance, even from the willing, which leads to the failure of an exhilarating and motivating mode of assessment. Stresses almost compel tutors to ask, 'Why not just tell them?' But we have been doing that for years with little effect. Some caring and conscientious teachers sincerely regard formative assessment as abdication of responsibility, although this reaction implies a picture of the teacher as inevitably possessing all the answers to learning problems, and pupils receptive to the direct influence of the teacher, grasping eagerly at the wisdom of the teacher in a dependent way. This is admittedly a caricature, yet one that probably highlights the relevant, unquestioned assumptions. Hard work will be needed to assure many good teachers that engagement in the co-operative activity of formative assessment can be founded in mutual respect without loss of professionalism.

The material in Chapter 3 on beliefs about the nature of ability, the relative contributions of luck and effort, the impact of predictions and the importance of self-management, contributes to this discussion of formative assessment. It seems helpful to create a positive atmosphere in which the student is encouraged to regard himself or herself as probably capable of a higher level of achievement, although higher expectations are not threat-free. Attitudes and emotions can then be considered as either hampering or enabling achievement.

There is sometimes the need to ask why some tasks, apparently within the student's ability, are seen as boring, irrelevant, impossible or distasteful. Fishbein (1967) argued that attitudes are evaluative aspects of beliefs: certainly values – and hence evaluations – and perceptions are at the heart of formative assessment. To deny them their place puts one in danger of acquiescing to sterility, or indulging in an empty process that has little which is educative and developmental. Beliefs about the abilities and legitimate preoccupations of the sexes; susceptibility to extraneous features in a learning task, e.g. its appearance, length or apparent unfamiliarity, are examples of what has to be challenged. Threat, and its product, anxiety, (Lazarus, 1966; Spielberger and Sarason, 1976), enter the formative discussions, particularly when the student is under stress in other areas of important relationships. Formative counselling attacks any fallacious assumptions that the learner exists in a social vacuum. Comparisons, not only those operated by teachers and parents, but self-generated ones, have to be tackled. Left untackled, they encourage a view of the world as hostile or lead to self-labelling as a failure, strengthening the 'theory of the impossible task' falsely held by many learners, which saps self-belief and initiative.

Staff development is essential, but it does not dispose of problems of lack of time and resources. Resources must be provided, but we can alleviate the problem by supplementing individual consultations with other approaches. Determined and consistent training of pupils, over the years, in target setting, self-evaluation of work and constructing their own profiles, almost certainly reduces time and effort expended in cutting away the undergrowth of ineffective learning in formative assessment in the fifth and sixth forms.

For many years we have incorporated formative assessment – without calling it this – into group counselling. Within the form or tutor group, self-help groups were formed, in which individuals kept learning diaries. The counsellors and students examined the reported experiences: usually the counsellors did not inspect the diaries, but allowed students to choose what they discussed in the self-help group of three or four chosen friends. This manifests respect, but also incorporates two principles of formative assessment. The first is an acceptance that students will be ready to be open and discuss problems at different rates; some will need more time than others. The second is that the structure for formative counselling should allow the student to do things at his or her own pace; to hurry them activates resistance or boomerangs by reinforcing their feelings of inadequacy. The small groups detected and alleviated problems through mutual support, developing a purposeful attack on them. This context of support, and establishment of legitimacy for the examination of learning problems and building on strengths, seemed as important as the development of simple tools such as the use of diagrams which met the needs of some group members for concrete, visual and active aids to their assessment.

Formative assessment which leaves out the peer group ethos and, more importantly, makes no attempt to harness the peer culture positively, will constantly be tripping over difficulties. Vorrath and Brendtro (1974) are among those who used peer culture positively for the treatment of delinquents. If it can be done in such unpromising circumstances, it can be achieved in the school context. Glasser (1969) showed how the class could be used to resolve educational and behavioural problems within it. From the experiences reported above, the probability is that it will be beneficial to use small self-help groups based on co-operation – without unrealistically denying the existence of competition – as part of formative assessment. Concrete, down-to-earth peer discussion of learning problems, conducted in a context where the tutor creates helping relationships between members of the group, leads to expectations of success, and positive approaches to learning which usually manifest themselves in improved attainment.

Competent students act as models for others – a positive form of comparison. They also help their friends examine their feelings and resentments in a constructive way, with a skill I have sometimes envied! Blind emulation does not occur; they use the helper and his suggestions as points of departure. Observation of the ways in which the helping roles shift with the subject or situation is fascinating, and part of the data of assessment. To know the areas in which someone accepts peer help and where he has the confidence to give it is illuminating. The climate of co-operation comes gradually, but the tutor can facilitate it by supplementing small group work with form discussions of topics which could be evaded by pupils, e.g. delineation of the conditions under which rejection of peer criticisms carry heavy costs, and those where passive acceptance of it maintains a false definition of reality.

It may be useful to highlight some of the issues the tutor could introduce through taped narratives, or playlets produced by a group of pupils. Discussion calls for the application of simple counselling principles by the tutor. Questions should be open ones which invite exploration; the positive responses of pupils should be positively reinforced; signals of acceptance should be given to pupils without patronage. Justifications which create irritability should be avoided: pupils may not voice their inner response to such remarks as 'At your age . . .' or 'If I were you . . .', but undoubtedly they are present. Interaction, particularly with parents, has conditioned them to immediate dismissal of both speaker and statement.

Formative assessment benefits from group work which encourages discussion of self-management, especially using time wisely. The poor planner perceives the demands of school and peer group in 'either/or' terms, not realising that he or she can be successful in both. Tutors should use group counselling activities to interrupt the defensive attitudes used by students to keep the educational process at a distance. Memorable sessions have resulted from discussions of

- the purposes of learning;
- current ideas held by students of the reasons for their successes and failures;
- the tendency to oblige teachers in the classroom by meeting their demands, but going away and forgetting them at home or in private study;
- the inability to see things from the teacher's viewpoint.

When a relationship of trust is established, behaviour even nearer to the bone can be tackled. For example, many students in higher education set out to impress their tutors, but I have noted fifth- and sixth-year students using this skill of impression creation successfully. A good tutor can help students look honestly at the motivation, ethics and later costs of such practices.

Irrespective of the organisation of formative assessment and methods employed, it is imperative that effort is directed to helping students move from sole reliance on a regurgitative approach to learning to one concerned with the development of meaning. Once this is achieved, the text not only provides facts, but is used to integrate or relate ideas derived from it with those already held, becoming a point of departure for new ideas. Obviously, a curriculum strongly orientated to a problem solving and critical appraisal is essential, but the pastoral programme must also responsibly reflect these trends and so enrich living in a post-industrial society. Josephs and Smithers (1975) describe the syllabus-bound and syllabus-free sixth-former: the former accepts the syllabus as both means and end; the latter is intolerant of convention. It is more practical to think in terms of tendencies rather than types; indeed, it seems foreign to the ethos of a pastoral programme fostering development to peddle ideal types for emulation. We can assist students to look at the dangers and strengths of both positions – evaluating the consequences of the caution, conscientiousness and persistence associated with syllabus-boundedness, or of the imagination, independence and possible self-indulgence of the other trend. Formative assessment seems to be a far-reaching developmental process which includes such considerations.

The future of education is as unknown, and postulates as many threats, as that of employment. The reaction to change is sometimes that of attempting to replicate or continue the structures of the past with merely expedient change of activities and ideas. While current debates on the reliability and objectivity of profiles are in order, it is just as important to look at profiles creatively, not merely as teacher assessment of pupils, but as the means of developing mutual understanding and new co-operative relationships between teachers and pupils. Welcome signs of this are appearing, but the nightmare of schools where pupils assiduously, but meaninglessly, tick questionnaire boxes in pastoral periods, and overworked tutors tick boxes in profiles cannot be eliminated. Misuse of comment banks could eliminate careful judgements and reduce assessment to the superficiality of which we have complained in the past.

Roberts (1984) states that unemployment is likely to impede, rather than aid, attainment of social maturity. What then is the function of profiles in an age when training courses could be used as an annexe to the stark reality of unemployment? History suggests that man has a well-developed capacity to ignore the lessons it teaches. The secondary modern school failed, in spite of devoted teachers, to attain the special form of excellence claimed for it – perhaps parallel dangers exist today. Profiles, even in the pastoral programme, could be misused to distort or build a shield against reality. Profiles could, in spite of earnest deliberations, incorporate the insidious shift from the descriptive verb to the labelling noun. In interpreting profiles, the employer's implicit ideas of causality operate to blame students' personalities rather than the educational or training situations. Careful assessments of persistence, reliability and initiative are transformed into statements about character and temperament, unnoticed by those who make the transformation.

Profiles should be welcomed because they contain possibilities for changing relationships in the school. But this depends on the inclusion of all pupils; to confine profiles to the allegedly less able would make them part of a pernicious labelling process, destroying the credibility of both pupils and profiles. Pupils' comments must be incorporated into them in a significant way. Token incorporation or total absence of pupil contributions would lead to profiles being treated with the indifference and incomprehension all too often evoked by current report forms.

In striving for acceptance there is the danger of creating a spurious appearance of objectivity similar to the rating scales described by Glassey and Weeks (1950). Five-point scales were used, each point being described in concrete terms, but the question was then raised whether the traits or characteristics could survive condensation and still reflect reality. Cyril Burt's injunction that each point should be explicitly and unambiguously defined and the different levels of it given concrete description, is still relevant, but equally hard to achieve. Problems of interpretation of apparently unambiguous descriptions abound.

Summative assessment follows formative assessments, giving evidence of achievement to employers or those selecting students for further education. All are busy, therefore the summative assessment must be easily understood and allow for valid comparison between individuals. Employers found CSE difficult to understand and compare with GCE. The difficulties are real and will not be resolved easily. It may require a computerised, national summative assessment to do this, bringing new problems of local autonomy, FEU (1984).

Some help may be derived from past work in guidance on methods of recording and assessing achievement and progress, e.g. Traxler and North (1966) who look at the appraisal of behaviour and personal qualities through rating scales, inventories, anecdotal and observational records and critical incidents. Cronbach (1966) examines self-reports, judgement by peers and supervisors or evaluation through systematic observation. School working parties will be unwise to ignore this legacy of past experience, but should adapt and build on it.

Psychologists have emphasised two aspects of tests which should be kept in mind: validity – does it actually measure what it purports to measure? and reliability – the degree of concordance between measurements obtained from the test with the same individual on different occasions. It has been argued by Nuttall and Goldstein

(1984) that the reliability of a profile could be more questionable than that of a public examination: the damaging consequences of this are apparent, providing hostages for the cynical. Pastoral and curricular heads have to take the issues of validity and reliability to the forefront of their considerations.

Profiling allows escape from norm-referenced methods of assessment which many teachers believe to be damaging. Essentially, this means a comparison of individuals: how far, positively or negatively, is the performance of the individual from the average for a relevant group? To many this seems to stultify endeavour, decrease motivation and foist a label, perhaps identity, on the pupil as a below average, above average, or average type. Negative expectations are then stimulated which could lead to under-teaching. Ethically, it seems odd to value or devalue a person, not primarily for himself or herself and his or her qualities, but on the basis of comparison with others. Ipsative and criterion-referenced assessment are more logical. In the former, the pupil's own performance becomes the baseline for assessment. Criterion-referenced assessment involves the concrete, specific description of different levels of performance and skill; the individual's attainment is assessed against them. IFAPLAN (1984) state, and Nuttall and Goldstein cogently argue, that profiles are not a substitute for conventional tests. Indeed the latter argue for profiles and graded tests being brought together to combine the humanistic and quantitative traditions of British education, giving a desirable rigour to humanistic assessment, and paying due service to validity and reliability.

There is also a need to accept the reality that profiles cannot conceal pupils' incompetence; statements of competence are also statements about what the person cannot do. Again, IFAPLAN (1984) highlight the danger of self-deception. Teachers in the Clydebank Project believed they were assessing pupils against the specified criteria, but although their assessments seemed to confirm this, investigation showed they actually had an image of an average student against which the comparison took place. Tutors could be bound to past practices despite willingness to change, finding it hard to discard their tenacious and long-held frameworks of judgement.

Teachers and pupils need to be involved in a dialogue about the nature of judgements if criterion-based assessment is not to be a sham. Indeed I would argue that the fifth- and sixth-year must be invited to help construct profiles. My experience suggests that they will do this with integrity.

Certain difficulties were discussed in Hamblin (1984), but the problem of comparability is urgent. Several forms of comparability present problems. Assessments of the same student made by different teachers may bear little relation to one another: selective weight may be given to different elements of the criteria; interpretations of what is meant may differ; teachers are likely to have very different images of the average pupil, swamping the criteria supposedly applied. A tutor's assessments of different pupils may lack objectivity, perhaps because he or she allows likeability to distort judgement; or is influenced by some characteristic dominant in his or her inner life. An unnoticed tendency in judgements comes from the value climate of the school; employers are well aware that some schools never permit themselves to acknowledge the presence of geese – all their pupils are swans. Staff development is essential if the problems partially illustrated above are not to devalue profiling, or make some tutors retreat to a defensive position from which they condemn it as impractical.

Validity is a major preoccupation in testing, as Buros (1978), and Johnson and Bommarito (1971) point out. We can question whether criteria can be defined equally validly in all areas. Nuttall and Goldstein ask whether criterion-referenced assessment can be totally independent of normative processes. The teachers in the Clydebank project seemed unable to avoid establishing a norm. Pastoral heads would do well to take the Nuttall and Goldstein paper as the basis for debate and staff development.

Stanton (1984) looks at records of personal achievement. Profiles form a structure for statements about what pupils can do, but supplementary forms of description and assessment are to be welcomed. Stanton points out that students should be able to record their dissent or ask for a second opinion: perhaps some fifth-year pupils concerned with current methods of resolution of pupil–teacher disagreements might cock a cynical eyebrow at this! Involvement and thorough debate are vital if distrust is to be overcome. Pupils do not take the statements about changed relationships in the sixth form seriously. Profiles used formatively could increase cohesiveness and affiliation with the school, not as ends in themselves, but as by-products of co-operation in assessment.

We have to justify ourselves as much as pupils if we are to combat the *anomy* coming from an ever-increasing delay of entry into a full adult role. What, for example, is it permissible for the teacher to assess about character and personality? It is equally important for pupils' beliefs about how teachers think, and how they assess pupils, to come into the open. Many pupils I have met question the teachers' knowledge of industry and their capacity to assess what is needed. Three different views of reality may be at work: the pupils', the teachers' and the industrial. What do such qualities as 'good working relationships' mean to each group? Do they need, and are they capable of, resolution?

Staff development is essential, but if the school is to be a democratic community, then pupils have to be active in the process from the first year upwards. Profiles afford opportunities for pupils to make a positive and satisfying impact on the school; responsible identity through self-awareness and identity by belonging go hand-in-hand. Fifth-year pupils' needs for participation and acceptance of their maturity can be met, indeed must be met, as part of reconciliation to changing realities. But the values and behaviours of formative assessment should permeate the pastoral programme and curricular activities. As teachers we need self-knowledge and the ability to support one another.

Problems abound. We may behave as if a profile could compensate for a poor curriculum, which is manifestly absurd. Impressive format could deceptively exaggerate the objectivity of a profile. Clearly, value judgements must be acknowledged as such, and those who make them have to be identified and accept the onus for justification. Comment banks may be useful, but they could lead to triviality or inaccuracy if coverage of each area is less than comprehensive, and even if satisfactory in this way, tutors have to be trained to select with precision. The temptation to select with an eye to the impact on the pupil – to punish or encourage – lurks behind the surface task. Students are wary of such aspects of profiling and become distrustful. The cool, calculating manager of impressions, moreover, is encouraged in his manipulations.

In conclusion, the task behind staff development is to prevent profiling degenerating into yet another form of unilateral assessment in which the pupil's role is unwilling, passive agreement. Activity and toleration are key themes: activity based on the institution of a co-operative dialogue; toleration of students' questions and disagreement as the grounds for trust.

5 Group Interaction and Peer Counselling

Teachers often ask whether a single period a week is sufficient for the pastoral programme. They forget that the pastoral programme is only part of the pastoral effort. It is both the guts and the backbone however, and like these physical essentials does not exist in isolation. A two way process is at work: ideas and capacities developed in the programme feed into school life, while the value climate, teacher attitudes and priorities operating in the school influence the pastoral programme perhaps more strongly than other curricular areas. Half a dozen periods weekly will be ineffective if the application of what has been done is not stressed. The question, 'What evidence is there of transfer of training?' is only meaningful if there is something capable of transfer. Transfer requires content and activities which relate to the classroom and general school life; something which is best achieved when heads of year or house work persistently to involve tutors in planning the programme and constructing activities, so that they can pick up the issues in their classroom teaching in an informed way. The argument is straight-forward: even a well planned and relevant programme has little developmental worth unless the values and principles underpinning counselling permeate relationships within the school. We often say that our problem is unmotivated pupils, without seeing that this can mean we are searching for a recipe which will push them into action or energise them. Essentially, we hold a view of man as passive or merely reactive. My own work (1968) showed that even difficult and failing pupils value and want success, but do not know how to obtain it, and so seek compensatory satisfactions.

The current emphasis on skills in curriculum innovation is welcome. Yet innovations are not immune to the process of trivialisation which has bedevilled pastoral care. A structured approach is not necessarily mechanistic, but due to lack of training and resources there is a danger of initiating a reductionism which denies the vitality and imagination of human beings. The principles of counselling are not only a safeguard, but a spur to development. They are:

1 The creation of a safe climate in which the pupil can look at his behaviour and attitudes openly without fear of exploitation.

2 The reinforcement of strengths rather than concentration only on weaknesses.

3 Helping the individual understand how he contributes to the events of which he complains and to his successes.

4 Developing in him a diagnostic orientation which allows him to detect the steps he has to take to solve the problem.

5 Using the skills of anticipation and inoculation (see *Guidance 16–19*), to increase his sense of power, by enabling him to break habitual, fruitless patterns of behaviour.

6 Increasing the sense of responsibility to others so that his behaviour yields greater satisfaction, not only to those figuring importantly in his life, but also to himself.

The last point reminds us that counselling is not loosely self-indulgent, encouraging the complacency that one is to be satisfied with what one currently is. Neither is its advocation of caring and co-operation endorsement of peace at any price. It is concerned with the social as much as with the individual. Counselling creates awareness of the ways we judge others. The need to ask what underlies our reactions and acquire insight into our motives is prime. What is true for the teacher as counsellor is just as true for the adolescent as learner.

How is this to be facilitated in a genuine and lasting way? How can valuable innovations be protected from degeneration into superficiality, perhaps sham? The answer seems to lie in modifying peer group interaction by creating a network of helping relationships and co-operative activities, bringing pupil and pupil, pupils and teachers, into a joint endeavour. Adolescents should not only be involved in their own guidance and the pastoral programme, but also take major responsibility for counselling each other. I described the counselling process in 1974 as a market place in which changes occurred; i.e. a two way process is at work, not a unilateral flow aimed at the pupil. Unilateral situations in tutor periods mean confrontations: exchanges mean the tutor as a good teacher can learn from pupils, receiving support as much as giving it. As we move towards the community school where different age groups work together – the elderly, middle aged and young – the irrelevance of many present relationships is obvious. Curriculum developments of worth, such as CPVE, will be semblance rather than reality if the nature of the relationships does not change.

The previous chapter began by showing how the individual represents, indeed makes, his own reality. We are impelled towards earnest pursuit of the capacity to take the standpoints of others, constructing their position imaginatively and accurately, so that we grasp the reasons for apparently awkward or irrational behaviour and understand the goals for which they strive. Hazards stem from our limited perceptions of peer groups. We tend to focus on the negative to the exclusion of the positive. From the vantage point of the adolescent the peer group is a source of help and protection. It is a long time since Sir John Adams remarked that one cannot teach John Latin without knowing John; today it is as true to say that John cannot learn without knowing his teacher. All concerned in education will benefit from questioning their perceptions and learning to understand the others' viewpoint. Pupils misinterpret the motives of teachers and doubt their sincerity; adults focus on the brashness, unforthcomingness and unpredictability of adolescents. Rutter (1976) argues that self-depreciation and other feelings of misery are not recognised by adults; not even by those who are in close contact with adolescents professionally. My basic argument is that peer groups contain positive elements which can contribute to pastoral work. The development of peer counselling will also minimise interaction which constrains or harms their members.

Counselling is based on trust, and that derives from open communication. Where there is little communication, trust is usually absent. It is time for a major shift in perceptions of guidance by the pastoral team; pupils will no longer be the passive recipients of our alleged wisdom. In profiles we attempt to assess such characteristics as initiative and reliability. May not genuine opportunities for involvement in their own and other's guidance and counselling stimulate responsible achievement in these areas? Authority relations are a proper focus for concern in pastoral work, but should not the outcome be that of bringing pupils and teachers into co-operative relationships? Fifth-year pupils in the work briefly reported in Hamblin (1984) stressed their impatience with trivia. They desired treatment as equals in the sense of receiving signs of respect and concern about the resolution of teacher–pupil difficulties in some schools. School could have been rejected as irrelevant to life, yet there seemed to be an honest desire for a more personal kind of interaction with teachers. A sound peer counselling scheme provides this.

Peer counselling uses friendship constructively: an obvious statement which conceals many complexities. Friendship gives a feeling of personal worth; yet it also increases self-knowledge, counteracting the omnipotence or illusions of peculiarity that dominate, or feature in, the adolescent's self-perception. Friends can size up motives, ability and character with intimidating accuracy. The relationship makes it possible for the recipient to accept the opportunity for looking at behaviour from a new perspective. The need for affiliation sets limits: the expression of anxiety or distaste by a friend is a cogent signal. Mutual controls and encouragement lead to the development of insights, not least when emotions run high. A caring friend acts as a safeguard against impulsivity or succumbing to undesirable group pressures. Emotive group situations invite abdication of responsibility and abandonment of standards. Friends can provide mutual support which allows young people to escape that trap. Stereotypes have to be questioned: it is likely that girls seek support from friends more noticeably than boys; but ambivalences are built into the relationship, which create tensions or sudden disruption of the friendship and vulnerability to character assassination and rumour. Boys apparently depend more on the group, but the best friend is used to mediate its influence, and this relationship then continues alongside heterosexual relationships. Relationships and emotions occupy boys as deeply, although they are defensively reluctant to admit it unless they are sure of the intent of the adult.

Peer groups present stable and clear expectations to their members, acting also as a setting in which participation is more likely to be as equals, rather than inferiors meeting superiors. They *can* make a contribution to mental health by providing relief from the pressures of adults' contradictory demands for autonomy and conformity, permitting confusions and tensions to be aired. In appropriate circumstances, they will reinforce social change by bringing together people from diverse backgrounds in pursuit of a unifying common cause; stimulating discussion and assimilation of new horizons and life styles. Yet, especially if largely composed of males from disadvantaged backgrounds, they reinforce prejudices, obscure possibilities and perpetuate tradition destructively. The salient fact is that peer group interaction is the means through which young people gain some sense of mastery of their environment: a fact which the pastoral team would be foolish to ignore.

Discontinuities increase with acceleration of social change, but they can be creative, as Adams *et al* (1976) show in their work on understanding and managing personal change. Peer groups cushion necessary breaks with tradition and the constraints of a person's past. The developmental stance urges pastoral teams to harness peer groups as a way of developing identity and effectiveness rather than deprecating their influence or pretending they do not exist.

Using peer interaction constructively does not mean we are attempting to abrogate parental functions, nor are we abandoning our professional values. The latter can be implemented more efficaciously; the former renegotiated. There is evidence, e.g. Lindley (1976) that older pupils see parental intervention in their school lives as an attack on their autonomy or as denial of their maturity. They protest at the perpetuation of earlier dependent relationships, although accepting the propriety of teacher contact with parents when severe trouble occurs. Again, let us beware exaggeration: some adolescents seem to be poorly equipped to meet parental demands and inflexibly reject their views, but they are exceptions. Kandel and Lesser (1972) and Coleman (1974) reveal that the significant fact may be similarity of values rather than deep-seated generational conflict. Conflict itself may be manifested as indifference rather than aggression, or more likely, centre on relatively minor issues such as dress or lateness. There is, therefore, evidence of coincidence of major values in parents and their children. When decisions carry important future consequences, almost inevitably pupils refer them to their parents. Reid *et al* (1974) showed parental influence as the prime factor in subject choice. Such findings, in conjunction with the experience of tutors that a cautious, provident and forceful professional father may distort his son's or daughter's A-level choices, again show the need for caution in dismissing parental influence.

Peer counselling

The movement towards experientially based methods of learning has been accompanied by growing recognition that, as I have argued, 'Counselling is only effective when it is part of the everyday life of the school' and that it is 'a joint enterprise involving other teachers.' (Hamblin, 1974). This integration demands increased professionalism from the tutor, who will have not only to make logical and methodological connections between different parts of the course followed by the student, but also accept the learner's experience as the fundamental data of counselling. Heathcote *et al* (1982) helpfully distinguish between evaluation and assessment: the former is concerned with the appraisal of a total situation; assessment is appraisal of the achievement produced by a particular educational experience. Evaluation, as just described, is a major element in counselling: counsellors are concerned with the total context. The FEU (1983) claims that the individual learner has the right to identify his or her learning needs, but also argues that tutors should be able to helpfully modify obvious misconceptions about those needs, and dispel prejudice about certain approaches to learning. The right may be legitimate, but does that guarantee that the ability or desire to assess one's learning needs is possessed? Counselling may have the difficult task of bringing both into being.

Prejudiced people try to achieve security by rigidly allocating people and experiences to simple categories of good or bad; strong or weak; active or passive; masculine or feminine. The sense of threat is ever present, and all-too-easily activated. Counselling will be necessary to help such a rigid person, who will tend to make up his or her mind instantly, stubbornly refusing to admit doubt and the need for further evidence. He or she will need counselling support as they learn to tolerate uncertainty and anxiety as they tackle the unfamiliar.

Let us now turn to wider issues. Mansell (1983) in introducing the document just mentioned, remarks that, 'Flexibility in learning is about optimising the autonomy of the learner'. Most teachers would agree that flexibility in learning is a necessary part of preparation for the technological explosion accompanying the approaching post-industrial world. But what can the pastoral programme contribute to the necessary adaptations? A clue is provided by Evans (1983) who illuminates the problem by reminding us that it is the learning from the experience which is valuable, rather than the experience *per se*. Objectives do not inevitably lead to neglect of processes, although over-reliance on them could encourage this. Experience has to be reflected on; well done, the reflection leads to new activity enriched by that reflection. This continuous process is the equivalent of developmental counselling described by Blocher (1966) as a search after effectiveness. It incorporates the assumptions that the individual is capable of making his own choices and taking responsibility for his own behaviour and future development. It is this which suggests that peer counselling can be used not as an expedient device, but as a necessity. The triple aims of integration, consideration of the total context of learning and the stimulation of mastery behaviour can be facilitated, through peer counselling which incorporates evaluation and productive reflection, into small group activity.

Williams (1973) and Hamblin (1974) discuss peer counselling but it remains a sadly neglected potential resource, although a few schools have successfully attempted it. The work at Abergele school described in *Insight One* (1985) demonstrates that different age groups can work together in mutually reinforcing and motivating ways. Little would be necessary to extend this into peer counselling. Vertical tutor groups, which presented difficulties when a pastoral programme was organised on a year basis, may come into their own with peer counselling and curricular development. There is, how-ever, no need for different age groups to work together as a requisite for peer counselling because it can be a logical extension of the co-operative self-help groups described earlier as a basis for formative assessment. It also makes sensible use of well-known facts: pupils talk more, and with greater ease, to one another than they do to their teachers; they offer sympathy when distress occurs, and take each other's perspective. They can, of course, intimidate, display selfishness and exploit as well as help, but they are less likely to behave like this in groups where responsibility is expected of them.

Withers (1976), in an experiment on peer counselling, argues that a preliminary programme of decision-making and problem-solving activities is a pre-requisite. Quite so, but this is the function of the pastoral programme. From the first year we should set out to encourage positive peer group interaction in these activities, bearing in mind that peer groups may insulate their members indiscrimi-nately against the demands of the school, producing informal, perhaps tacit, agreements about investment of effort and the nature of learning. Perhaps this sounds negative, almost contradictory to the earlier discussion, although it merely calls attention to the need for early and positive intervention.

After the honeymoon period following entry to the school, old tendencies reassert themselves. Limited methods of coping with demands, or the use of evasive techniques, are rewarded with peer approval. Early positive guidance on successful coping with learning problems and managing peer pressures should be paramount. Pupils derive short-run benefits from 'playing the system' and wriggling out of trouble, but the long-run costs of 'robbing Peter to pay Paul' and staving off trouble, are ignored both by pupils and pastoral activities. I have wondered if this accounts for the fact that vulnerability to peer group influence is strongest amongst those with the lowest achievement.

The thrust of guidance in the early secondary years will be towards creating legitimacy for the exploration of behaviour and motives. The experience of counselling and training counsellors for years satisfies me that extension of pupils' understanding of behaviour produces both greater self-control and increased sensitivity to the needs of others. This then leads to the realisation that if, as outlined above; peer groups function to make life tolerable (by insulating members against external demands, and also by supporting patterns of behaviour seen by pupils as rewarding and desirable) then attempts at imposing change from outside the group will involve an uneconomical investment of effort at least, or prove abortive. Is this yet another reason why we end the term exhausted?

Changes are most likely to be induced in the context of the peer group by those who have credibility with other members. Those who lead and benefit from peer structures possess sufficient status to act as agents for change. The engagement of opinion leaders in peer counselling seems to be almost inevitable if apathy is to be dispelled, and the opportunities afforded by curriculum change used to the full.

Teachers often comment on the closed groups created by the tendency for pupils holding similar attitudes and values to associate together. Affiliation with, or dissociation from, school is then reinforced. 'Roughs' and 'respectables' form extreme populations displaying antipathy to one another. One questions whether peer counselling can be a reality in such circumstances. From experience I know that it is. Obviously, pupil groups founded in affiliation to school present fewer barriers to the development of support strategies which encourage responsible initiative in learning; but the others, despite their low expectations of success and suspicious attitudes, will question their predictions and modify behaviour when counselling is offered in a climate of acceptance rather than blame, and respected friends and liked teachers are the source. The key is the attitude of the tutor.

Counselling research, such as that of Truax and Carkhuff (1967) and Carkhuff and Anthony (1979), suggests that empathy or the capacity to take the standpoint of the individual and comprehend his feelings, is essential for effective helping. Spontaneity – the skill of making constructive adaptations to the perceived and expressed needs of the counselled, rather than sticking rigidly to preconceptions of what they should need – is something which has to be fostered in both students and teachers through staff development.

Genuineness, honesty and the concern which allows the counsellor to admit his mistakes are safeguards against unintentional harm to the pupil. What does this mean to us? First, we have to strive to ensure that our response is to the pupils' behaviour and not to the labels acquired by the individual or group, with the consequent dubious attribution of motives and meaning. We have to ask what functions the behaviour serves for the individual. The questioning of our judgements and interpretations of behaviour has to be at the forefront of in-service training. Second, we have to pay attention to pupils' perceptions of our roles and motives. If I cannot see that a pupil regards me not as benevolent, but as an interfering Nosey Parker, or that he feels my underlying motive is that of labelling him as abnormal; if I fail to see he interprets my actions as harrassment, then I hamstring myself as a counsellor. If I do see it, but lack the courage and skill to bring these perceptions construc- tively into the open and make them part of the counselling, I almost certainly perpetuate that pupil's destructive assumptions, and harm has been done. Third, I must be practical, helping pupils take one step at a time, recognising that while instant change is improbable, this is not the end of the matter. Constant monitoring, support and adaptation to changing circumstances yield results.

Preliminary work includes discussion of the tutor's role as organiser and supporter, and of the purposes of peer counselling. Questions of trust, confidentiality and the limits of peer counselling are explored, while misconceptions about the responsibility asked of pupils must be corrected. We want no distorted versions of being one's brother's keeper. Willingness to work together supportively crumbles as soon as a tutor conveys the impression that one person is necessarily inferior because he receives some help, rather than presenting peer counselling accurately as the mutual reinforcement of confidence and achievement through pooling resources. These remarks are necessary because pupils, especially in the fifth and sixth years, are highly sensitive to loss of face, and comparisons wreak havoc. An example is provided by the girl I met this week who refuses to take two years over her A-level mathematics as strongly advised by caring teachers. Why? Her father felt she would lose status with her sixth-form group; she agreed that she would probably fail doing it in one year, but that if she did not make the attempt, the others in her group would have no time for her.

Girls seem more open-minded and ready to try; boys appear more defensive initially, but individual differences outweigh any apparent sex-linked trends. More important is the fact that peer counselling cannot be introduced without consideration of the legacy of earlier pastoral work. If the school has created conditions in which pupils believe the pastoral heads are punishment-orientated, dealing only with those 'in trouble', and that tutors are agents of this system, scepticism is likely to be high initially. Sometimes a phenomenon such as that reported by Wills (1971) emerges. Some of my former students had gone into a school where pastoral development was sponsored by a new head, but the old regime continued because a sub-culture had developed amongst groups of pupils which reflected, even caricatured, the earlier teacher attitudes and formal disciplinary system. This mitigated against peer counselling because mutual respect had been replaced by exploitation and 'putting down' of each other. Insecurity then resulted in testing out the adult: attempts at forcing him into false positions or turning the situation to their own account had to be worked through patiently.

Similarly, pupils have sometimes been left feeling that pastoral activities are trivial. Fifth-year pupils have reported honestly that they feel nothing has been achieved by pastoral care in their school, nor is it likely to be. In such circumstances they will approach peer counselling with mixed feelings. Insecurity created by staff–student relationships accentuates the tensions felt by pupils between what they seem to others, and what they seem to themselves. Even the competent student may not see himself as such, being entangled in self-depreciation and inner insecurity which is strengthened by the network of interaction in the school. Isolates (by this I do not mean the healthily independent, almost self-sufficient introvert), seem to treat friendship as a superficial thing, finding trust difficult. To expect peer counselling to overcome such deep-seated tendencies is asking too much.

Staff development is crucial. Difficulties abound: teachers who

developed a survival kit in their early teaching, and who have
maintained it, perhaps increasing the social and attitudinal distance
between themselves and their pupils, will find such procedures a
distasteful attack on their beliefs about what works in teaching.
There are still teachers who see the pupil role as passive and
inferior. Yet a post-industrial society requires pupils to choose
responsibly, and teachers who know they cannot impose. Staff
development brings anxieties and uncomfortable feelings into the
open, relating them to peer counselling. Tutors may feel their role
is eroded; that pupils will be vulnerable to the negative influences of
their peer group if the tutor encourages peer support. The belief
that peer involvement in tackling problems diminishes the teacher
leads to the cry, 'But what if they make a mess of it?' as if the
teacher has a monopoly of wisdom.

Next, pupils have to be gradually introduced to their helping
roles. Time must be available for adjustments and modification,
e.g. some pupils have to be protected against over-enthusiasm. Too
sudden and intense demands will foster dishonesty because pupils
believe they must deliver the goods. Time is necessary to foster the
mutual ability to give and take criticism. Imposition and passivity
are both foreign to peer counselling: the helper chooses to give it;
the helped decides to receive and use it. Our concern is with
friendship, not artificially created relationships. I have noted that
the best counselling usually occurs between friends of the same sex
although peer help by a member of the opposite sex can productively
lessen feelings of rivalry, comparison and consequent inadequacy.
Problems occur in cross-sex counselling when one partner wishes to
extend the relationship, but the other does not. Yet this is part of
everyday life with which young people have to come to terms, and
scarcely a convincing reason for abandoning peer counselling.

The following steps were usually involved in peer counselling,
although each team will have to work out its own procedures:

1 The contractual elements are defined so that the helper or
   small group is aware of the nature of the task. In this initial
   stage I found it useful to look at the danger of emotional
   blackmail on both sides, the danger of improper pressure by
   helpers and of imposing their point of view.

2 Clarification is essential in counselling because the 'client' may
   not know what the problem really is. Emotions may confound
   understanding, or family influences may give it idiosyncratic

or odd meanings. The tutor need not be present, indeed it is often better for him to withdraw as the helper's view of the difficulty is compared with that of its holder. The tutor may be called in to assess or extend. To dispense with this clarification brings the risk of focusing on a false definition of the problem.

3 A diagnostic approach equivalent to that of formative assessment should be adopted once the dimensions of the problem are known. Small groups or partners are alert to the presence and impact of predictions, the fear of loss of face if failure is a possibility, and the presence and reactions of others who will form the audience for the changed behaviours. Barriers, hazards and sources of support are identified, and plans made for dealing with them.

4 Regular reporting back of progress will be necessary. This need not always be to the tutor directly; he can be called in as a consultant. The self-help groups can be used as a source of evaluation and ideas. Helper and helpee can validate their perceptions of what is happening against those of others. These progress reports then motivate further activity and change.

Since beginning this chapter I have assessed a dissertation and interviewed a student whose project employed a version of peer counselling. Sixth form students were involved – the details do not matter, but the outcomes do. They assessed the improvement of those they helped, maintained a sensible confidentiality about what they were told by their 'clients' and demonstrated the ability to win their confidence, talking them through periods of doubt and frustration. The counsellors gained from the experiences, taking the responsibility maturely, gaining great benefits from the new mode of interaction with their tutor. Interestingly, the progress checks undertaken in conjunction with the helpee seemed to deepen the relationship: again we see that appraisal conducted in an atmosphere of liking and responsibility is motivating.

Let me now assess the difficulties. Boys tend to be less apt than girls, perhaps reflecting their slower rate of maturation or different learning in the field of social relationships. Same sex helpers may evoke feelings of rivalry or inadequacy, but opposite sex helpers could introduce inappropriate notions of sexuality and obligation. Realism is essential: there is no guarantee that peer counselling will always work. Indeed, there are times when it is harmful. For example, friends may profess to be in a helping relationship, when in practice it is one of pairing, where each insulates the other aginst the constructive influence of the tutor and larger peer group. Immediate interruption of this mechanism is imperative. The tutor's perceptions or fears are vital: e.g. he or she may predict that the helper will not achieve results or resent what they see as infringement of their status. Unmodified, such attitudes have obvious implications: the negative expectations are conveyed to the students, influencing their investment in peer support, therefore the activity is abortive.

The essential requirement is for a practical and concrete approach. Goals should be defined explicitly once values and the problem are clarified, then alternative ways of reaching the goals examined and the first steps spelt out. Tutors may blanch at this, claiming they will not have enough time. Obviously they must be allowed sufficient time: but the point is that they do not have to do it all; they act as consultants for the pupils who actually carry out the step-by-step analysis.

Tutors might well initiate the counselling process by using the life space diagram. The peer counsellor helps his partner construct the equivalent of a 'snapshot' which describes his or her current life space. Pressures, strengths, weaknesses and sources of support are all included. The pupil puts himself in the centre of the paper, making statements that he considers relevant to the goals he pursues, and his academic progress and social relationships. He then systematically looks at other areas of life, relating them to his goals. This simple technique provides both a framework and orientation for later peer counselling. Tutors themselves will shape their interventions and support to facilitate movement from external to internal sense causation, e.g. from 'This is too difficult for me,' to 'How do I change the way I study so that I can succeed?' The plaint, 'They don't treat me fairly' has to be changed. 'What do I have to do to make them stop pushing me around?' is likely to be productive.

Many so-called unmotivated pupils are victims of their perception of an impossible task or helplessness from which they find no escape. Peer counselling may provide some solution because it both changes peer group interaction and relates to the developmental tasks concerned with puberty and the accompanying experience of more complex social relationships. Key issues will include the need for constructive self-assertion and for resisting the influence of the peer group when it erodes identity or foists an unwanted one on the individual. These are the realities of life which enhance or confound the lives of young people; given concrete examples as an anchorage, even the allegedly less able pupils tackle these topics maturely.

Group discussions should also study the forces which reduce individual responsiblity. Expectations have a compulsive hold on people; heads of year or house often feel trapped by them but so do adolescents, to whom they almost seem contagious. All of us feel insecure when we cannot share our expectations with people important to us, but the pressures of expectations force adolescents to abandon a desired position for the reward of acceptance. Sixth-form pupils often retreat into a cynical compliance which masks a retreatism best put as, 'Well, I do as they want, then I go home and try to be myself, wondering what the hell it's all about!' Simple group mechanisms will have to be examined, e.g. the 'gatekeeper' who is the individual, not necessarily the obvious leader, who controls incoming information because he is seen as having a special credibility. Processes of filtering out certain information and distorting or amplifying other messages usually emerge. Informal feedback is admittedly patchy, and often comes from those for whom the experience came at the right moment and who developed a positive relationship with the supervising counsellor. Nevertheless, it indicates that peer counselling acted as a springboard for professional creativity or set them on the road to successful artistic, commercial or industrial initiative and innovation.

I would argue that self-appraisal in a peer group context orientated toward support is important for identity through self-awareness. The acceptance coming from friends has a special poignancy which allows discussion of vulnerability to emotional blackmail from parents or peers; exploration of feelings of ineffectiveness or being manipulated; dissatisfaction with running one's life on the basis of expediency; or the fear of being seen as deviant. It has struck me that we are unwilling to accept that loss of the fear of being deviant is most likely to occur in a group setting where acceptance is immediately given. I have dealt with techniques in *Guidance 16–19*. It seems appropriate here to look at general topics. If the tutor encourages pupils to look at their tendencies to interrupt, put others down, attack, support or show warmth in their discussions, personal effectiveness will improve and so will the learning climate. Strategies such as setting up smoke screens of sarcasm or superiority to hide inadequacy; attempts at intimidation; scoring points to reinforce a precarious ascendancy are most helpfully reached through peer counselling. The argument is simple: if such things constrain pupils' performance, reducing the impact of our hard work as teachers, then it is sensible to do something about them. There is no need to seek out the pathological or dramatic: reactions to everyday embarrassments, disappointments and novel situations merit examination because they cause pupils to stumble. Trust fundamentally relates to the perception of the other person as potentially beneficial or harmful. Often such attributions go unnoticed, or are merely regretted, when they could be the material for guidance. The criteria for trust in varied situations and with different individuals and groups should be brought to the fore, beginning with simple, immediate situations, e.g. 'If your friend is broke, how do you know he will pay back a loan?' Trust is a necessary ingredient of human intercourse, but a pastoral programme does not blindly endorse trust as a virtue. Deutsch (1973) comments that trust can be a form of innocence carrying a dangerous lack of appreciation of the consequences. Distrust may be seen as morally more flagrant than credulity: an evaluation unhelpfully encouraged at times by counselling and psychological treatments. Trust is possibly most dangerous when it is a resigned response to uncertainty motivated by a sense of hopelessness. It is seductive when used to bring commendation and acceptance, as a form of immediate gratification without regard for future consequences. Pastoral programmes should shun the romanticism of trust: insisting that while it is at the heart of development and mental health, it must be submitted to tough criteria.

Staff development should include greater understanding of group interaction and functions. Increased volume of communication is not necessarily improved communication, neither can we take the fallacious viewpoint that it will inevitably lead to better understanding and co-ordination. It may lead to awareness of discrepancies of objectives and motives. One head of year or house should acquire knowledge based on sound academic work which he brings to bear on the problems of group interaction. Communication does not necessarily produce co-operation (Baron *et al*, 1974; Berkowitz, 1980), although Deutsch's findings suggest that communication is better in co-operative groups.

Members of a developmentally orientated pastoral team should address themselves to the problem of applying some of this knowledge to their pastoral activities. For example, to alert pupils to the nature and functions of rumour, and how it flourishes in conditions of ambiguity, is surely a sensible anticipation of life. Even self-fulfilling prophecies are talked about as if they were uniform, when in practice they vary in their impact according to the nature of the group. Where the orientation is toward rejection of authority, or suspicion of the intent of outsiders is strong, then they will be ignored or will strengthen existing attitudes. There is well established evidence (Cartwright and Zander, 1968; Shaw, 1971) that conflict between groups sharpens members' group identity, defines the boundaries of the group more precisely, and increases cohesiveness. The pastoral principle of harnessing even the ostensibly negative in the service of development still applies. Sherif (1966) summarises his work on conflict and co-operation which showed that superordinate goals with compelling reward value have an integrating effect. Why? They could not be achieved without co-operation between the competing groups, therefore, they function as powerful agents for attitude change. A pastoral team should search for such superordinate activities and incorporate them as part of the programme. CPVE, TVEI and other vocationally based courses provide such goals, but others can be developed through community work and helping projects. The climate of co-operation is extended through peer counselling and support in the small groups. Even the unwilling then find it hard to deny that pastoral work is concerned with the realities of life.

6 The First Year

The nature and purpose of the activities

The activities are not presented as a complete programme to be followed without modification. That would block the dialogue between pupils and tutors about pastoral activity, resulting in lowered commitment on both sides. What is presented has been carefully selected from the materials tested out by all involved. Activities have been eliminated which, although successful in the hands of teachers who had followed an intensive one year full-time training course, make heavy demands on the tutor for preparation, or are liable to misinterpretation by pupils and their parents. Many other ideas for activities will be found in the preceding chapters.

Ideas and points of departure are provided, but their integration into a package suited to a particular school requires exercise of curriculum development and leadership skills by the pastoral head. The fact that activities have been tested does not mean they are tutor-proof. Fortunately, the tutor who has the knack of taking anything and make it not work is rare. There are some however, who cause tutor activities to founder because they do not understand their purpose. In-school training and the support of the pastoral head in encouraging tutors to select only activities which he or she sees as purposeful, are safeguards against misuse, although pupils may then be denied helpful experiences. More dangerous is the apparent enthusiast who grabs materials eagerly, but does not consider how he will adapt them to the needs of the form. Pastoral heads must face the dilemma created by those who will use the materials as a means of occupying the form while they get on with something else. After such experiences pupils are left saying, 'So what?' and tutor work is condemned as a waste of time.

Tutors' perceptions cannot be ignored; not only are they surprisingly varied, but they incorporate idiosyncratic factors. Topics should not be imposed because they may have a personal relevance and import for the tutors which makes them incapable of handling them objectively. In a CFPS couse, a well respected head of year was testing out material and getting feedback from tutors. She was shocked by a religiously determined rejective response from a tutor who labelled very ordinary decision-making material as Anti-Christ! Difficult to understand, but acceptance of the reality of those feelings was essential. The impact on the tutor, even more on the pupils, would have been profound if the tutor had been coerced.

In evaluations of 40 schools I found class teachers were unconvinced of the value of a pastoral programme, but even more worried about failing or harming pupils. Discussion of difficulties may be hampered by tutors' feelings that they ought to be able to cope. Respect for tutors' anxieties is essential. Provision of early feedback and opportunities for immediate discussion help tutors see the truth of the old adage that the fantasy is often worse than the reality. Teachers correctly perceive that it is easy to take off the 'emotional lid', but then more difficult to deal with the real or imagined discontent and self-dissatisfactions that are unthinkingly stimulated. Readiness to scapegoat and blame others is part of the mild paranoid fantasy which lurks below the superficial compliance of some adolescents. Others, conditioned to see defeat of authority as a way of consolidating their prestige with peers in their 'us against them' upbringing, welcome any chance of displaying hostility. Creation of states of arousal is far from therapeutic: activities have therefore been scanned to eliminate those which invite excitement of this kind. More positively, we believe the activities selected will act, as part of a long term programme, to increase pupils' sense of responsibility.

Elaborate activities not only frustrate the tutor, but can impede attainment of the desired learning. The situation is akin to that of over-complex simulations where the original objectives get lost. Sometimes the procedures and interaction are powerful forms of learning which contradict stated aims. I have ruefully seen that pupils have learned to compete rather than co-operate! The emphasis therefore has been on simple activity and subsequent discussion focused on concrete problems.

We earnestly hope that, in the ways indicated in earlier chapters, pupils will become increasingly active in the choice of topics and the manufacture of materials for their own guidance. This is the reverse of the caution given in the preceding paragraph. Autonomy and independence only assume problematical form when unintended reinforcement of adolescent omnipotent fantasy has been built into the activity or encouraged by an immature tutor. We, however, see teachers as professionals of integrity, capable of inducing responsible pupil co-operation in the development of a pastoral programme. This joint enterprise produces mutual understandings which feed into classroom interaction. Critically, the involvement of pupils provides insights which make it easier to maintain a balance between present needs and the future identities of pupils.

The first-year pupil

All guidance is basically concerned with the development and implementation of identity. First-year pupils suffer a sense of discontinuity in the transfer from primary to secondary school. The picture presented by pupils in their first few weeks seems to be a curious parody of reality, in which pupils and teachers are not quite themselves. Identities which were well articulated in the primary school in relation to peers, teachers and schoolwork seem to be suspended during the transitional honeymoon period of the first six weeks or thereabouts. The functions of a traditional honeymoon include separation from, and often closure of, past relationships; coming to terms with new demands; and tolerating unpleasant realities associated with intimacy.

Elsewhere I have reported activities and ideas which allow tutors to cope with the needs and tensions of the first few weeks (Hamblin 1978; 1984). A first year pastoral programme should use the honeymoon intensively to give pupils the immediate experience of success and being cared for. Their expressed needs are usually about coping with the demands of new methods of teaching and learning, discipline and peer relationships. If a good start is to be made, then the school should give the first year the best tutors. Realism, however, acknowledges that not every caring and competent tutor can relate to first-year pupils. They present a facade of virtue, can be unduly fussy, blame others for their misfortunes, and adopt a surface appearance of 'pleasing teacher', while quite skilfully testing out the limits of acceptable behaviour as a prelude to middle of the road performance. In some, underlying anxiety is cloaked by conformity and the semblance of coping.

Even a casual glance reveals striking differences in physical development. The tutor quickly discovers that these are accompanied by parallel variations in social and emotional development. Some pupils are over-dependent, some already strive for dominance provocatively. Fashion and sex role behaviours already preoccupy some. Girls show dependence upon the best friend: the relationship may, however, incorporate petty jealousies and attempts at manipulation. Girls seem more vulnerable to psychological aggression, i.e. rumour and character assassination. Boys are developing defensive fronts of toughness, taunting one another about their masculinity, and the problems of puberty are given expression in competitive comparisons of bodily development.

Schools are no longer barren wildernesses of pitchpine and concrete. First-year pupils are concerned with their comfort and the quality of daily life. I am impressed by the efforts made in many schools to provide comfort, colour and effective display of pupils' work. Intensification of these exertions will create the context for meaningful pastoral care; not just to overcome unfavourable comparisons of the secondary with the primary school; but as acceptance of the fact that a physical environment incorporates an evaluation of those who use it. The transition from primary to secondary school evokes insecurity which is reduced by the signals of worth inherent in a pleasant environment.

The first-year tutors have to adapt flexibly if they are to cope with the range of attitudes and behaviours which confront them. Pupils' responses to the transition will depend on the ethos and methods of the primary school, family and cultural background as well as personal development. The content of pastoral work is equally varied. First-year pupils are aware of unemployment and will wish to discuss it. Gender stereotypes will have to be examined, and learned helplessness brought to pupils' attention. Much of this will be done as the opportunity arises, the tutor providing a model of open-mindedness. Self-evaluation of learning and school work have to be introduced; problem-solving based on consideration of the evidence reinforced. Activities must break into conventional, unquestioning responses which prejudge the issues.

We have accepted the maturity of pupils in subject areas such as computer work and mathematics, but is this matched in the fields of social learning and emotional development? A final point: some teachers will say, 'Why bother with active learning? Why not save time and just tell them?' My rejoinder would be that we have been telling them for years, but the upshot has been that they seem to take little notice, or conform without understanding. Is this adequate preparation for an uncertain future? Professionalism demands empathy with the pupil who is in a situation where he has to protect his personal integrity, creating the means of preserving individuality, simultaneously balancing the legitimate demands of teachers against the need to maintain a good face with peers. Inevitably, there will be the teacher who says, 'Well, I didn't have all this, but I coped all right.' I wonder?

The induction phase

First-year guidance is concerned with feelings and perceptions at least as much as with behaviour. It is the product of professional assessment of the discrepancies between the resources of individuals and the legitimate demands of the school. This assessment should include consumer research which involves first-years: examples can be found in Hamblin (1978) where almost 2000 pupils were involved, and in Hamblin (1984). The induction programme is concerned with creating the conditions for success, and not confined to overcoming anxieties. It could be argued that there is no need for an induction programme because pupils settle down. The reply must be, 'Yes, but into what?' Superficial adaptations can occur which obscure the fact that pupils are moving into apathy, ritual performance, underfunctioning and growing dissociation from school. The transition reveals weaknesses which may not have been evident in the primary school. Primary school records and information from primary teachers, although very important, do not reveal all potential difficulties.

Some pupils have the latent resources with which to cope, others do not. For example, some pupils cope with, even enjoy, the sudden expansion in the number and range of social relationships inherent in the move to the secondary school. A minority fall into confusion or are chronically ill at ease. Even the apparently well-adjusted pupil may be less competent than appears at first sight! Small group activities allow pupils to chat freely; the alert tutor quickly picks up clues about difficulties, assessing with the pastoral head whether a pupil is likely to be at risk. The induction course should be designed to create enthusiasm for learning and build confidence in pupils, creating a positive image of teachers and the school. It should communicate the fact that the school is a caring community. A full description of an induction programme is given in Hamblin (1978), but some of the activities below may be included.

1 Several sessions should be given on the role of the tutor, the purposes of pastoral care and the job of the head of year or house. It is important to establish the parameters of pastoral care immediately, if pupils are not to begin to see the pastoral head as one who solely deals with those in trouble. Associated activities could include:

a Writing down questions they will ask the year or house head. Individuals' questions are then discussed in small groups and one is selected by each small group. The pastoral head then comes in to each tutor group to answer the questions.

b Second-year pupils describe the tutor programme and the way in which pupils can contribute to it. After a general presentation, each second-year pupil works with a small group, giving examples of activities they found interesting.

2 Second-year pupils can be put into a helping role. There is a tendency for some second-year pupils to perpetuate the myths such as 'head down the lavatories' or create tensions as they boost their own status. One or more tutor periods can become 'helping periods' where:

a Second-year pupils work with small groups telling them about the way they coped in the first few weeks.

b They discuss the best ways of coping with homework.

Second-year pupils benefit from this: it allows them to re-work problem areas and increase their sense of competence. Affiliation with the school is increased.

3 Simple decision-making exercises on the theme 'What happens to me if . . .?' will be useful e.g. losing one's dinner money, getting lost when sent on an errand or message, being late for school. Pupils are asked to make a list of situations they want to know about. Small groups share ideas about what will happen, and how they would cope sensibly. They then ask the tutor questions and ask for further ideas. It is crucial that the skills of constructive working in small groups, which are a matter of course in the primary school, are not lost. A positive tutor group climate means that pupils feel confident that they can ask questions and be taken seriously.

4 School rules need to be explained and justified. They should be presented in a way which highlights their rationality, and their

contribution to the well-being of all members of the school community, e.g.

- Rules about situations of danger, swimming baths, workshops and gymnasium. The element of responsibility in not creating hazards for others should be stressed.
- Rules about pupil–pupil interaction. Standpoint-taking and awareness of the feelings of others will be stressed: an element essential for responsibility in a social climate where the threshold for the appearance of aggression has been lowered and courtesy devalued.
- Rules about teacher–pupil interaction; showing that the rules are as binding for the teacher as for the pupil, and that they are rooted in mutual respect and concern. Pastoral heads should discuss with tutors how they will grasp a particular nettle. Hamblin (1984) reports the concern of first-year pupils about teachers who could not control unruly pupils. Teachers who were late for classes, leaving pupils exposed to the forces within them, or who seemed unaware of school rules created insecurity. Understanding of the unpredictable events which may delay a teacher breaks into the self-righteous stances of certain pupils; understanding how bossiness or priggishness attracts unwelcome attention will also help. The main aim is, however, to stress that the tutor has positive expectations of the group in such situations.

[5] A useful session is one where the group debate the criteria for staying at home or coming to school. Initially, focus is provided by considering events, e.g.

- having a heavy cold;
- the unexpected early arrival of a grandparent from Australia;
- mother's illness.

Rational criteria for attendance or absence should be established, taking into account the cost of a particular action.

[6] Several sessions on coping with teasing and aggression presented as decision-making activities are useful. Discussion will centre on *one* of the following:

- ways of defusing the situation;
- methods of not giving the bully the payoff he wants, e.g. by using humour or remaining calm;

– the level of risk and possible consequences of their reactions, e.g. escalation of conflict.

Examples can be found in Hamblin (1981 and 1984). Another example is:

Bill has a rather fussy and loud-voiced mother who not only walks with him to school as it is on the way to her work, but gives his uniform a final check, straightens his tie and questions him about whether he has forgotten anything. All this happens by the main school gate in front of older pupils. Several of them have started mocking his mother and call Bill a 'nance'. Imagine you and your partner are Bill's best friends. What advice would you give him? How could you help change what is happening?

After partner work the tutor instigates some class discussion. Then the tutor asks the group to evaluate the likely success of the following tactic of the friends:

'Arrange to meet Bill on the way to school, all three of you going ahead of the mother, and going through the school gate before she arrives.'

Among other things, they should consider the mother's feelings and reactions and how they will cope with the name callers. (Pupils often confess to a fear of contagion, i.e. if they help, then the labels will also be attached to them.)

7 A tape is prepared, perhaps most effectively by pupils, in which two pupils are heard coming up to a teacher. One is highly agitated, and says, *'Miss, Miss, Peter Brown keeps picking on me, and he's just taken my new football boots!'* His friend confirms this.

Pupils work in groups of three or four, discussing the following questions. Before they proceed from one to the next, the tutor has a brief discussion with the form, listing the main points on the blackboard.

Questions:

i What do you think the teacher should say immediately? Why?
ii What questions should he or she ask? Why?
iii Why do you think some boys or girls make things worse when they get 'picked on'?

The tutor in the final discussion emphasises the issues they feel are important, e.g. when to complain to the tutor, recognising our own contribution to the unpleasant event or the role of the tutor in these situations.

8 Understanding the bully. First-year pupils are surprisingly mature in their discussions of such topics once they are given the chance of exploring them. Pupils from another year have prepared a tape in which they describe the bullying tactics of a boy in their form. The tape ends with the statement of one pupil, *'You know, when you meet him outside school at the youth club, and get to know him, he's all right. Why does he have to be a bully at school?'*

The tape then stops, and the tutor asks pupils to develop their answers to the question, writing them down on a sheet of paper. They then join up with another group and share ideas. After this, they return to their original group, working out how the bully could change his behaviour and reputation at school. If he stops bullying, what will happen to him? The final discussion led by the tutor focuses on the need to understand why people behave in certain ways.

9 This activity is taken from the Clywd package of First-Year Materials undertaken as part of the Professional Development Programme in Pastoral Care. It is presented as a taped narrative or as a duplicated sheet.

In this example of physical bullying, the bully, Ginger, picks on the unfortunate victim, Pongo, on the way to school. Ginger dislikes Pongo because Pongo never seems to be in trouble, involves himself in lots of societies and clubs and always obtains good marks for his work.

'Hey you, come here!' shouts Ginger. Pongo continues to walk towards school, trying not to take any notice of Ginger. 'Hey creep, I told you to come here,' yells Ginger. Pongo, still pretending not to hear, carries on walking. Ginger becomes annoyed, runs up to Pongo and grabs him by the coat. 'Who was that stupid looking girl I saw you with last night in the Youth Club?' demands Ginger.
'Let go of my coat,' yells Pongo, obviously frightened. Ginger tightens his grip. 'Who was she?' he growls.
'I don't know what you're talking about, I wasn't with any girl last night.'
'Are you calling me a liar, you creep.' says Ginger angrily.
'Get off.' screams Pongo, terrified, 'You're always picking on me.'
Pongo manages to get free and begins to run.
'Come here, chicken,' growls Ginger, 'you're not going to split on me to a teacher.'

Ginger strikes Pongo in the face, cutting his lip and making his nose bleed. At that moment, Mr. Dawson, the Geography teacher, pulls up in his car. Ginger disappears among the crowd of pupils entering school.

What does Pongo do next?

i　Get some friends to help him get his own back on Ginger?
ii　Try not to be alone and keep away from the bully?
iii　Talk to a friend to see if he has any suggestions?
iv　Go straight to a member of staff?
v　Tell his parents when he gets home?

10　This script is also drawn from the Clwyd Project materials. It could be recorded by fourth- or fifth-year pupils who are taking drama.

The Bullies

Cast:　　Victim – A very thin girl with glasses
　　　　　　Bully 1
　　　　　　Bully 2
　　　　　　Bully 3
　　　　　　Victim's best friend

SCENE 1: *The School playground at morning break*

1st Bully:	Oy! You with the red bag.
Victim:	Who me?
2nd Bully:	Yes, I can't see anyone else with a red bag and as skinny as you.
Victim:	I'm not skinny!
3rd Bully:	Yes you are, and you're a specky four eyes.
Victim:	At least its better than two.
3rd Bully:	Do you want a fight?
Victim:	No (*starts crying*).
1st Bully:	You're a coward, aren't you?
Victim:	No I'm not a coward.
2nd Bully:	Alright, we'll fight.
Victim:	If you lay one finger on me, I'll ask my dad to come to school.
1st Bully:	If you do we'll get you out of school.
All Three	Skinny, skinny, who's a little coward.
	(*A fight begins. They pull the victim's hair and have her surrounded. But the bell rings for the end of break so the victim can escape back to class.*)

SCENE 2: *The School canteen at lunch-time*

Friend: What shall we do when we've had dinner. Shall we go outside?

Victim: No, I don't want to go in the playground – I'm going to the medical room.

Friend: Are you sick or something?

Victim: No.

Friend: Why are you going to see the nurse?

Victim: Because I want to.

Friend: That's silly, you must have a reason.
(Victim begins to cry quietly.)

Friend: What are you crying for, what's the matter?

Victim: *(amid sobs)* I'm afraid of meeting those bullies again. They'll tease me again about my glasses, and about being thin. Then they'll chase me again. I want to hide in the medical room.

Friend: You can't go to the medical room every day.

Victim: I can keep finding different places to hide.

Friend: Don't be silly, you can't forever. You'll get fed up.

Victim: What else can I do?

Stop tape for groups to consider what they would say if they were the friend.

Friend: Don't be afraid, I'll be with you all lunch time today so they won't get you.

Victim: But there are three of them, and they're bigger than us.

Friend: We'll get some other girls from our class to go around with us. They won't touch you if we're all together.

Victim: But what about tomorrow.

Friend: We'll stay with a group for the rest of this week, and by then they will have forgotten all about you.

> i   What would/could the victim have done if she hadn't got a particular friend to help her in this way?
>
> ii   How do you think the bullies respond to the victim's threat of bringing her father to school?
>
> iii   Look at the last statement. (Tutor has written this on the blackboard.) Do you think it is true?

Activities on personal and social development

11   *a* Pupils fold a piece of A4 paper into half. They will need felt pens. They are given four minutes to draw themselves as accurately as possible, as they are now. Then on the other side of the folded sheet they draw themselves as they would like to be in five years time, again taking four minutes. They then open the sheet up so that both pictures are visible, discussing the changes they have shown with a friend. What do they hope people will be saying about them in five years time?

  b The tutor gets the class to give him words associated with bodily appearance, e.g. tall, strong, good looking. As many words as possible are collected. Pupils label one page on the reverse of the pictures *I would like to be* and the other *I would not like to be*. Words are selected from the board and placed under the headings with any other words that the pupil wishes. Again, discussion occurs between friends.

  c In groups of four, pupils explore the advantages and disadvantages of:

    i being tall, e.g. people notice you or expect you to behave as if you were older;

    ii being attractive;

    iii being strong.

The tutor ends the session by getting two or three well-liked pupils to introduce a discussion on fashion and self-presentation. Both sexes should be given the leadership positions of initiating discussion.

12 Emotional blackmail from friends is not the problem of first-year pupils exclusively, but they seem to be especially vulnerable to it. Friends simultaneously give mutual support and strive to be in control of the relationship. Some pupils experience helplessness in the face of a friend's attempt to manipulate them into doing something they are uneasy about. An initial exercise could be based on this:

Your best friend had a birthday last week. Today, on the way to school he surprises you by showing you his birthday money, and suggesting that you come with him into town and spend it, rather than going to school. You say that you would prefer to go to school, but he then taunts you, saying that if you don't come with him you're not a real friend. You value his friendship, but you like school and want to do well. How would you deal with this situation?

 a Pupils discuss this situation in groups of three for five minutes.
 b The tutor then produces a flip chart with the following possibilities:

> *i* Offer to go with him after school, if he comes along with you to school.
> *ii* Tell him you will still be his friend if he wants, but you are not going to do what he asks.
> *iii* Explain to him why it is not a good idea, and then leave it to him to decide what he does.
> *iv* Suggest he gets somebody else to go with him.

 c The small groups explore the likely response of the friend to each of these actions. Partners then discuss the way they would act in this situation. Tutors should avoid asking pupils to say what they would do in front of the class. This could stimulate socially desirable answers or other forms of dissembling, e.g. bravado. Both would inhibit further honest involvement in associated activities.

[13] A follow-up is to get partners to write about the incident; one writing as the 'birthday boy or girl', the other as the friend who received the invitation to truant. They are encouraged to give what they believe might be the inner thoughts of that person. Two couples are chosen to read their stories to the form. After the first pair have given their readings, the teacher initiates general discussion on the discrepancies between viewpoints. After the second reading, the partners in the form assess the likelihood of the friendship continuing.

[14] Pupils should be encouraged to identify and explore situations of peer pressure they have met earlier or are currently coping with, e.g. being forced to be unpleasant to somebody they quite like or having to accept a 'dare' because they fear shame more than the risky activity. Why? The malaise that some sixth-form students experience because they feel a false self has been foisted on them partially – I wish to stress the word partially – stems from enforced adaptations to peer group pressures. Older pupils working with first-year pupils can help small groups prepare activities which they present to the tutor group. Other age groups can be involved as

helpers equally profitably. This reminds us of the need for co-ordination and co-operation between members of the team. Tutors of the helping group will have to brief them on the nature of peer forces and provide ideas for the development of the decision-making activities.

|15| Embarrassment is usually associated with social shame and loss of face. The feeling of being unable to cope is an experience which disturbs many first-year pupils when they want to say something sympathetic, but somehow can't. A basic situation might be:

Your friend's dog has died. He has looked after it well through a long illness. You want to tell him how deeply sorry you are, but you can't find the right words and are afraid he won't believe you.

Pupils work out in pairs how they would cope with this. The tutor then encourages them to think of other situations where they would like to show sympathy and caring, but are afraid to, perhaps because they think they may be repulsed, or that this might provoke strong emotions in the other person. This may be especially significant for boys because male expression of emotion and caring is still regarded doubtfully. Tutors list the situations, selecting for further exploration one or two they deem to be especially important.

|16| The idea of denying oneself immediate pleasure for the sake of long term gains has an aura of virtue, although it is becoming less important to many adolescents. Simple decision-making and dis-cussion around down-to-earth situations bring the issue into focus, e.g.

Jim never seems to have enough money because he is always scrounging from his friends. In fact, he has as much as most of them, and more than some. His problem is that he spends his pocket money as soon as he gets it. What advice would you give him?

Pupils work on this in small groups. They then divide into pairs where one plays the part of Jim and the other is the adviser. The adviser gives his advice, but Jim has been instructed to be critical, and look for sensible reasons why the advice will not work. The adviser overcomes them as far as possible by reasoned argument. The tutor circulates, noting the counter-arguments produced by those playing Jim. Two or three are selected for discussion, e.g.

– *'I've always been like it.'*

– *'Well, if I don't spend it straight away, I'll end up losing it.'*
– *'It's my money!'*

Role reversal is useful. The second role play is often very productive. This activity opens up discussion of other behaviour: robbing Peter to pay Paul; staving off trouble in the short run. These ways of coping allow pupils to create a distance between themselves and school work, reducing involvement, and strengthening negative attitudes which began in the primary school. They are responsible in part, I suspect, for the apathy against which we exhaustingly battle.

Learning

Decision-making should be introduced as soon as possible, encouraging first years to take responsibility for their learning. We tend to underestimate first-year pupils' capacity to discuss their learning styles and evaluate their progress. In decision-making approaches to learning, the tutor should concentrate on one aspect of the decision, e.g. the likely costs.

17 A first exercise is usefully related to homework:

It is Thursday night, and you have two subjects to do for homework. You like one of them and are good at it; the other you do not like very much, and always seem to do badly in. Which will you do first? Why?

Pupils are asked to discuss their way of coping, looking at possible consequences. The tutor then begins discussion with the whole class emphasising there is no single right answer; that what works for one pupil may not work with another. Pupils are more aware of personality and its link with style of learning than we think. Therefore the tutor draws attention to such possibilities as the anxious pupil feeling he has to do the 'bad' subject first because he feels it will be 'on his mind'. This is fine in one way, but he may fail to appreciate the danger of spending too long on it, then getting 'fed up', and scamping the liked subject. Crucially, this activity also leads to pupils expressing their need to talk to teachers and fellow pupils about difficulties in learning.

18 This homework decision-making exercise is most effective when presented on a tape as a dramatic excerpt, although it works if put on a flipchart or duplicated sheet:

You have homework which you want to tackle – indeed, you want to do it well – but you don't understand what you have to do. Dad takes a look, but you are suspicious that he hasn't understood it – somehow his advice doesn't seem right. Dad keeps referring to what he did at school but after all it was a long time ago! When you voice your doubts he becomes more insistent that he is right.

Pupils undertake the following activities:

i   Work out with a partner how you could explain your doubts without making Dad angry – he wants to help.
ii Write a short ending to the situation *as if you were Dad* describing his feelings.
iii Write a conversation between Mum and Dad about the incident, after you have gone to bed.

More than one period is necessary. Discussion should be full, as much will emerge about the way tensions develop over homework and pupils' perceptions of parental views. Both may need to be tackled.

19 Homework must be justified, and its purposes understood, if pupils are not to conform passively. The teacher writes on the blackboard: Why is homework set in our school?

a   Partners work on clarifying their views, writing down on a sheet of paper divided into three: *Parents' views; Pupils' views; Teachers' views.*
b   The tutor collects ideas from the class, putting them on the blackboard under headings as above.
c   Partner role play then takes place:

   i   One of the pair plays the teacher who is explaining to a parent the reasons for homework as positively as possible.
   ii Next, the one who was the parent is a son or daughter explaining to his father or mother how they could help with homework without undue interference.

d   Finally, the tutor collects ideas from the form about homework problems they would like to discuss in form periods. Again, older pupils could be involved as helpers.

20 Adjustment focuses on two areas. First, relating to teachers who have intermittent contact with pupils and who therefore appear unpredictable. Second, adaptation to different teaching styles, some of which devalue implicitly the activity of the primary school. Adjustment is facilitated if the pupil can take the standpoint of the teacher rather than regard the situation egocentrically. A simple activity is illustrated below:

a A short tape is prepared in which a teacher is heard handing books back to pupils. After a brief introduction the tape focuses on one pupil to whom the teacher makes positive yet critical remarks, e.g. 'I liked the beginning of the essay, Jim, because it was interesting and clear, but what a pity that . . .' (Tutors will obviously put in problems that they have noted in the form's work.)

b Pupils then work in pairs, imagining that both of them are teachers. They have to teach this pupil. What help and advice would they give him?

c The tutor then gathers ideas from the form, selecting some for further discussion. Pupils are still encouraged to look at the situation from the teacher's position. The concern of the teacher for the pupils' progress is also made clear.

The tutor could get instances from pupils of situations they think might annoy or concern teachers, e.g. the pupil who is always coming in after the lesson or tutor period has begun, or who never has his books or pens. (If tutors doubt the need for standpoint-taking it may be useful for them to consider their perceptions of the examiners if they have recently taken a B Ed or higher degree.)

21 Another exercise associated with this is set out below:

a Why set homework? This is written on the board. The tutor then gets pupils to estimate how many pupils a teacher teaches in a week. Then he or she takes a particular subject and works out how many books a teacher will mark in a week. They then assess how long it takes to mark a book (unrealistic answers come at this stage, therefore the tutor may have to supply a sensible figure); how many homework assignments have to be marked; and how much time this will take.

b The following question is then posed: As it takes so long for a teacher who is already marking many books, it seems sensible for them not to burden themselves with homework. Why then do they set homework?

Answers can be obtained by brainstorming a discussion in groups. The answers can be discussed drawing the pupils' attention to the contribution made by carefully-done homework to their progress and capacity to take responsibility for achievement.

22 General problems of adjustment complicate or exacerbate anxieties about new learning demands. Phillips (1978) called attention to the high proportion of individuals who fear making mistakes under conditions of visibility and who feel they cannot understand the teacher. Reading aloud in class, answering questions, errors in translation should be discussed. It is even more positive to help pupils gain an understanding of the factors comprising a good classroom climate. The exercise below provides an introduction.

A flipchart cartoon is prepared by an older pupil who, with several others, comes into the form to lead the discussion. The cartoon shows a classroom where one pupil is saying, 'What does he mean?'; another is asking anxiously, 'What if I'm wrong?' The task of the older pupils is to help relatively small sub-groups look at their feelings when they can't understand, and how they react. Suggestions are put forward by the helpers which the groups evaluate. They then discuss the embarrassment and loss of face involved in public errors. They draw on their own experience as they see fit, but the gist of the messages is, 'There's nothing wrong with making a mistake, provided you learn from it'. Helpers and tutor end the session by becoming a panel who answer questions from the form.

One useful follow-up activity is to get the form to produce as many reasons as they can to explain why the teacher asks questions in a lesson. They then rank them in order of importance. After this they discuss with a partner what makes for a good answer. A very healthy extension of ideas usually occurs.

23 We have tended to ignore learned helplessness and the beliefs about sex based differences in ability and aptitude in first-year guidance. The following activity seems to lead to lively discussion without confirming existing prejudices or attitudes.

    a The initial stimulus consists of incomplete sentences which are written one by one on the blackboard or read out by the

teacher. (It seems less effective to present them all together.)
  – Boys are usually good at . . .
  – Girls like . . .
  – Girls do well when . . .
  – Science is . . .
  – Most boys find it hard . . .
  – Important jobs . . .
  – Teachers always say . . .
  – The best marks . . .

b Groups of three, composed of pupils of the same sex, are formed, and asked to consider their completed sentences. Do they, for example, suggest that the pupil has fixed ideas about what each sex is likely to be good at? Is this a sensible viewpoint? Then a group of boys and one of girls join together to discuss the proposition that 'There are no differences in what boys or girls can do well.'

c Tutors invite questions from the form about the existence of sex-determined ability. Questions about physical strength, attitudes towards dirty work or future careers will arise. Tutors of both sexes must watch themselves carefully for any hints of distasteful patronage towards females, or premature interruption of pupils, as this effectively stifles comment.

24 Straightforward discussion in which the tutor moves between the use of small group work (including partner discussions) and work with the whole form is very productive. It sounds simple, but is not easy. The skills of counselling are employed to create the climate of acceptance in which pupils express, question and, if helpful, modify their views. Attitude change and personal development require tutors able to show warmth, and whose behaviour is manifestly genuine. I have found that male teachers can be very threatened by the revisions of judgement demanded by equality of opportunity. Even in the first year of the secondary school there is evidence of a legacy from childhood which leads to the adoption of unthinking assumptions of superiority in certain fields of learning by boys, and an over-readiness by girls to accept the evaluations of themselves conveyed by boys. Topics for discussion usefully include:
  – Why do people expect girls to be tidy and neat in their work and boys to be careless?
  – Is it really true that women do not make good scientists?
  – Do you believe that women do not want a lot of responsibility in their work?

– Girls are not such good athletes as boys! True or false?

25 A learning problem which concerns the first year is catching up after absence. Obviously, a pastoral team needs an effective policy for helping pupils. For example, a mathematics or English 'clinic' operates in some schools, allowing pupils to receive individual help. Pupils should be encouraged to discuss their responsibilities for coping. One activity is outlined below:

A tape is played in which a pupil is heard asking his friend if he can copy what he has missed in the science lessons. The friend agrees: both feel satisfied. Later that week the first pupil is asked a question during the lesson by the science teacher. It becomes clear to him that he has not understood what he copied. Partners discuss the situation, trying to construct a sensible plan of action. They then link with another pair. The strategies are explained, and subjected to critical scrutiny. The tutor leads a final form discussion, highlighting helpful points by writing them on the blackboard.

26 Listening has to be developed as a skill, pupils understanding that they should know the purpose of listening, e.g. to distinguish fact from opinion, to detect a step-by-step argument, to isolate cues of salience and thus distinguish between what is marginal and what is peripheral. *Readers Digest* provides excellent, well written, clearly structured material for a training programme in listening. Pupils are given examples of the way key points can be extracted from a passage. The tape is presented in two parts. They listen to the first section. As soon as the tape is stopped, pupils write down the key points. Pupils are instructed to write down any key fact they did not recognise, putting a box around it. This procedure is repeated for the second part of the tape. Then:

a Pupils discuss with a partner the reasons for not recognising certain key facts.

b The tutor begins a 'signposts approach' to cues of salience, e.g. 'Were you alert when you heard "first" because second and third followed it?' (See Hamblin, 1981)

c Supplementary exercises such as a quiz where pupils have to listen to a narrative and answer questions support the 'signposts' approach.

27 Formative assessment requires skills of self-evaluation which are established early in the secondary school. Pupils should be given frequent experience of self-assessment through constructing

simple profiles, talking about their strengths and weaknesses as learners, and target setting.

A simple activity is given below and the tutor can relate it to his or her subject.

a Pupils apply a simple checklist, e.g. that on pages 34 and 35 of *Teaching Study Skills*.

b With a partner they then set targets for improvement in the next three days. The targets must be concrete and capable of achievement. It is not acceptable to say, 'Work harder in English', nor is it sufficient to say, 'Improve my spelling.' If it is in this area, the target would be defined by looking through the English book, selecting three words which frequently have red marks against them.

c Friend helps friend decide how they will work towards their targets, turning difficulties into a supportive dialogue.

Simple problem-solving exercises

28 *Sally's grandmother comes to live with them. Sally has to share her little sister's room because of this. Her sister moves all her things making it difficult for Sally to find anything, including her school books. Worst of all, she scribbles all over them if she gets the chance.*

i What do you think Sally can do to cope with these problems?

ii What further information would have helped you make the decision?

The value of these simple problem-solving activities depends on the way the tutor approaches them. Standpoint-taking could be stimulated by this way of setting about it:

a With a partner imagine that one of you is Sally and the other is her form tutor. Sally is explaining the situation to the tutor. What suggestions will the tutor make?

b In a group of three work out ways in which Sally can teach her sister not to touch her things.

c Now imagine you are Sally's father. What do you think he will say about the situation?

29 *Stuart works hard and gets good marks so the tutor thinks highly of him, and believes him to be responsible. A new boy arrives in the form, and the tutor asks Stuart to look after him. After a few days, the new boy does not do his homework, borrows Stuart's book and copies from it. They both get into trouble! A week later the new boy again asks to*

borrow the book to copy from it, but Stuart refuses. He then hits Stuart and threatens to get him after school.

   i Where do you think Stuart made a mistake? Why?

   ii What should Stuart do now? Make a list of possible actions before you decide.

30 *Your father has arranged a family holiday during the school's examination week.*

   a Fill in, after discussing the problem with a partner, the boxes below:

Reasons why I should carry on revising as usual	Reasons why it is not worth carrying on revising

   b Now imagine that your decision was to give up revising, and that the day before you are due to go on holiday, your father has an accident, breaking his leg. The holiday has to be cancelled. How would you explain your decision to the head of year or house? What will he say? Write down the conversation (pupils work in pairs). The tutor then selects one pair to read out the conversation which leads to general discussion about the level of risk, e.g. when can we afford to take a risk?

31 This simple problem-solving exercise deals with the experience of feeling isolated.

   a Pupils work in groups of three.

   b They are asked to produce a list of kinds of behaviour which are likely to increase isolation. A starter idea is given, e.g. 'pretend not to notice other people'.

   c Next, they produce a list of ideas about the behaviour that would allow them to help the lonely person. As before, a starter idea is given, e.g. 'ask them their name'.

   d They are then asked to imagine they have moved to a different area of Britain. It is a rural area, but they have always lived in a bustling city centre before. The groups are given the task of deciding the steps they will take to make themselves feel at home and gain acceptance in their new school.

32 The following exercise will obviously use up more than one period. It only has minimal value if treated as a questionnaire. Pupils should give reasons for their choices. The tutor should select items for general discussion by the form, showing that he realises their significance for first-year pupils. The context and consequences of the incidents and pupils' reported reactions should be explored.

Situation	Possibilities
You are in the dinner queue when an older boy takes your dinner money out of your hand. *Reasons for choice:*	1 Go without dinner and do not tell anybody. 2 Borrow from your best friend. 3 Tell mum when you get home. 4 Tell an adult at once. 5 Other (say what it would be).
You need a bus pass, but you were away when they were given out. *Reasons for choice:*	1 Go to the office and ask the secretary. 2 Put off doing anything. 3 Ask mum to ring up. 4 See if your elder brother or sister will get it for you. 5 Other (say what it would be).
Your parents want to make an appointment to talk to somebody about your progress. *Reasons for choice:*	1 Pretend to forget. 2 Ask your best friend what to do. 3 Tell them they must write a note. 4 Tell the tutor your mum wants to see him or her. 5 Other (say what it would be).

Situation	Possibilities
You are playing rounders in the playground at lunchtime and accidentally break a window. *Reasons for choice:*	1 Keep quiet about it. 2 Tell a dinner lady. 3 Tell your best friend. 4 Tell mum when you get home. 5 Other (say what it would be).
It is first thing in the morning and an older pupil has just come up to you and pushed you out of the way. When you protest he thumps you and kicks you hard. As he goes away he says he will give you worse than that if you tell anyone. *Reasons for choice:*	1 Tell a teacher immediately. 2 Do not say anything. 3 Cry in the lavatory. 4 Tell your best friend. 5 Other (say what it would be).
Suddenly you realise you have lost your new coat. *Reasons for choice:*	1 Hope mum does not notice. 2 Ask your best friend to help you look for it. 3 Go to your form tutor. 4 Other (say what it would be).
Dad wants you to go out of school at lunchtime to renew your fishing licence. *Reasons for choice:*	1 Get Dad to write a note. 2 Pretend to forget. 3 Ask your best friend to go with you. 4 Just go. 5 Other (say what it would be).

Situation	Possibilities
You have left your bag containing your games kit at the bus stop.	1 Telephone home from outside school. 2 Go to the school office. 3 Borrow your friend's kit as s/he is excused games today. 4 Dodge games. 5 Other (say what it would be).
Reasons for choice:	
It started to rain at lunch time and your shoes got very wet.	1 Do nothing. 2 Tell your tutor. 3 Take them off, and hope nobody notices. 4 Put on your plimsolls. 5 Other (say what it would be).
Reasons for choice:	

33 (This activity is partially based on a Summer School activity by Sheila Toms' Group. Here it is presented as a single session. In practice, two or more tutor periods will be required.)

Decisions about friendship:

a Pupils are asked to tick the qualities of a good friend from the list below. (It can also act as a basis for general discussion.) They select the two most important ones, explaining why they see them as such.
   – somebody you can tell when you are upset
   – somebody who is useful because he/she will do things for you
   – somebody who lives close to you
   – somebody you can trust
   – somebody who is tough
   – somebody who does not mind being pushed around
   – somebody who can make you laugh
   – somebody who likes the same things as you

- somebody who is clever
- somebody who lets you copy their homework
- somebody who will lend you money
- somebody who is always cheerful
- somebody who will protect you from bullies

b Pupils now write a brief description of themselves as they hope they appear to friends.

c Groups of three then discuss the limits to friendship, starting with statements of what they would not do, even if their best friend asked them.

d Pupils take the standpoint of parents, writing a description of the kind of friend they think their parents would like them to have. (Usually a fair number of references are made to 'not getting them into trouble'. This seems to reflect the reality of parental concern, and it is usually worth taking up in general discussion.)

e The tutor may find it helpful to end by looking at ways in which friends can support one another in school. This could be a preliminary to stimulating simple peer counselling activities.

7 The Second Year

We almost take it for granted that a fair proportion of pupils will show increasing disenchantment with school. In institutions the second year is often marked by frustration or disillusionment: this seems to be true of the 11–16 or 11–18 school; the problem being compounded by the tensions of puberty and the stresses of inter-action within some families. Evidence for the growth of negativism in the second year comes from attitudinal surveys towards learning, school and teachers carried out by experienced teachers during their training in pastoral care and counselling, for example, Edwards (1974). A strong tendency for antagonism to school or apathy to become manifest in the second year was a common finding. Such studies had to be cross-sectional and not longitudinal, therefore age-related trends could only be extrapolated, but it was difficult to escape the conclusion that at least 20 percent of pupils were becoming increasingly malcontent and resistant to teacher influence as they moved through the school. Some individuals displayed negative responses in the attitude scales in the second year, but did not attract teacher's attention until the third year. Truancy appeared in some pupils who conformed in the first year, but were testing the system, noting opportunities for evasion or sizing up the chances of outwitting adults. Guidance which leads to integration with the school reduces the likelihood of these pupils absorbing teachers' energies without effect in later years.

Attitudes, however, do not inevitably lead to certain types of behaviour. Antagonism can be expressed by superficial performance and direct conflict or indirectly through passive resistance, where pupils force teachers to adopt a hectoring or nagging role. In 1980, experienced teachers coming to the end of a one year full-time training course investigated the problem in more depth. Eight hundred and fifty pupils in 13 comprehensive schools were studied; care being taken to avoid provoking socially desirable responses or conveying expectations. Unexpected, yet helpful, indications of problem areas and points of intervention resulted.

Irritability was a major source of concern for the second-year pupil. It seemed to stem mainly from physical growth or anxiety about social relationships. Subsequent discussions highlighted the pupils' strong awareness of the demands school was making, and unease that more would be asked of them. In certain individuals, uncertainty about meeting those demands was equally likely to be accompanied by doubts about wanting to meet them. A few bluntly acknowledged they were already psychological truants: present in the flesh and absent in the spirit; viewing the years of schooling ahead with distaste. What was striking was the way loss of control preoccupied them. The form of this was irrelevant: temper, tears or inadequacy appeared equally threatening. Energy was invested in forestalling loss of face.

Pastoral heads of the second year need a keen awareness of the impact of learning within the family on performance at school. Family relationships are mechanisms for the allocation and maintenance of identity. Struggles over identity and independence spill over into the second-year pupil's school-life. Pupils sometimes complain their families will not let them grow up. Clumsy self-assertion evokes sanctions and the consequent ructions leave parents and children rueful, but no wiser. Some parents encourage their children's development but deny themselves the rewards of new interests outside the home. They then feel taken for granted, periodically reacting by reminding their children of the sacrifices they are making, or creating insecurity. The frustrated ambitions of parents are foisted on the submissive daughter or son as ideals to be pursued: a false identity is then in the making.

Once trust is established in the tutor group, the opportunity to air such tensions is used sensibly. The most troubled area of family interaction is with younger brothers or sisters who are viewed as pests and intruders into the territory of the second-year pupil. Let us remind ourselves that pastoral care is about the identities of belonging and self-awareness. The second-year pupil is approaching what Erikson (1968) calls the 'identity crisis'. The link between identity and territory has probably been neglected in pastoral care, although its importance has been recognised in studies of adolescent gangs. Self is invested in possessions: territory is both a possession and a statement about identity. (Questions about where one comes from are almost as frequent as those about one's job in adult life. Both act as identity probes.) Concern about territory probably heralds the development of a personal space to the invasion of which the individual responds by embarrassment, aggression or anxiety.

To return to the significance of possessions: we know how a teddy bear or cot blanket is permeated by emotional significance, preserving a young child's unique relationship with the mother, yet also making a bridge with the wider world. I speculate that the preservation and care of personal territory and possessions has a somewhat similar significance at this critical point in adolescence: they encapsulate identity, providing a means through which the individual insulates herself or himself against the damaging elements of current demands, comes to terms with inner fantasies and works through doubt. Pastoral heads will deal more sensitively and helpfully with pupils if they are alert to such possibilities.

Awareness of the demands made by school comes at a time when the effects of inadequate and faulty learning within the home become manifest due to the insecurity, the mingled excitement and tensions of physical development. What is understandable – indeed welcome – in retrospect, is sometimes disturbing while being experienced. Key skills are developed within the family: the vital personal and social skill of empathy is one such product. Communication and interaction within the family either facilitate or check a child's capacity for standpoint-taking, and his ability to detect, and then where proper, meet, the expectations of others. A pastoral programme has to provide opportunities for development for pupils who come from homes where maladaptive experience is the norm, noting that this is as likely in affluent homes as in poor ones. A neurotic parent, wearing a mask of rationality, denies the validity of a child's perceptions of reality, creating fundamental self-distrust. Such a pupil may grasp eagerly the over-simple formulae offered by the production of 'right answers', but find questioning and problem-solving intimidating.

In pastoral work we sometimes deplore the defects of a family, when it would be better to ask how we can compensate for distorted family communication which stunts intellectual and social growth because it provides negative identities, e.g. 'he has always caused trouble'. If pupils have learned to predict failure or see aggression as highly desirable, we have to deal with it by thinking in terms of re-education rather than punishment which merely inhibits, and does not teach new behaviours. Pastoral activities concerned with beliefs about altruism, co-operation and the individual's responsibility for his destiny allow pupils to correct misconceptions about the world fostered by family interaction. Ideals are purveyed by the family, but we have to be alert to possible contradictions or difficulties. At first sight the ideal for behaviour may be laudable, stressing the desirability of achievement, responsibility and the acceptance of legitimate authority; yet with it may come injunctions to avoid, even despise, those from 'rough' backgrounds – even though the vast majority of pupils come from such backgrounds. The pupil either has to reject the home's standards or may be in danger of attracting counter hostility.

Aston and Dobson (1972) show how imbalanced patterns of communication at home are reflected in the pupil's response to learning. Some parents undermine their child's statements without explanation, or cut off what they are saying without justification. This unilateral imposition of meaning may create difficulties in the small group discussions, e.g. the pupil compensating by trying to dominate the talk, or feeling too insecure to put his own point of view. Dominant ideas emerge in family communication which, when transferred to the classroom, influence the pupil's response; indeed the interpretation he or she places on school activities. I have met families dominated by anxiety around the theme of 'things getting out of control'. Where pupils had been conditioned by the strong reactions of the parents to any hint of this they tended to be perfectionist in spelling and writing, studiously polite, but avoiding exploration and risk, consequently restricting their learning. Confusion existed where the two parents held different interpretations of 'in and out of control'. Tutors and pastoral heads have to be compassionate and cautious in dealing with difficulties which emerge in pastoral activities when such family factors seem to be the cause. Gender stereotypes have to be tackled, but one has to be alert to complications which exist for the occasional pupil. Let me illustrate: a family emphasised to their only child the idea of 'not right for a girl' which masked both parents' suppressed desire for a son. The result of their pressure was determined rejection of their ideas about female behaviour and adoption of an aggressive and delinquent lifestyle. These extreme cases are used to show the need for observation of tensions and the provision of counselling for pupils displaying them.

Joking is not straightforward. In some families jokes are used to confuse or belittle a child. Jokes can be a way of gaining power. Messages are sent in a joking way, but the recipient is left uncertain. To have a parent refuse to treat a situation seriously by making fun of it almost certainly leaves the child humiliated. Some second-year pupils are adept at using jokes to confuse others and to assert their superiority. They then evade responsibility by saying, 'it was only a joke' but the damage has been done, and is not easily repaired. Pupils have to accept leg-pulling, but the vulnerable have to be helped cope with cruel jokes.

In the study the strongest concern was voiced about the prospect of being laughed at because of physical deviance, e.g. being too short or having funny voices. Livesley and Bromley (1973) showed a preponderance of statements about bodily appearance at the age of 15, but this study shows the second-year concern with the physical. Two factors are of particular import for a second-year programme: obesity and the social comparison process. Self-depreciation closely accompanies comparisons: the second-year pupil actively experiencing this. Obesity is probably the most disliked form of social handicap as Richardson (1961) suggests. Jersild (1969) associates obesity and self-blame, whilst I have frequently counselled adolescents who because of obesity have felt compelled to take up clowning roles, become bullies or felt figures of fun. They tended to see their bodies almost totally as inferior, holding the belief that others judged them in the light of cultural taboos against greediness and self-indulgence and the desirability of slimness.

Anxieties about competence centred around self-organisation and the presentation of work. Learning about learning seems to be a key area in developing the second-year programme. While the mechanics of learning must be given attention, motivational and judgemental elements of learning have greater importance. Predictions shape behaviour, and predictions of failure already operate in some second-year pupils, producing the defensive reaction of 'the school is no good' or the apathy of learned helplessness. In the study and subsequent work it became clear that part of second-year tutor work is concerned with teaching constructive assertion in the face of frustration, especially in learning.

The principles of anticipation and inoculation play as great a part in the pastoral programme as in individual counselling. The second-year work includes decision-making as preparation for third-year subject choice. Pupils should be encouraged to build up their own model of decision-making; therefore the tutor systematically calls attention to elements such as level of risk, assessing the credibility of sources of information, and protection against illicit or irrelevant sources of influence. Closely linked factors are reactions to frustration and susceptibility to audience anxiety.

The materials which follow are not presented as a programme: they are points of departure for the school's own development of a programme. Their value depends on the way pastoral heads explain them, and encourage tutors to change or branch out from them.

Personal and social development

1 It shouldn't happen to anyone. (This activity stems from an original idea by Peter Lindup of what formerly was Matlock College of Education.)

a The tutor recounts the following story, holding a large sheet of paper in his hand. At the completion of each stage, he divides the paper in half, obviously ending up with a very small piece of paper. This conveys the impression of someone being diminished by events. The tutor holds up the paper and says *'This is Douglas. Today he woke up late to find his Mother pulling the bedclothes off him angrily, shouting, "Douglas, get up you lazy creature, I'm fed up with you being late for school."* (The paper is torn in half.)

Douglas eventually gets downstairs. Now the only thing he likes for breakfast is cornflakes, but his greedy younger brother has drunk all the milk. A row starts; his mother intervenes angrily; and Douglas sets off for school without breakfast.

He is a cheerful fellow, so he soon joins his friends, and they have a good knockabout on the way to school. Unfortunately, he lands on his face in the mud, and ends up looking a mess. He delays a little to tidy himself up, and goes into form where Mrs McGovern his tutor is waiting for him. She takes one look, points to the door, and roars, "Douglas you disgraceful lout, go and wash immediately!" *Douglas sets off for school without breakfast.* (Tutor tears paper in half.)

Now, I'm afraid Douglas isn't too well organised: so he didn't check his bag to see whether he had everything when he finished his homework last night. And this morning – well, you know what happens. In technical drawing he finds he has no set square, compass or ruler. Result: "Detention for you tonight, my lad!" (Tutor tears paper in half.)

Douglas gets through the morning without more trouble. But the first lesson of the afternoon is French. He likes the teacher, but not the subject, so he starts talking to his friends. When the teacher says "Who is talking?" Douglas, being an honest lad, puts up his hand, but his friends don't. So he gets all the telling off. (Tutor tears paper in half.)

Now they have a silly game in Douglas' school, hiding one another's property. He goes to get his bag before going to detention, and it isn't there. The result is that he gets home very late. His mother is waiting at the door!' (Tutor tears the paper in half.)

b Holding up the small piece of paper, the tutor asks the form to discuss in small groups why all this happens to Douglas. Pupils are encouraged to look at ways of coping when they feel things are happening to them, and how they can get back in control. Attention is drawn to the need to assess their contribution to the events of which they complain. They are quite interested in the idea of contagion between one situation and another, e.g. that because trouble has occurred in one lesson and they feel frustrated, they then create difficulties for themselves in the next.

2 Boasting and bragging are sources of difficulty for the un-certain second-year pupil. The message the tutor gives can usefully be that we *all* tend to exaggerate how well we are going to perform at an activity to boost our confidence, and then we still do badly. Although it is sensible to avoid boasting, it is very important to cope sensibly afterwards if you are teased, avoiding making matters worse.

a The situation

Imagine that you have been selected to play in a netball or football match. In your excitement you meet a group of friends, and brag about how well you are going to do. In fact you are a dismal flop. Next day you see them coming towards you, and you realise they are likely to tease you. What do you think will be the best way of coping?

b The tutor introduces the small group discussion by enlarging the range of possible behaviour. It is a good idea to anticipate by making a joke about your performance: say they must be laughing at you, find excuses for your poor performance; say you are ashamed of yourself.

In the second year it is important to enlist peers in constructive evaluation of decisions and activities. In each group of four, one member becomes a peer judge who provides feedback about the riskiness, sense or impact of the decision on relationships.

c The tutor ends with general discussion, raising the question of whether the assumption that the others would tease them is necessarily justified. What factors would inhibit or reinforce the tendency to tease the bragger?

3 Embarrassment:
Adults dislike being over-dressed or turning up in casual clothes to find themselves conspicuously different from others. Second-year pupils also dislike this kind of limelight and are easily humiliated.

a Situation (It can be presented as a flip chart cartoon):

Jim, who is keen on sports, had to visit the doctor to have a slight rash looked at. He dislikes having to miss games, so he dashes back to school, changes and starts to rush off to the field. He looks immaculate in his kit. As he is going out of the building he meets a PE mistress who says, 'Your group is in the gym'. Jim unthinkingly dashes there; throwing open the door to see the group unchanged, sitting on benches, listening to a general talk on caving given by the Deputy Head as the PE master is unwell. The class inspects the immaculate Jim, bursting into ironic cheers. When the noise subsides, the Deputy Head reprimands him for wearing football boots on the wooden floor.

  i Pupils write down what they think will be in Jim's mind, discussing it with a partner.
  ii They then decide how Jim's friends could ease the situation for him.
  iii The tutor collects ideas about situations that cause embarrassment for members of the form. Each group is allocated a topic and asked to give a 10–15 minute presentation on it. Tape recordings can be made as part of the presentation and the help of older pupils requested.

4 Resisting pressure:
A tape is prepared in which a pupil is heard being asked to lend

money to someone. It becomes clear that the second pupil has borrowed money on two previous occasions, and failed to pay it back. The sums involved were not large, but of importance to the lender. The question put to the class is how the first pupil can refuse to lend the money without making an enemy of the other person.

a Pupils discuss this in small groups. A peer or third-form pupil then evaluates the discussion.

b The tutor introduces questions about the criteria for trust, e.g. *if* you do decide to lend someone money, how do you know they will pay you back?

c General discussion follows in which the tutor helps pupils distinguish between a proper readiness to help and impulsive lending. Many other issues, amongst them the problem of coercion, usually appear.

5 Coping with being laughed at:
Western films present no moral challenge to pupils because the good and bad characters are clearly defined and there is no ambiguity to be resolved. The complexities of real life are denied, and little learning occurs. Presentation of clear-cut, socially desirable solutions to problems is unlikely to lead to real discussion. In the exercise below pupils are asked to evaluate two positive solutions of approximately equal desirability.

Fourth- or fifth-year pupils taking drama could be asked to write a script which deals with two positive ways of coping with a persistent and malicious practical joker. They could present it on tape to the form.

a The first solution emphasises the importance of the teaser's not getting his pay-off because the victim laughs heartily, responding with a joke of his own.

b The recipient of the practical joke quietly ignores it, but immediately links up with friends, consolidating his position in the form.

Follow-up activity consists of evaluation of the advantages and disadvantages of both courses of action, listing them on a sheet of paper. The tutor ends the session by gathering ideas from the form about the courses of action, inviting the form to produce more ideas of their own.

6 Coping with difficulties:

a Pupils are asked to consider a problem that concerns them, e.g. how to cope with a brother or sister who interferes with their possessions or prevents them getting started on their homework. It is emphasised that:
   – they must want to do something about the problem;
   – they feel they could do something about it if they tried.

b They are then asked to imagine that they are somebody else who is older and who is tackling the problem. They write down exactly how they think the older person would tackle it. They then discuss the plan with a friend who makes suggestions. They are then asked to play a game of 'make believe', imagining that they are that person, trying out the solution during the next 24 hours.

c The next day, in the tutor period, they discuss how they felt: what worked and why; what did not work and how it could be made to work. The tutor then helps the form clarify their ideas about behaviour change. Pupils use what they learned in the trial 'make believe' exercise as the basis for planning their attack on the problem.

d The tutor follows up the activity in the way he or she feels to be most appropriate. This activity is concerned with orientating pupils to problems they wish to tackle. The major gains come from helping pupils recognise that problems do not have to be passively endured and that even a small inroad into the worrying situation changes it. These simple approaches to behaviour modification contribute to the development of feeling in control that is vital for the second-year.

7 Coping with stress and tension cannot be avoided, but we may give insufficient attention to the situations which create insecurity in the second year. Waiting to see if they have been chosen for a part in a play or given a place in a team is one situation. There is the subsequent disappointment which has to be faced and which is made worse by the comments of both friends and enemies.

a A simple tape could be prepared in which a pupil is being questioned by other pupils about what part he or she hopes to get, or if they expect a place in the team.

b The tutor then asks partners to discuss the best way of coping with such questions without pretence or taking undue risks by boasting. Ideas are then shared by the whole form.

c The tape continues with the pupil discovering that he or she has not gained a part in the play or a place in the team. Loss of face is involved: another pupil jeers at him or her; two reactions from friends are also included. The first consists of over-done sympathy or 'cheering up'; the second is an invitation to join in devaluing the successful person, e.g. 'She's always creeping to the teacher' or 'What do you expect, he's always showing off!' Pupils discuss, in pairs, ways of coping with the teasing. Then groups of four are formed and pupils decide how they would deal with the reactions of friends. One member of the group is appointed as a peer judge, evaluating the discussion. (This activity can take two periods to cover thoroughly.) In this case, the tutor ends the first session by asking pupils to think about the reactions of friends if the character in the tape is disappointed. Ideas are then collected before the second part of the tape is played and included in the final discussion.

$\boxed{8}$ Body image:

This is an area of great concern to the second-year pupil who fears, for example, being too short or having 'a funny voice'. Comparisons with others are strong, therefore the tutor has to be sensitive to the danger of reinforcing some pupils' negative self-evaluation. Equally important: the issue must not be treated negatively. Adolescence is an unparalleled time of grace and agility for most pupils; the problem lies in insecurity in relationships which then affects self-evaluation in the most rapid area of change. Discussions and activities are centred around the constructive theme of making the most of yourself. The PE teachers can visit the tutor groups to initiate the theme by talking about the development of physical skills in adolescence, and presentation of self.

Activities can include:

a Drawing up a balance sheet of good, poor or indifferent body characteristics and discussing them with a friend.

b Evaluating the image presented to others. Pupils write about themselves as they think they appear to others. Friend works with friend looking at:

   – exaggerations or unjustified anxieties;

    – what could be improved;
    – what has to be accepted.
c The tutor encourages pupils to explore their ideas of masculinity and femininity, helping pupils appreciate the inadequacy of crude gender stereotypes.
d Other discussions could centre on:

    i what fashions do I follow? Why?
    ii how can I build on my physical skills?

9 Communication:

a This first activity can be undertaken in different ways to suit the tutor:
    – all pupils are involved in the tutor group;
    – two pupils demonstrate the activity to the form who make notes on the difficulties;
    – it could be a group activity undertaken by the drama specialist in the studio or hall, the tutor visiting the drama teacher's form.

The basic situation is this:

You are two survivors of a plane crash. Clinging to part of the fuselage, you have been washed up on to the beach of a tiny island. No source of water exists on the island. Rain is falling. Your task is to make a container to collect it. Unfortunately, one of you has severe facial injuries and cannot see. The other has sight, but cannot use his hands because of severe burns. The sighted one therefore has to instruct the blind one how to make the container. (The blinded pupil shuts his eyes, the other clasps his hands behind his back.)

b Pupils discuss the difficulties of giving directions and understanding them. The tutor develops the theme in ways he or she considers helpful to the form.
c Tutors divide the class into pairs, giving one partner a duplicated map or pattern, taking care that the other does not see it. The other partner has paper and ballpens/felt pens. His task is to reproduce the map or pattern from the directions given by the other. They sit back to back, which not only ensures that the drawer cannot see the map, but also means that the other cannot give help if his instructions are misinterpreted.
d When the time allocated expires, pupils compare the original and the copy. Difficulties are then discussed generally, the

tutor drawing attention to the need to put oneself in the place of the person receiving the instructions, trying to anticipate their difficulties.

Decision-making activities

Decision-making in the second year anticipates the choice of subjects in the third year, although it is primarily concerned with events of daily living that bother second-year pupils. Tutors emphasise one aspect of decision-making in the follow-up discussion, e.g. level of risk, sources of pressure, credibility of the information used. Pupils should be given real life decisions to make in organising fund raising, community work and tutor group activities. The subsequent activities have been used successfully to promote awareness of decision-making.

10 Constructive assertion: refusing to lend money.
The following situation is put on tape as a short playlet or as a 'Stop, wait, go' activity (Hamblin, 1981).

A pupil who travels with you on the bus to school asks you to lend him 50p as he has lost his dinner money. You lent him money before when he said he had lost his bus fare home and he didn't pay you back. You want to avoid trouble, but neither do you want to lend him the money.

a In groups of three, pupils discuss ways of dealing with the situation.
b When they have reached a decision, the tutor asks them to consider the steps they may have to take to avoid unpleasantness on the way home.
c The final tutor-led discussion is about constructive assertion: how to refuse courteously and steadily; not allowing the pitch of one's voice to rise as the other presses; to be able to express regret, while firmly stating that there is no point in pressing.

11 Providing an explanation in a difficult situation.
The basic situation is:

You are a keen member of your youth club. You have promised to be part of the group who will entertain a visiting party from Germany tomorrow. Tonight, Dad comes home and announces unexpectedly that he has decided the family is going out tomorrow and that he has made all the arrangements. You protest and explain, but to no avail. He is adamant that you will go.

   a Partners discuss how they would deal with the situation.
   b Tutor led discussion then evaluates the ideas produced, looking at the level of risk in suggested action.
   c The tutor then calls attention to the need to telephone the youth leader and explain the difficulty.
      Partners role play the telephone conversation, the youth leader expressing disappointment, although accepting the inevitability of the situation.
   d In a final discussion the tutor encourages pupils to look at the temptation to avoid the difficult explanation, and explore similar situations in their real lives.

[12] The dog:
Fears of wild animals and the dark are not admitted easily by second-year pupils. Indirect discussion and searching for ways of coping with imaginary situations have a therapeutic effect while preserving the privacy of the pupil. The situation is:

You are on the club committee. Once a week you go to the club early, on your own. A house nearby has a ferocious dog which comes out into the lane and snaps at you menacingly. You are quite terrified by it. The owner normally has it chained up at the time the club opens. There is no other way into the club so you have to go along the lane. You value your position on the committee and do not want to give up the duties that take you to the club early. What is the best way of coping?

   a After discussion in small groups the tutor brings in questions about what prevents us from telling people about such difficulties and from getting help.
   b The tutor group then discusses situations where they feel they may have to do something they dislike, in order to get something they want. A decision may be made for small groups to follow up some of these situations, turning them into activities which they present to the form.

[13] Managing one's spending:

   a A small group prepares an amusing brief playlet on Freddie Hardup who never has any money because he spends his pocket money immediately. They then ask the class for ideas about such behaviour, e.g. Does Freddie hope to extract more money from his parents? Does he rely on his friends to give him sweets or lend him comics?

b The tutor then invites pupils to discuss in small groups their spending and saving habits, working out ways in which they could improve their money management.

14 The costs of smoking:

a Pupils work out the cost of smoking 20 cigarettes a day for a whole year. They then discuss alternative uses for this money.

b Small groups then look at the reasons why people smoke. The tutor encourages them to question these reasons, producing counter-arguments.

c Older pupils have prepared a tape in which a small group tries to press one of its members to smoke. He or she resists successfully. They then lead a discussion on, 'Because you find a group attractive, do you have to do everything all its members do?'

d The tutor ends by getting the class to look positively at the non-smoker, and consider the other costs of smoking. (More than one session will be needed for them.)

15 Dealing with neighbours.
The basic situation is:

You are at home by yourself one evening when a neighbour calls. He is not, as far as you know, friendly with your parents, although they greet one another when they meet. He says your father promised to lend him his electric drill and rotary saw. You know nothing of it and cannot contact your parents. You know they will not be back until late. He says he will come in and wait for them. What is the best way of coping?

a Small group discussion follows where they explore possibilities.

b The tutor then gets the class to consider the consequences of different lines of actions.

c Pupils sometimes produce other situations which have made them uneasy, and valuable learning results from a well handled discussion.

16 A decision-making quiz:

a *Instructions:*

  i No names to be written on quiz sheet.

ii Pupils complete sheets in about five minutes without discussion.

iii Tutor collects papers, and asks pupils to form groups of four or five.

iv The groups then discuss the situations again. One of the group records the responses to the group discussion of each question, e.g. 1a:2; 1b:1; 1c:0; 1d:1.

v While this is happening, the tutor collates the answers from the individual sheets, recording them on the score sheet below.

vi Results from the group discussion should be collated.

Score Sheet	INDIVIDUAL	GROUP
1. a. b. c. d.		
2. a. b. c. d.		

b A second tutor period will be needed in which the tutor leads form discussion on the implications of choices, and of the significance of discrepancies between group and individual choices.

Situations:

1 *While the teacher's back is turned in the laboratory, the person next to you turns on the gas tap.*
   Would you: *a* Tell her to turn it off?
                b Tell the teacher?
                c Turn it off yourself?
                d Take no notice?

2 *During a lesson two of your closest friends begin to flick pellets.*
   Would you: *a* Laugh, but not join in?
                b Laugh, and join in?

        c Tell the teacher?
        d Ignore it?

3 *You know Maths is important, but you dislike the lesson because you feel you can't understand it.*
  Would you: *a* Switch off, trying not to attract the teacher's attention?
            b Make the effort to concentrate?
            c Talk to your parents about it at home?
            d Explain what is happening to the teacher?

4 *The PE teacher has said the 'trampette' is not to be used unless she is present. Your friend is somersaulting on it.*
  Would you: *a* Tell him to stop?
            b Join in?
            c Ignore it, but wish you had the nerve to join in?
            d Make an excuse, and go into the playground?

5 *Your friends are bullying someone in your form.*
  Would you: *a* Join in because they might turn on you if you don't?
            b Join in because you think she deserves it?
            c Ignore it, and do nothing?
            d Ask someone for advice?

6 *Your class has been asked to prepare a year or house assembly.*
  Would you: *a* Take part willingly?
            b Take part, just because you don't want to let your friends down?
            c Refuse to take part because you are afraid of being laughed at?
            d Say it's stupid?

17 Decision-making should be related to the daily lives of pupils. School trips and holidays can be prepared for by decision-making activities which allow pupils to cope with situations of potential danger. Teacher warnings and instructions often do not cover the complexity of situations. Imaginative coverage through role-play and decision-making is extremely helpful. It creates awareness and the capacity for responsible action. Coping with situations of emergency, e.g. a chip pan catching fire when the pupil or a younger sibling is cooking chips for their tea. Accidents where electricity is involved or when on a weekend trip with a friend are

obvious examples. The following have led to useful discussion and greater awareness of dangers.

Situation 1:

You have just come to the area, and are beginning to make friends. You have met a group at the youth club who are slightly older than you. You like them because they are always good for a laugh, they like sending people up, and will try anything. Last Saturday you unthinkingly told them your parents would be out: so they all turned up and there was a bit of a party. Nobody got drunk or did anything too silly, but they did get at the sherry and wine . . . During some fooling about, a bottle of red wine got knocked over, staining the new cream carpet. Your parents were furious, and are deciding what to do about you and your friends.

- *a* Role play can extend appreciation of the standpoint of the other person. Pupils work in pairs, one being father or mother, the other being the son or daughter. They work for about ten minutes putting their viewpoint. Then they change roles, again tackling the problem.
- *b* The tutor then opens a general discussion.
- *c* In the next tutor period, the tutor reminds them briefly of the problem. The form is divided into groups of five, one pupil in each group becoming a peer judge who evaluates the decisions they make about appropriate action.
- *d* The tutor leads a discussion based on questions the pupils ask him or her. Through 'referring back' pupils begin to answer their own questions, the tutor merely calling attention to difficulties or discrepancies.

Situation 2:

This uses role play, but creates added awareness of communication because pupils have to pretend to be using the telephone.

People living in three isolated cottages have been cut off by heavy snowfalls from the outside world. The weather forecasts are warning that more snow is expected, and that the long-term forecast is unfavourable. They live in a mountainous area of great beauty, therefore the telephone cables are underground and they can talk to one another. The electricity supply has been disrupted. They are making plans over the telephone for self-help. Below is a list of occupants and some details which may be important. The houses are between half a mile and a mile apart.

House one
Man, his wife and a son on leave from the army
A deep-freezer full of food
Calor gas cooker with gas canister in caravan
Shovels and ropes

House two
An old lady over 70 who has lived in the area all her life
Coal fires are used for heating, and she has about half a ton of coal
in her shed
Six packets of candles (60 in all)
She has a few sheep which she keeps in her barn during the worst
winter months
It is a large house, but very cold and draughty

House three
Young couple and a baby of three months. The mother is develop-
ing 'flu and is really ill
Bread – four loaves
Tinned food – about ten days supply for a family of three
A storm lantern and a gallon of paraffin

    a Pupils work in groups of four, one of whom is an observer.
       They telephone each other constructing a survival plan.
    b The observer comments on the plan, pointing out other
       possibilities or drawing attention to difficulties the participants
       ignored.

18 Learning about learning

Learned helplessness, comparisons with others and the impact of
predictions upon success and failure in learning should be thoroughly
explored in tutor periods. Pupils need to be equipped to attack
these tendencies which diminish them. Simple tutor activities
include:

    a Discussion of the influence of predictive statements on be-
       haviour, e.g.
       'I know I'm not going to do very well in my examinations.'
       'None of our family are good at that sort of thing.'
    b Third-year pupils could prepare a simple taped narrative in
       which a pupil compares himself or herself negatively with
       other pupils. He also predicts he will not do well in a certain
       subject. Three or four third-year pupils lead a group discus-
       sion on ways of overcoming these tendencies.

19 Visual skills are becoming increasingly important with the growth of technology. The following activities create awareness of, and interest in, visual memory. Some preparation is needed and the head of year or house could involve a small group of pupils in this. A stopwatch or wristwatch showing seconds is required.

a Two large sheets of manilla card are needed with a number of pictures on them. Each card carries the same pictures, but the second sheet has the pictures stuck on in different places *and* one is missing.

   i   The first card is held up high enough for pupils to see it, and they are allowed 60 seconds to scan it.

   ii The pupils are then told that one picture is missing on the second card. They are allowed 60 seconds to look at the card. When they discover which one is missing they write it down.

   iii The tutor then opens a discussion on the use of diagrams and pictures in text books. A stimulating ending is the presentation of pictures for 10–15 seconds. The tutor then asks particular pupils questions about the details of each picture.

b This exercise requires about 40 thin manilla cards of A4 size. Each has drawings of 12–15 different objects. (Thin manilla card will go through a spirit duplicator successfully. It is useful to write 'Top' at the back of each A4 card.) A watch will be needed.

   i   Students work in pairs, and should sit facing each other. Forty seconds is allowed for this. The card is then turned round so that the 'holder' can see the pictures. The 'looker' then tells the holder which pictures he can remember. A mark is given for each picture recalled. At the end, the 'looker' is allowed to inspect the card, identifying the pictures which were not recalled. The activity is repeated with a different card and the pupils change roles.

   ii A variation is to ask the looker to not only describe the picture, but state its position on the card. A mark is given for both.

   iii Pupils discuss why they omitted certain pictures or put in something that was not there.

iv Suggestions for games they can play at home using television can be collected. Arrangements are made for reporting back.

[20] Auditory recall is obviously influenced by interruptions or other instructions. This activity can lead to helpful discussion of memory, especially improving listening ability.

a The tutor prepares a list of seven-figure numbers, avoiding any combinations easy to recall, e.g. double nine or two followed by three.

i The tutor calls out a number, and immediately gives an instruction which is unrelated, e.g. 'sit up straight'. Then the pupils are asked to write the number down. It is then checked.

ii Another number is called out. This time the tutor makes a joke. Pupils are then asked to write the number down and check it as before.

iii After two trials, most pupils are determined not to be put off by the tutor. This time the number is called out, and the tutor immediately instructs them to write it down *backwards*.

iv This time the tutor calls out a nine-figure number. Pupils are instructed to write down the last six numbers only, and then the first six numbers.

b Follow-up discussion explores the nature of interference, the effect of expectations and immediately processing what you have heard.

[21] Other listening activities include:

a Listening to a narrative which is followed by a quiz. Groups of four are formed; each member in turn writing the answer down in turn. No communication is allowed. Marks are assessed at the end. The discussion focuses on the tensions which interfere with recall when a group is involved.

b A tape of a telephone conversation in which a large order for DIY materials is given. Certain items have to be ordered specially, some are temporarily out of stock, different qualities are discussed, prices are given and suggestions for alternatives are made. A misunderstanding between the person ordering and the sales person occurs about a third of the way through the conversation. Pupils are then asked to write down the answers to about 20 precise questions.

22 Self-evaluation should be developed in as many ways as possible. Second-year pupils can take steps towards formative assessment. The first is constructing their own profile. A simple bar profile based on five steps ranging from 'Do badly in this', to 'Do very well in this' can be constructed. Pupils seem to find it easier to make the profile on the basis of specific subjects, e.g. English, mathematics, physical education. Fifth- and sixth-year pupils can help small groups of five or six pupils answer the questions:

i Why am I good at it?
ii What steps can I take to improve?
iii Which subjects do I see as important for me? Why?

The interaction between the different age groups has many gains for both. Older pupils have their sense of competence improved, and look at the skills of formative assessment from a new perspective. Younger ones are provided with a glimpse of more mature attitudes towards learning.

23 A next step could be the comparison of the pupil's own profile with the last report they had. Discrepancies are examined, and small group discussion of the steps to be taken in a particular subject occurs. Pupils spell out what they will do in the next week. The tutor encourages them to work with one another, showing that he or she has very positive expectations.

24 Pastoral effort often concentrates on improving the image and weakening stereotypes about the non-smoker and non-drinker. Changing the image of the pupil who works is even more important.

a Pupils draw up two lists of words – one describing a successful pupil and one a pupil who does not do well in school.
b Partners then critically assess the accuracy of their lists, e.g. 'Is it really the case that a successful pupil is a creep?', or 'Is the one who does badly necessarily tough or lazy?'
c The tutor then encourages pupils to look at the way they judge successful individuals and at the excuses for failure, perhaps 'They don't teach us properly here!'

25 After these activities it may be appropriate to introduce some group counselling which explores gender-based beliefs about ability in an open-minded way.

26 Pupils should be encouraged to question their judgements and become aware of the evidence on which they are based.

a Pupils are shown pictures of two different rooms. One is full of glass and chrome and has a futuristic atmosphere; the other is cluttered, and contains antique furniture and curtains and upholstery with large flower patterns. They are asked to write brief descriptions of the people who use these rooms. Some are read out. The tutor opens a discussion in which he or she urges caution about lightly assuming that one can necessarily come to conclusions about people on the basis of such evidence.

b Fourth- or fifth-year pupils produce two flip-chart cartoons. The first shows a supporter of any well-known football club waving a fist in the air, face distorted into a scowl, and generally looking tough. Pupils are then asked to assess what sort of person he is. That done, they are shown the second cartoon where he is seen courteously helping an old lady across the road. They are then asked to re-assess him. Interesting replies emerge, providing grist for the tutor's mill, e.g. 'He's doing it because his team won!' or 'He'll get her across the road and then mug her!'

c The old game, 'What's my line?' can be used. First-year sixth-form pupils bring in items which suggest they follow a certain occupation. They are questioned by the panel in the usual way, while the rest of the form write down their suggestions. Some of the items, e.g. a chef's coat, may be ambiguous or misleading – cooking may merely be a hobby. A general discussion is then initiated on the use of evidence and following up cues.

d Pupils are told they are detectives involved in solving the case of the abandoned suitcase.

The suitcase was found inside the door of a city church. It seems to be almost new, very expensive and without any identifying labels other than the maker's name. The usual price for such a case is not far off £100. When opened, the contents are:

– a pair of jeans, almost new, but obviously worn;
– two sweatshirts; chest 36";
– a tee shirt with University of Arizona on the front;

- *a lady's nightdress in its original container from Marks and Spencer;*
- *a pair of boxing gloves;*
- *a paper-back thriller by a very well-known author – his latest!;*
- *an asthma spray;*
- *three pairs of nylon pants, waist 28″, rather jazzy in colour and pattern;*
- *a bottle of sweet white wine (Spanish); used toothbrush and a well known brand of toothpaste;*
- *a map of the area;*
- *a quarter pound bar of fruit and nut chocolate;*
- *a pair of good quality binoculars.*

Something strange has obviously happened. The owner of the suitcase may be in trouble. Work out a description of the person you are going to look for. Where will you begin the search? Why?

Partners work on this. They then give ideas to the tutor who questions them closely about how they arrived at their conclusion, and explained certain items.

8 The Third Year

Third-year tutor work obviously focuses on subject choice, treating it as one of the critical incidents which determine affiliation or disassociation from school. Readers should note that the material included in this chapter does not replicate the programme provided in *The Teacher and Pastoral Care*. Subject choice is part of the long-term process of guidance which, if systematically and conscientiously implemented, can have a real effect on pupils' development, facilitating intellectual, social and emotional growth and contributing to ego strength. But pupils must have a real sense of choice: something which can be more problematical than we care to acknowledge. Reid *et al* (1974) are among those who examine the constraints imposed by earlier curricular organisation, and the strong influence of parents. Both factors, in conjunction with pupils' immaturity; lack of knowledge of later rewards and stages of subjects; and frequent rigidity of timetabling, constrict choices and reduce involvement.

Poor pastoral work in the second year may have strengthened attitudes of cynicism and habits of expediency. Even if pastoral care has been good, some pupils are asking what is the point of schoolwork if they are unlikely to get a job. An energetic, yet realistic, attack on apathy and despondency has to be mounted. Ideas about success have to be examined critically: this, with the beliefs of third-year pupils about the nature of ability and the style of learning which is productive for them, will form an important area of dialogue between tutors and pupils. Stereotypes about occupations obviously come to the forefront in third-year guidance. Pupils have strongly held, but unsound, beliefs about gender differences in ability. Equally important, although strangely neglected in some pastoral programmes, are false perceptions of the nature of subjects, and stereotypes about the kind of person who is good at them.

Peer relationships and comparisons with friends – who always seem to have more liberal and understanding parents and access to more privileges – are examples of topics in the social field. Individual differences are becoming marked. Pastoral heads should guard against bias in activities, which could lead the introvert to assume his make-up is pathological and that he is a deviant. We may be deceived by the attraction of the noisy, jostling disco for the third-year into believing that such social situations are their ideal. Group counselling and discussions with the third year reveal that a number of them experience unease in crowded places, while the sense of being visible, 'Everybody seems to be looking at me!', provokes anxieties. Social skills concerned with stress situations are welcomed provided – and it is an important proviso – that pupils do not feel patronised, judged or given superficial advice. Pupils at this age are struggling to achieve identity and a measure of autonomy. They need to learn skills of coping in situations where the pride or reputation of the individual is at stake or put into question, e.g. incidents of wrongful accusation or public reprimand; or the escalation of conflict or violence in contexts of group hostility.

Within the family the issues of mutual consideration and responsibility seem to centre on meal times, tidiness and undertaking chores. Discussion of a family budget creates greater awareness of 'unseen' expenditure on overheads. There are still adolescents who believe that child benefits keep their parents in undeserved luxury. The issues of part-time jobs and parental attitudes to pocket money often emerge as a source of tension; some pupils feel that their parents are penalising them for initiative in finding a spare-time job.

Learning about learning is obviously linked with subject choice. It seems banal to call attention to the importance of pupils understanding the processes by which the content of subjects is learned. Yet, in very recent work with the sixth form, it seems that some teachers have not recognised that the more aware pupils are of how they learn, and the more suggestions they can make about tackling what they have to learn, the more interested they will be in facing the challenge. Third-year pastoral work profitably encourages exploration of the self as a learner. Building their own profiles and other aspects of self-evaluation should be incorporated. For much of this, help can be derived from the relevant sections of earlier chapters. The skills of formative assessment should be given a further boost. A final note on method: group work on these topics is essential but tutors should see that better self-organisation is the desired outcome of an initially co-operative venture.

Activities related to learning and subject choice

1 A simple method of evaluation is the use of incomplete sentences. Pupils complete the sentences honestly provided that the sheets bear no names. The results give a very clear picture of trends within the form although the tutor will need to analyse the responses of boys and girls separately. A *caveat* is necessary: the initial phrases should be scanned to ensure they do not invite undue self-exposure or focus on a particular subject. Pupils can be asked to discuss generally, but there is an unacceptable level of risk in asking them to read their completed sentences aloud.

Tutor could read the initial phrase or write it on the board.

Sentence beginnings:

1 For me the second year was . . .
2 When I got my last report I . . .
3 The third-year seems . . .
4 I worry about . . .
5 I would like to change . . .
6 My friends . . .
7 I would like the school to help me with . . .
8 I would like to ask the teachers to . . .
9 It is difficult in school when . . .
10 Things that make it difficult to learn are . . .

There is material for several sessions in this activity. Discussion in small groups initially focusing on what pupils feel to be important is productive. This can be followed by class discussion where the pupils raise issues and ask questions of the teacher. In the subsequent session the tutor can give his impressions of the trends revealed by the responses.

2 Achievement motivation is associated with the incentive values of success and the predictions of success or failure. The discrepancies between preference, desire and expectation have to be examined to make inroads into apathy.

  a Pupils discuss the success they would like to achieve by the time they reach 40. Ideas are written on large sheets of paper, and each group compares their ideas with another group.

b Small groups discuss what they *expect* to have achieved by the time they reach 40. Again entries are made on the sheet of paper, and comparisons occur between groups.

c The tutor then puts forward the idea that if you really want something you can get it. The form discusses this, then one small group is invited to present their ideas to the form, and look at ways of closing the gap between wish and fulfilment. The rest of the form are asked to make suggestions that are both helpful and realistic.

3 | Analysis of success:

a The tutor gathers ideas from the form, building a description of a successful person. The description includes both achievement and personal qualities.

b Pupils then discuss the importance of luck, perseverance, intelligence, effort, friends, teaching or whatever, in achieving success. The tutor challenges them to criticise their ideas.

c With a chosen friend, pupils explore the qualities they possess: it has proved helpful to begin by each partner describing the strengths of the other. (In some schools pupils are unused to talking about themselves positively, and the tutor should anticipate their embarrassment.)

d The tutor encourages pupils to ask him questions about the nature of success.

4 | Target setting:

a Pupils work in groups of three, discussing the way they would like to improve in some area of learning, making sure that physical education, art and the crafts are considered as important fields of achievement.

b Each member of the triad is asked to choose what he believes would be easiest to improve in himself. Then they discuss in turn the practical methods of achieving this. The tutor stresses the need to concentrate on behaviour and set clear, observable targets. In turn, the other two members of the group act as helpers.

c The tutor ends by building up a list of points about target setting and helping on the blackboard.

|5| The self as a learner:

a Tutors collect ideas, through 'brainstorming' by the form, about the characteristics of the effective learner.

b A ladder is drawn on the board and the tutor asks for ideas about the most important characteristic. He then enters this on the top rung of the ladder. The second characteristic is then selected allowing pupils to understand the procedure. The tutor then points out there is no single right order: pupils have to take responsibility for their own selection.

c Pupils then draw their own ladder, adding any quality they feel important, to those listed on the board.

d Discussion follows based on consideration of the three qualities seen as least important and the three seen as most important. Within the triads, pupils are encouraged to question one another's choices.

|6| Lifestyle:
The theme underlying subject choice is that of self-assessment plus lifestyle.

a The tutor may begin by writing the major fields into which work can be divided on the board, e.g. scientific, outdoor, mechanical, medical, social service, literary, aesthetic, computational, practical, persuasive. (Tutors should teach pupils the meaning of 'aesthetic' or any other unfamiliar word, or substitute an equivalent.) The form contributes job titles which are placed under appropriate headings.

b Pupils then select the fields they think will be attractive to them and discuss their choices in groups of four.

c The tutor then draws attention to the fact that it is possible to work at different levels in each field, e.g. in the medical field there are many levels, ranging from hospital porter to the specialist consultant. Pupils again discuss in small groups.

d The tutor ends with a brief summary discussion.

|7| Beliefs about gender differences in abilities:
(This activity should be undertaken only after careful thought. It should not be used until pupils have become accustomed to thinking about the topic).

a The tutor carefully introduces the topic of learned helplessness and alleged gender differences in aptitude and ability. He or she may ask the class to debate:

- Why are girls supposed to like making neat notes, while boys are expected to be more careless, perhaps slovenly?
- Why do some girls quite unnecessarily see physics and chemistry not only as difficult subjects, but too difficult for them?
- What makes some boys opt for the sciences, when they would be happier doing something else?

b The pupils then write a brief essay entitled, 'The life I would like.' They write it, however, *as if they were a member of the opposite sex.*

c In groups of four, composed of two boys and two girls the essays are read by a member of the sex whose viewpoint they are supposed to represent. General discussion about the accuracy of the viewpoints put forward in the essays then occurs.

8 Stereotypes:

Stereotypes are not confined to beliefs about the abilities of the sexes. Pupils often have rigid and unquestioned beliefs about the nature of subjects and the kind of person who does well in particular subjects.

a The tutor helps pupils construct a list of questions they would like to ask about:
  - the later stages of a subject;
  - the career relevance of a subject;
  - the qualities needed to do well in a subject.

b Subject teachers or heads of academic departments are then invited to answer questions.

   Sometimes they can be accompanied by a small group of fourth-year pupils who join in the discussion.

c An alternative is for sixth-form students to work with groups of four or five pupils answering their questions. They end by making additional comments, highlighting issues which have been ignored.

9 Self-evaluation can take several forms:

a Pupils write about 'themselves as a learner'. They write as if they were somebody else, but this person knows them better than even their best friend could. They are asked to be as honest as possible, looking at strengths as well as weaknesses. They then form self-help groups, looking at ways of building on their strengths.

b Sixth-formers can help third-years develop simple profiles. The assessments will include the following if the profiles are to be useful:

   i *Oral skills* – debating a point of view; stating one's position clearly; describing events; giving instructions or directions clearly; formulating questions; giving a clear and accurate report of what has been heard or read.

   ii *Listening skills* – the emphasis being on listening for particular purposes, e.g. detecting the steps in an argument; picking up cues of importance; isolating key facts from interpretation of them; looking for cause and effect.

   iii *Visual skills* – using diagrams to process what has been learned; extracting information from pictures; using films and television; drawing as an aid to learning.

   iv *Reading skills* – speed of reading; breaking assignments down into sections; use of Robinson's (1962) SQ3R; using an index; preparing a list of questions about what has been read; constructing a counter-argument.

   v *Collecting data for projects etc.* – library skills, locating information and evaluating information culled from different sources; interviewing skills, e.g. asking questions; putting relevant facts together, processing information into a new form.

   vi *Note-taking skills* – creating a sensible balance between the writer's or speaker's arguments and putting them into one's own words; making what is important stand out; using space and colour to help give a structure; getting things in a logical order; understanding the purpose of making notes.

   vii *Presenting information* – in projects and assignments; the use of diaries; making audio tapes; using sketches.

   viii *Thinking and problem-solving skills* – see earlier chapters.

   ix *Self-management skills* – e.g. planning; use of time; checking up on oneself through target setting.

The head of year can use the headings above as a basis for preliminary discussion of approaches and giving the sixth-form helpers a briefing.

c Friends can write careful descriptions of one another as learners. They then assess the validity of the report.

10 Case histories:

Case histories can be developed which highlight the consequences of poor subject choice, the effect of predictions and comparisons, and the influences of friends and parents. The team developing and testing materials found the following simple exercise of value in provoking discussion.

Jim is quite clever, but does not work hard unless pressed by his teachers. When he leaves school he would like to have a technical training in a local large firm. For this he will need good O-levels in physics, mathematics and a craft subject as well as English. He has a group of close friends who care little about school, school work or the people who try hard. These friends are in the same class, but do little work, spending their time in relatively harmless 'mucking about'. Jim values their friendship, but he is worried about his future.

i What are Jim's needs other than the O-level passes?
ii Of these, which are the most important needs for Jim if he is to change? Give reasons for your choices.
iii Take one need, and suggest as what he could do to get what he wants.
iv Take two of the actions you have just listed and look at the immediate results and possible long-term consequences.
v What advice do you think a good friend of Jim would give him?
vi How do you suggest Jim could change without alienating his friends or getting himself into a humiliating position?

11 Discussions will have to include fear of failure and learned helplessness. Topics could usefully include:

a The costs of not doing a subject, e.g. a girl leaves out physics at O-level but then decides to go into television production and finds she needs the subject because of the technical nature of production.
b Family influences – e.g. parental statements such as, 'None of

our family were ever any good at that'. (The implications and associations which pupils perceive are surprisingly wide.)

Other aspects of decision-making

12 Reactions to having to make a decision:
A simple exercise is to discuss the implications of:

a Avoiding the responsibility. Statements are written up on the board and then discussed, e.g.
  – 'What do you think?'
  – 'I'll leave it to you.'
  – 'Anything you say.'
  – 'It's up to you.'

Group discussion explores what is likely to be the reaction of the avoider to the decision they allowed to be made for them. The purpose of this discussion is to sensitise pupils to thinking about risk levels, sources of influence and personality factors which shape the response to decision-making.

b Next the idea of the confused decision-maker is presented. The key responses can be written on the blackboard or put on tape:
  – 'I can't think what to do!'
  – 'I don't know who is right.'
  – 'I get bewildered, there are so many ideas.'

c The delayer is then considered:
  – 'I'll leave it, then perhaps I won't have to bother.'
  – 'I'll think about it tomorrow, when I may have more ideas.'

d Other approaches are:
  i The intuitive, e.g.
    'It feels right' but is intuition enough?
  ii The fatalistic, e.g.
    'It's all in the stars.'
    'I'll do whatever I'm asked to do.'
    'I haven't any choice really.'

Pupils are then encouraged to think about the way in which they made a recent decision, what their approach was and, in retrospect, whether they could have used a more effective approach.

13 The menu:
(The basic idea is taken from the materials produced in the Clwyd Project.)

 a Pupils are presented with a menu from which they select a four course meal. Some of the dishes are familiar, others are strange because they are written in French. The meal is chosen: the tutor then initiates discussion about the reasons for selection and rejection. Attention is given to the influence of familiarity in restricting choice; or choices made blindly, without thinking of the consequences – what happens if you end up with snails or oysters which you detest? The way in which the likelihood of embarrassment or fear of appearing inferior inhibit the seeking of information is also explored.
 b Pupils are then asked to relate the menu situation to subject choice. They work in small groups, then report back to the tutor who constructs a blackboard summary. (It is important that the tutor allows pupils to make the associations for themselves.)

14 What are the consequences?

 a The importance of looking beyond the immediate situation to consequences is briefly mentioned. Then pupils tackle the following exercise in groups of four.

 A friend of yours has taken an evening job because she is saving up for her holidays. She knows she is lucky to have the job because jobs are scarce. There are many other people who would be delighted to take over from her. Her boss, Mr Jones, is rather strict about punctuality.

 Your friend's form is organising a disco for the local school for handicapped children. She usually helps on such occasions, because she knows how to work the lights, also, the caretaker at the local hall (where the disco is being held) is a friend of her parents.

 What would you advise her to do?

 b Below is a list of things she could do; discuss each one in turn and suggest what might happen or what could happen in each case:

   i She could see Mr Jones and ask him to let her have the evening off.

What might he say?

ii She could ring Mr Jones, say she is ill and then go and help run the disco.
What could happen if she does this?

iii She could arrange for a friend to work for Mr Jones for that one evening.
Can you think of any consequences?

iv She could go to work instead of helping with the disco.
How will she feel if she does this?
What will her friends think?
What will the caretaker feel about this?

v *Is there anything else she could do?*
What would you advise her to do?

15 Sara's day:

a Pupils are asked to read through the passage below and identify the decisions Sara makes by putting a coloured mark against them.

Sara was lying snugly in bed when her mum called her. She knew if she stayed in bed for an extra five minutes she wouldn't have enough time to wash and clean her teeth, so she got out of bed and looked for her clothes. 'Which shoes should I wear today?' she asked herself. She looked out of the window, saw it was raining and picked up her black shoes, which were waterproof. Then she went downstairs for breakfast. She grabbed the nearest packet of cereal and poured some into a bowl. She ate quickly while working out which books to take to school. She put her English book in her bag but left her History book at home because she didn't have History that day. She couldn't be bothered to take her Geography book, although she knew she might need it, because it was too heavy.

On the bus, which was crowded as usual, the conductor forgot to ask for her fare so she kept the money to spend in the tuck shop at breaktime. Sara got off the bus and ran towards school; she saw her friend Jane ahead and dashed up the stairs to catch her up but she almost knocked over the deputy head. She had to stand there red-faced while she was told off for unladylike behaviour.

At breaktime Sara went to the tuck shop and took so long to make up her mind what to buy that they had sold out! After break, she had to sit quietly while the Geography teacher told her off for not having her book, then gave her extra homework as punishment.

Poor Sara! It isn't lunchtime and she has already had to make several decisions. Some things haven't worked out very well for her, have they?

It isn't only during the school day that Sara has to decide what to do, or when to do it. Later on that evening, at the Youth Club, Sara had to wait for a game of table tennis and hadn't finished at 9 o'clock when she knew she ought to leave to catch the bus. 'Stay and finish this game' said her partner, 'you'll still have time to catch the bus'. They played on and as soon as they finished Sara rushed out to the bus stop. She was halfway across the car park when she realised that she had left her bag in the Youth Club. Without thinking she ran back to get it and so missed her bus. She was late in and her mother was very cross. 'If only I hadn't stayed to finish that game', she thought.

Not only do we make decisions but we do so in many different ways. Discuss each of the decisions you think Sara made, with a partner.

b Pupils are then asked by the tutor to discuss the decisions and put them into one of the following groups. (It seems most effective when they work in pairs.)

    i   The easiest way out.
    ii Spur of the moment.
    iii Careful thought.
    iv Making a balance between different ways of behaving.
    v Relying on others.

c The tutor then initiates general discussion on decisions which are problematical for the pupils.

16 The barbecue:

a This longer exercise asks pupils to consider how others influence our decisions. The tutor points out that we do not always have a simple choice between two possibilities, although even that needs careful thought. Pupils are told they will have to think carefully about:
    – The things they will want.
    – What might happen.

The pupils are instructed to write their answers in the boxes at the end of each section on the duplicated sheets.

The Barbecue

This decision-making game is to help you see the ways in which others can influence you when you are making decisions. It also encourages you to consider the costs and consequences of the decisions you make.

Work in groups of four. You will need to discuss each situation carefully. You must come to a group decision – that is, you must all agree.

Write your decisions in the boxes provided.

1 You are planning a beach barbecue. Decide how much money you need for food. How much is each person going to contribute?

```

```

2 Decide (and remember, you must all agree) what you are going to buy with your money.

```

```

You cannot overspend. You must all have enough to eat. Do you all like the same things?

3 Decide where you are going to hold the barbecue, *and* how you are going to get there.
   Consider bus, walking, bicycle, father's car.

```

```

Having decided where you are going and how to get there, you need to make sure you take *all* the things you need.

4 From the list below choose the things you think you will need. Each article has a number of points. You can only use 50 points.

Matches	5	Four forks	2	Extra matches	2
Paper napkins	1	A sharp knife	1	A barbecue	10
String	1	Four plates	5	A saucepan	3
Charcoal	10	Plastic beakers	3	A tin opener	2
Four knives	2	Skewers	2	An anorak each	5
First-aid kit	10	Fire lighters	5	Two umbrellas	3
A swimsuit each	2	Change for the		Tongs to turn food	5
A towel each	2	phone	3		

List the things you have chosen below:

Consider the following situations. For each one, decide what you would do, and state whether or not you were prepared to cope with it – had you got the things you needed?

1 It starts to rain.
   What can you do?
   What do you need?
2 One of you cuts a finger badly – it obviously needs some stitches.
   What are you going to do?
3 Someone slips and drops the matches in the sea. Have you any spares?
4 One of you slips on the rocks and gets wet; it is too cold to leave him to dry off.
5 A friend arrives and wants to join in, but hasn't contributed to the cost. Decide as a group what you will do.
   Follow-up questions
   Answer these without discussing them.
   1 Was it easy, as a group, to decide on the amount of money to collect?
      Did one person seem to take charge?

> Did the group agree to compromise?
> Did you agree with the final decision, or did you just go along with what others wanted?
> *THINK* How much do other people influence you?
> 2 Did you decide to take all the things you needed?
> Did you consider the consequences of *not* taking certain things?
> Would you change your choices now?
> If so, what would you take (remember, there is a 50 point limit)?

b Where possible the tutor should immediately help pupils relate what they have done to a real life decision, e.g. planning a trip.

[17] Truancy and absence:

This exercise helps pupils comprehend the social and organisational issues which accompany absence – whether illicit or legitimate. Material for several sessions is given below:

a The return:

Robert, a 13-year-old boy, has returned to school after being away for six weeks due to illness. In pairs, discuss how he should deal with this situation.

   i What do you think he will find difficult at first?
   ii What action do you think he should take?
   iii What could Robert have done when he knew he was going to be away from school for a long time?

b Help Ann to help herself:

This activity highlights the possibility of peer support, develops standpoint-taking and looks at self-management in such situations.

Pupils are asked to discuss Ann's problem in groups of four. They are asked to imagine she has talked to one of the group and this is what she said:

She has missed a lot of school lately, and is worried about it. She is in the fourth year and is lagging behind in her courses in Child Care and Biology which she does not like. She has kept up in English and Social Studies which she likes. She also says that she does not get on well with many pupils at her school, as most of her friends are older and go to another school. She finds it difficult to come to school, but she feels all right when she gets there.

Discuss:

  i   What do you think is her main difficulty?
  ii How can she catch up on her work? Make out a plan for her.
  iii How would you help her with her friendship problems if you were in her class?
  iv What do you think will happen if she does not do something now?

c Missed bus:

You and your friend have missed the bus to school. Your friend's parents are both at work and she suggests that you do not wait for the next bus, but go back to her house, and watch her new video film.

Pupils divide a sheet of paper into half. On the left-hand side they make a list of all the actions they could take in this situation. On the right-hand side, they write what they think would be the consequences of each action.

Social skills and stress

The issues of audience anxiety (especially fear of the limelight); loss of control (including bodily control); and fears of revealing in-adequacy which may create adverse impressions in authority figures, all play an important part in third- and fourth-year guidance. The situations below have led to interesting discussions, and tutors and forms have identified useful ways of coping.

[18] Incomplete sentences:
This technique can stimulate useful discussion, but pastoral heads must help tutors react sensitively. Probing will activate defensive reactions in the pupil, and bring challenges to the claim that

pastoral activity is founded in respect for the pupil. Carefully used,
it can be a tool for constructive discussion of emotions; badly used,
it can be a form of psychological rape. The following statements
have been used constructively as a basis for small group and form
discussion:
- I find it difficult when other people . . .
- When I do not understand . . .
- On my own . . .
- A room full of people . . .
- Making a mistake . . .
- It makes me angry . . .
- When I am worried . . .
- I like . . .

In using such techniques, the tutor must be non-judgemental,
creating a climate of acceptance in which pupils can look at their
feelings safely. Pastoral heads have to take the responsibility for
steering certain tutors away from such approaches: we cannot risk
damage to pupils.

19 A questionnaire about change:
This simple questionnaire offers a basis for discussion in self-help
groups. It encourages pupils to cast a suspicious glance at themselves without discounting the possibility of change. The tutor
could act as a consultant to the self-help groups. (Reference to the
sections on formative assessment and peer counselling will be
helpful.)

Questionnaire:

1 What are the things that could prevent you from succeeding in
   school?
2 Are there some groups of people you cannot get on with in
   school? If so, why is this? It may help to look at their view of
   you, and compare it with your view of them.
3 What would you like to get out of school in the next two years?
   Be as precise as possible.
4 If you could change anything about *yourself*, what would it be?
5 If you could change anything you do in school, what would it
   be?
6 What could the school do to help you be more successful?

20 'Trio' problems with girls:

A great deal of ambivalence exists in the relationships between girls in the third-year. This is obvious in the three-cornered relationships which are often the context in which problems appear. Simple decision-making activities could centre around:

a She's taken my friend.

Patricia has been friends with Jane since they met in the primary school. Jane detests netball, but Patricia enjoys it and is a key member of the team. Linda is the netball team's captain. She has become increasingly friendly with Patricia who doesn't bother much with Jane now. Jane picks a fight with Linda in the playground, getting her down on the ground and kicking her viciously. The teacher on duty intervenes and pulls Jane off who screams, 'She's taken my friend.'

    i Discuss in groups of three how you think the teacher will deal with the problem.

    ii What advice would you give to Jane? If you were Jane would you follow that advice?

    iii Think of another situation where three girls have a similar difficulty.

b The gossip:

Mary, Colleen and Ann have known one another for several years, although their relationships are sometimes stormy. Ann has just told Colleen that Mary has gone out with Colleen's boyfriend.

    i What action should Colleen take?

    ii What were Ann's motives for her action?

    iii The tutor initiates a general discussion on 'threesomes'. Pupils are encouraged to assess the form such problems take with boys, e.g. 'pig in the middle'.

c Fights:

Similar activities could be developed around:

    i The 'big fight' promoter who conveys the message that somebody wants a fight. Will the recipient oblige?

    ii Dealing with the excuse for aggression: 'She looked at me!'

21 Wrongful accusation:

a Pupils discuss in small groups of three or four the situations in which false accusations could be made.

b Each group produces a short play in which somebody is wrongfully accused. After planning it, a volunteer group presents their play to the class. They stimulate audience participation by stopping at crucial points and involving the audience:

 i What do you think will happen next?
 ii What could he have done instead of what he has just done?
 iii What do you think he should do now?

Discussion can focus on the dangers which arise when the accused one becomes aggressive, e.g. does this convince the accuser of his guilt? What could inhibit the accuser's admission of his mistake? Fourth- or fifth-year pupils taking drama can be producers, helping each group refine their playlet.

22 Other social situations:
Useful discussion can centre around:

a Comparisons with others, e.g. My friends are allowed to stay out later.
b Coping with situations in which the pride or reputation of the individual is at stake or is challenged, e.g. refusing a 'dare' in front of an audience.
c Feelings about crowded places, especially coping with jostling and random punching.
d Feeling the need to report something to a teacher, but also fearing condemnation as a sneak by other pupils.

23 Situations of discomfort:
Useful exploration can occur of:

a Sensible reaction to receiving disappointing marks.
b Saying 'no' to teachers or parents.
c Making a complaint.
d Coming into a classroom when the pupil has been unavoidably delayed.
e Handling provocation when acting as a prefect or monitor.
f Refusing to join in an activity without seeming critical.

24 Constructive assertion of a viewpoint:

a A tape is made which highlights the dilemma of a pupil.

A boy is earning £3.50 at his part-time job. His parents will only give him 50p pocket money because he has the job. All his friends get at least £1.00 from their parents.

   i Should he ask for more?
   ii Should he give up the job?

In groups of four, one pupil takes the role of the boy, who has made up his mind to argue with his parents because he feels they are unfairly punishing him for having the energy to work. As he produces his arguments, the other three try to persuade him that his arguments are invalid. He has to maintain his viewpoint by countering their arguments.

b A general discussion is initiated by the tutor on constructive forms of assertion.

(It may be important to allow the 'part-time workers' to share ideas for supporting their position outside the class. The others try to anticipate what the arguments of the workers will be. The section on role play provides ideas for pastoral heads who wish tutors to introduce role play.)

9 The Fourth Year

The key themes in fourth-year guidance can usefully be self-management and value clarification. The latter will stem directly from discussions embodying the principles and techniques of counselling, see Hamblin (1974; 1983 and 1984). The experience provided by the activities contributes indirectly by encouraging considered discriminations about the intent of self and others. Self-management means recognition of the different facets of the self:

1 *The self as a learner* This is more than the possession of skills. Attitudes to success or failure, motivation, and awareness of self-defeating behaviour have to be explored.

2 *The self as a potential worker* Lifestyle; the matching of personality and occupational demands; recognition of industrial change . . . have to be included, without evading the doubts and problems posed by economic uncertainty and unemployment.

3 *General beliefs about the nature of the world* Is the individual able to control his destiny or is he a hapless pawn? Is ruthless competition an inescapable norm or can altruism play a part?

4 *The self in social interaction* Has the individual the ability to engage in interaction without being manipulative or passively accepting the expectations of others?

5 *A sexual identity* This should be satisfying and not based on crude, unquestioned gender stereotypes which glorify one's own sex and devalue the opposite sex.

Fourth-year guidance is truly developmental when it gives pupils the means of understanding, and subsequently modifying, the forces which constrain and distort their interaction with others. Pressures are denied: a mask of bravado or indifference is adopted as a way of contending with pressures. The pastoral programme creates awareness of self-defeating forms of behaviour which carry penalties not fully comprehended by those who feel marginal about school and success. Confusions about what they should, can, or even want to do, are manifold; often being resolved by resort to attitudes which dismiss adult demands as meaningless. Clumsy forms of self-assertion complicate the situation further and the adolescent is unsure whether he or she is 'waving or drowning', to use the potent images of Stevie Smith's poem.

Our aim is to remove the false distinction some pupils make between school success and peer group success. Pupils can be successful learners and still enjoy themselves; but far too many fourth-year pupils behave as if the two were irrevocably opposed. We should be disturbed by the fact that learning is amorphous – perhaps a profound mystery – for so many fourth-year pupils. It is seen in black and white terms as either something you can do, or something at which you have no success. Pastoral systems can operate to reinforce passivity in learning, but pupils themselves find it convenient to adopt an inert approach if they are orientated to avoid shame or punishment. Such learners see the demands of the school as hostile forces which have to be circumvented, perhaps outwitted. They are quick to attribute negative intent to teachers, while their tendency to compare themselves with others tempts them to see successful peers as threats or dismiss them as snobs. The use of peer counselling, the stimulation of co-operation, and the inculcation of responsibility through formative assessment, can overcome these tendencies, although pupils will be resistant at first.

If pupils are deprived of support and the skills for coping with social anxieties, then they may adopt one of the two extremes of retreatist or crudely assertive behaviour. Our main tool will be inducement of purposeful discussion which encourages more precise discrimination and interpretation of the pupil's interactional world. In the fourth-year, social inadequacies are compounded by worries about unemployment. Tutors may recognise this in boys, but be unaware that unemployment has a greater impact on the girls, who are more vulnerable to social pressure. Girls' accelerated rate of development, relative to that of boys, creates sensitivity to devaluation and appreciation of the more subtle aspects of unemployment.

Self-management and learning

Tutors should realise that the specialist study skills of an academic subject are not the concern of pastoral effort. They are the responsibility of the subject specialist: they reflect the research procedures of professionals in the field and embody the basic concepts and style of thought which undergird the subject. Pastoral work is concerned with the broad-based skills and attitudes necessary for success in school and with creating awareness of the style of learning that is productive for each pupil. There is no right way and pupils must take responsibility for their own learning. (Heads of year or house should refer to *Teaching Study Skills*.)

[1] During the secondary school pupils learn to reject responsibility for their learning and blame others for their lack of success. This simple exercise interrupts this mechanism:

a The tutor writes on the blackboard:
  'If you did all that the teachers want you to do, you would have no life of your own.'
  Pupils discuss the truth of this statement for two or three minutes. The tutor suggests that it might be a good idea to get some facts.

b A duplicated sheet is then handed out in which the 24 hours from midnight to midnight are shown. Pupils fill in the space against each hour showing the major activity undertaken. They then work out the time they spent in working, sleeping, eating, enjoying themselves or just drifting.

c The form discusses the results in small groups, looking for ways of managing their use of time more effectively. The tutor ends by introducing pupils humorously to 'the theory of the impossible task', i.e. 'we don't have enough time; they don't teach us properly'.

[2] This exercise links self-management to beliefs about control: are we responsible for what happens to us? Is what happens shaped by luck or forces outside us? The best materials I have seen have often been constructed by pupils taking drama. The example below is based on the work of two pupils.

a A tape is constructed in which two pupils are talking. They appear to be of equal ability: but one has done very badly in her exams while the other has done quite well. The first begins by saying:

'I was shattered when I got my results! Dad went berserk and hasn't spoken to me all week. Mum has been crying. I didn't want

to upset them, but I couldn't help it. You won't believe it, but every time I tried to get some revision done, one of my friends came round, and I had to let them in, didn't I? Then they wanted me to go out with them, and I had to, otherwise they'd turn nasty on me in school or I'd be on my own. I couldn't have that could I?'

The second girl interrupts, pointing out that she has some of the same friends, and that she also has a Saturday job which the other has not. She then goes on to explain how she managed her time.

b The tutor draws attention to the first girl's reliance on implicit appeals for sympathy which function to absolve her from responsibility for what happened. The form usually gets absorbed in the discussion providing the tutor moves quickly from tape to group discussion. Too many comments from the tutor seem to reduce the impact of the tape. After group discussion, the tutor structures a form discussion by drawing attention to the importance of beliefs about success.

3 Other tapes can reinforce the self-management and control issues, e.g. a boy or girl discussing the reality of the fear of being labelled a 'swot' or a girl examining her belief that society has many subtle and indirect punishments for the able woman.

4 The tutor writes two or three excuses for not working on the blackboard, e.g.
- I would work if only my mother did not nag so much.
- I somehow can't settle down to my homework.
- The house is always so noisy.

The form supplies other excuses which are added to the list. Partners then work out ways of dealing with the situations they feel are particularly relevant to them. The tutor then asks some pupils to put their ideas to the whole form.

5 Self-defeating strategies are a phenomena often ignored in guidance. Humour can be used to prevent pupils from feeling attacked or activating dismissive responses. The tutor draws two pin boys or girls on the blackboard. The speech bubble of one reads, 'I quite liked this girl/boy up the road, so I went to talk to her.' He draws a line across, beginning the second frame in which the other girl or boy is saying, 'So?' The other goes on, 'But when I got there I was so embarrassed, I couldn't say anything to him/her.'

In the third frame the 'punch line' is, 'So I hit her/him.' When the merriment has subsided, the tutor points out that similar self-defeating strategies occur in learning. When do we undertake the equivalent of cutting off our noses to spite our faces?

Provided that they feel what they say will be treated with respect, pupils welcome the opportunity to discuss the self-defeating tendencies of which they are usually uneasily aware. Other topics are:

a The tendency to predict failure gloomily, and then work without direction and energy.

b The belief that they know how to study, coupled with the feeling that there is no need for urgency because they have plenty of time before they take their exams.

c The possibility that discontent with performance is transformed into aggressive behaviour or a cocksureness which not only hides inner insecurity, but which progressively alienates them from those who could give support.

6 If self-help groups are not already operating, they can be developed from evaluation of the self as a learner in the fourth year. Pupils write a report on their strengths and weaknesses as a learner. They write as if they were someone else who is very concerned about his or her future progress, so the essay is written in the third person. They are asked to imagine, however, that the person knows them better than even their closest friend. Pupils are told that these essays are for them to use, and not for the tutor's information. Self-help groups are formed. The tutor leads a discussion on their functions, pointing out that a number of factors have to be taken into account, e.g. motivation, friendship and interest in the same subjects. The last factor is especially important as a basis for mutual support. The first step is for the groups to examine their strengths, deciding how they can support one another in an attempt to build on them in the next three days.

The ladder technique is used to analyse weaknesses. The easiest thing to correct is put on the lowest rung, the next easiest on the next rung, the process continuing until all the problems have been arranged in order of difficulty. Then the self-help groups look at ways of tackling the problem on the lowest rung of their ladders. The tutor ends the first problem-solving session by pointing out the effectiveness of the principle of graduation in inducing change.

[7] Self-management involves many things, but a neglected area may be discovering the pattern of learning best suited to the individual. We are aware of rhythms in biological fields, but we may be insensitive to their existence in study. The question is, 'What is the best time of day for me to do certain things?' The tutor distinguishes between receptive and active forms of learning, that is, between the assimilation and retention of new facts or ideas and processing, applying and considering the implications and development of those ideas and facts. It is made clear that there are no recipes and pupils have to take responsibility. Some are unable to learn after eight in the evening, some cannot begin until ten o'clock. Some find it more effective to deal with the reading tasks first and then write later. Some find the reverse is more productive. I have found that pupils welcome the opportunity to discuss their learning style, and use it well within their self-help groups.

[8] Standpoint-taking:
It is useful to provide pupils with the opportunity to take the standpoint of the tutor in investigating a learning problem. The example below provides the basis for the exercise, although the tutor may prefer to use a situation he has experienced.

a *Imagine you are a fourth-year tutor. Jane, who is in your form, comes to you shortly after the Christmas examinations, and asks if she can change two of her options. She wants to give up Chemistry and Physics and replace them with Home Economics and History instead.*

b Partners or small groups discuss how they think the tutor should deal with the request and how he or she will investigate the problem.

c Pupils are then asked how the tutor would react to the discovery that Jane's marks in Physics and Chemistry were high.

d They then discuss the tutor's likely reactions to a statement made by Jane when he or she is discussing the problem with her. She says that despite the good marks, she feels 'useless' at these subjects, especially disliking the practical work in Chemistry.

e The tutor could follow this activity with a session in which he or she answers questions from the class about the way he or she would deal with such a problem.

9 Ideal pupil and ideal teacher:
Behind classroom interaction and judgements are models of the good pupil and good teacher. This is as true for the pupil as it is for the teacher. This exercise encourages pupils to question their judgements and also take the standpoint of the teacher.

- *a* Pupils work in pairs and build up a description of the ideal fourth-year pupil. This is not confined to study, but includes relationships and activities outside the classroom.
- *b* The pair then joins another pair, sharing their ideas. They are then asked by the tutor to discuss whether they think that tutors would totally agree with the picture. In what ways would their ideal pupil differ from that of the pupils?
- *c* The next step is for the pairs to construct a picture of the ideal teacher. (Work by my students showed that pupils younger than this had well-defined ideas about the attributes of the good teacher.)
- *d* As before, pairs share ideas. Then the tutor requests them to discuss the ways in which their ideal teacher picture might differ from that of teachers. What considerations might the teacher have to keep in mind, which might not seem important to the pupil?
- *e* A follow-up session could be held in which the form tutor is joined by the head of year or house, deputy head or head teacher to answer questions as well as raise them about the ideal pupil and teacher.

10 Anxiety and learning:
The following checklist is handed to pupils who are asked to identify the situations which make them worry:

Checklist:

1 Being asked a question by the teacher.
2 Not understanding instructions.
3 Being praised by the teacher.
4 Explaining that I could not do my homework.
5 Having to work with a pupil of the opposite sex.
6 Finding I have left a book I need at home.
7 The teacher reading out marks to the class.
8 Being promoted to a higher class.

---

9 Having to read aloud in class.
10 Coming late into the class.

The self-help groups are used to discuss why particular situations are threatening, and the ways in which pupils could cope better. Pupils then work out the steps they will take during the next three days to cope with *one* situation that worries them. They present their proposals to the group, who evaluate them and make useful suggestions.

Social and personal development

The previous section touched on both the self as a learner and beliefs about the nature of transactions between the individual and his environment. This section provides ideas for materials related to sexual identity and the self in social interaction. Pastoral heads will find much that will spark off ideas for additional activities in the appropriate parts of earlier chapters.

11 Why does she behave so badly?
Standpoint-taking has to be related to judgements of peers. The activitity does this through the use of a life space diagram (see *The Teacher and Counselling*).

a The basic situation:

Alison seems to quarrel with everyone. She snaps even when people are nice to her. Today, she hit and kicked your best friend for nothing, and then dashed out of class. The teacher sent you to find her. She is sitting in the cloakroom crying. She tells you her father has been hitting her, and that she is afraid to take her report home. She wants to leave home as no one there cares about her.

Pupils then try to imagine that they are Alison. They do this in silence for one minute. Then partners discuss the following questions.

i What would you say to Alison?
ii How will you tell her you have been sent to bring her back?
iii How do you feel about her now she has told you this?
iv Will you say anything to the others in the class?

The tutor ends with general discussion on coping with such situations.

b In the next tutor period, the tutor produces the life space diagram which is on a large sheet of paper (24″ x 30″) or a transparency.

Dad and Mum:
Fed up with her. Say she is a bad influence on her sister. Cross about letter from school and truancy and poor work. Her mum feels very depressed and tired because her baby is due very shortly.

Sister:
Little sister is at junior school: teachers and neighbours often say she is a sweet little girl.

ALISON: AGE 15

Teachers:
Cross because she doesn't pay attention – dreams in class. Plays truant. Doesn't do homework or project work.

Classmates:
Fed up with her bad temper and borrowing their work to 'copy up'. Sometimes afraid of her because they don't know how she is going to behave. They know she used to be spoiled. Dad gave her anything she wanted and she boasted about it.

The groups then assess:

i the reasons for her behaviour;
ii what Alison could do to improve the situation.

The tutor selects one group to come to the front of the class and explain their views, answering questions from the rest of the form.

12 Teasing:

a The situation:

You tell your best friend that you would like to go out with a boy or girl whom you fancy. In the dining hall a small group of classmates

*laugh at you for this, also making fun of the person you want to go
out with.*

b The groups 'brainstorm', producing as many ideas as they can
about ways of responding.
c They then evaluate the likely consequences of different courses
of action, trying to identify the most sensible one.
d Each group then gives its idea, the tutor commenting on the
strengths and weaknesses of each proposal.

This activity can be the basis for a subsequent discussion on
trust. How do you know you can trust someone? The tutor shapes
the discussion around concrete situations, e.g.
 – How do you decide that if you lend a friend money s/he will pay
 you back?
 – If you tell someone a secret about yourself, how do you know
 s/he will not tell somebody else?

13 Do you all have to do the same thing?

a Four of you have gone to the seaside for a day trip. It has been
a gorgeous, hot day and you have all enjoyed yourselves. Three
of you are good swimmers, and enjoy bathing. The other
dislikes the sea although he can swim. He prefers to sunbathe.
The others want to make him come in for a final splash about.
 i Have they the right to make him?
 ii Although he enjoys their company, does he have to do
 everything that they do?

b After small groups have discussed these issues, the tutor opens
up a form discussion on the limits to membership of a group.
As the discussion develops, the main points are summarised on
the blackboard.

14 Leadership:
The fourth-year pupil often relishes challenge, yet may have
undeveloped ideas of leadership. There may be over-emphasis on
forceful personality, and insufficient recognition that different
situations call for different qualities and approaches. The comparison
of different situations is helpful.

Situation 1:

a *The youth club committee entrusted you with the task of producing
the annual pantomime. You welcomed the responsibility, although at*

*the moment the project is almost a nightmare. Some players have
failed to learn their lines. Strong rivalry has developed between the
two main characters who spend their time putting each other down.
Parents and others who are responsible for scenery and costumes are
not taking their task seriously. You have to keep the whole effort
together, but . . .*

   b Pupils discuss in groups the skills of leadership needed by the
producer. How does he deal with the rivalries and motivate
actors and helpers?

Situation 2:

   *c You are leading a small group on a mountaineering course. You are
out on a very hazardous and exposed peak when there is a sudden
and unexpected change in the weather. A blizzard blows up, the
temperature falls below zero. One of the group has badly sprained
his ankle when walking on scree in search of shelter. It is obvious
that you will have to spend a night out in the open. You have to
take control.*

   d Small groups discuss the leadership skills needed in this
emergency where rapid action is required and the consequences
of a wrong action could prove dangerous, perhaps fatal.

   e The tutor gathers ideas about the different skills required. The
question of confidence often arises: the leader's confidence in
himself or herself; and the way in which he boosts the
confidence of those he leads. The problems of fool-hardiness
and unrealistic confidence in the ability of the leader are
sometimes raised by pupils. Discussion can be refreshingly
direct and rewardingly mature.

15 Aggression and the skills of defusing a situation:
A false accusation produces intense anger in many adolescents,
leading to hasty and unwise reactions. A sense of being demeaned
or devalued leads to aggression in the attempt to restore self-
respect. We have used many situations to encourage adolescents to
explore their reactions to false accusations, e.g. not paying for their
drink, pilfering in the first job, cheating in a game or examination.
The elements of visibility and the presence of an audience are
usually considered.

   *a A group of four friends are buying Christmas presents in a large
store two days before Christmas. The whole world seems to have*

left its shopping until late: there is jostling and the assistants are quite frantic. One of the group purchases two video tapes. Instead of wrapping them properly, the assistant just drops them into a thin paper bag. The boy pays for them, but as he picks them up, the bag splits, so he discards it, dropping the tapes into his plastic carrier. Ten minutes later, he is approached by a store detective who is courteous, but asks if he has paid for the tapes. He then asks to see the receipt. Unfortunately, it was inside the paper bag. The young man who bought the tapes loses his head, becoming very angry and threatens the store detective. Obviously, a very unpleasant situation is developing, unless the heat is taken out of it.

b Small groups discuss:

  i   the feelings of the falsely accused person;
  ii the impact of his behaviour on the store detective;
  iii the feelings of the companions of the one accused.

c The tutor then *briefly* discusses de-fusing this type of situation. Groups then look at the way they would attempt to deal with the situation and take the heat out of it.

d Ideas about coping with false accusations are then shared by the form.

In a subsequent session the tutor examines the part played by loss of face and the presence of an audience. The form considers:

a What the effect is of a rise in the pitch of one's voice in a potentially aggressive situation.

b What part is played by eye contact.

c The wisdom of holding or touching someone in a state of anger.

d How to detach oneself from a difficult situation without ignominy or attracting violence.

With this age group it has proved useful to discuss the situations which are likely to trigger aggressive reactions. The danger of invading the personal space of an aroused person can be discussed. The rule of thumb is that personal space is approximately an arm's length, therefore one keeps that distance, plus a hand's length away from them. The cumulative impact of tense bodily stance, rise in pitch and volume of voice and provocative eye contact can be discussed, leading to a realistic appreciation of the ways of defusing tense situations.

16 Rules and authority:
Material for discussion activities is present in an earlier chapter. More direct experience is provided by the production of a simple game within each group of four. Simple materials such as thin coloured card, felt pens, scissors, paper clips and stapler should be available. Each group is asked to construct a simple game for others to play. The one prohibition is that it should not be a game where chance plays a major part. Pupils are allowed to choose their own topic.

The tutor points out the importance of clear instructions. They:

i   provide order by ensuring that people do things in the right sequence;
ii deal with difficulties and prevent arguments;
iii say what the penalties and rewards will be, and when, and to whom they apply.

Pupils test their games out in their own group. In subsequent sessions, they select another small group with whom they will work. Each tests the other's game, providing feedback about the clarity of instructions, the adequacy of the rules and possible improvements. The tutor could develop this topic by looking at the nature of rules in the world of work. A small project could be undertaken in which pupils enlist parents and relatives to give information about rules in work places, looking at safety rules, procedural rules and rules emanating from different sources, e.g. management or trade union. The function of industrial etiquette, such as the unwritten rule that one does not go over the head of one's superior to a higher authority, except in rare circumstances, can be considered.

The need for authorities to justify the rules they produce and the relation of rules to personal responsibility can be studied. It has proved useful to look at the difference between rules aimed at prevention of pilfering, e.g. – that parcels and carriers must be handed in at the security lodge in the department store at entry and collected when leaving – and the rules of professional behaviour for the lawyer, teacher and doctor in relation to their fellows and clients.

Another useful ploy is the well-known 'castaways' exercise, in which the survivors of a shipwreck have to construct a mini-society, evolving rules and authority positions. Rules about division of labour, defence against danger and allocation of leadership roles have to be drawn up. Nuclear disaster and its aftermath provide an even more compelling setting. Pupils often display considerable knowledge and develop insights about authority and rules which can illuminate their everyday lives.

17 Social models:
The earlier chapters referred to processes of prediction, attribution and intention, to which those responsible for the pastoral programme must be sensitive. The following exercise has created greater awareness in pupils of their judgements of others and the models they emulate.

a The first steps are concerned with those of the same sex, therefore pupils work with a partner of the same sex. Two large sheets are presented each of which bears eight to ten pictures of adolescents. One sheet carries pictures of males and the other of females. They are differently dressed: some formally, others casually. Hair styles and bodily characterics differ. Pupils are then asked to select one they think they would like, and one they feel they would not like. They write brief stories about each character, based on answers to these questions:

  i What does he or she like doing?
  ii What are his or her friends like?
  iii What do people say about him or her? (This refers to parents, teachers and other adults as well as friends.)
  iv What will happen to him or her after school?

b Groups of four then discuss their stories and choices. Ideas are shared without tutor intervention.

c The tutor ends by brief discussion of the importance of the models on which pupils fashion themselves or with whom they identify. A subsequent session then allows discussion to develop freely. The function of the tutor is to highlight issues, directing attention to them in a non-judgemental way, providing a summary and raising points at the end.

d If the tutor decides it is appropriate, the exercise can be repeated with evaluation of pictures of the opposite sex. The structuring questions remain the same, but the discussion looks at the significance of the judgements for friendships between the sexes. The tutor should consider the danger of activating stereotypical judgements, especially in the male, before introducing this second stage.

18 Coping with disappointment:
Pupils will only talk honestly about their reactions to disappointment if they have learned that the tutor is trustworthy, and that their feelings are not likely to be dismissed as trivial. The tutor can set the scene by talking about Christmas. In counselling adults, I am never surprised when they recall it as a time when they had to be grateful for something they did not want; or for things which never quite came up to their expectations. The tutor calls attention to the complex feelings involved: feelings of guilt or sadness, minor jealousies or inflated expectations. The intent is to show that there is nothing wrong in experiencing such feelings, but the pursuit of maturity demands we face and accept them.

a Pupils make a list of situations about which they have experienced disappointment in the preceding six months. They then decide which one they would like to discuss in the self-help group.

b After this they look ahead and identify future times or situations in which they feel there is a danger of disappointment for them. They assess:

   i   Is the prediction realistic?
   ii Is there any way of changing the situation?
   iii How can they cope with the disappointment maturely if it does occur? Could they use it to understand others better? Could they use it to change their own attitudes and behaviour?

   (A skill of pastoral work is to use negative experiences to induce maturation. In pursuit of this, we never obscure the pupil's contribution to creating the disappointment of which he complains.)

c The tutor structures the discussion by building a balance sheet of positive and negative ways of dealing with disappointment. Negative reactions include bravado, denial of the disappointment, or gross exaggeration of it.

19 Frustration:
This is experienced, but many fourth-years feel they are not expected to discuss it, or they fight shy of expressing their feelings. One of the most frequent sources of frustration seems to be the feeling that their parents neither listen to them nor take seriously what they have to say. The tutor encourages them to talk, intervening as little as possible but acting as a model of a good listener.

He then makes explicit simple aspects of good listening, e.g.
- not interrupting;
- sending a signal that you understand;
- encouraging the speaker to continue if he stops;
- helping when he seems lost for words.

He asks pupils to discuss how they frustrate one another in the self-help groups. Can they listen more carefully to one another? He then suggests they work on more effective listening and on helping one another during the next three days. There is a general discussion on frustration and methods of reducing it after the three days' experiment is over.

Vocational development

Ideas and activities can be drawn from the section on vocational development. The pastoral head should consider the implications of the changes accompanying the move towards a post-industrial society, and then discuss their significance for the pastoral programme in the school. Regional differences in unemployment and the rate and nature of economic changes obviously influence the content of the pastoral programme. The careers teacher, careers officer and the guidance department have to be consulted: to devise the programme without consultation is to provoke tensions and invite loss of credibility.

20 Discussion of major features of a job:
Vocational development in the fourth year should widen horizons and encourage exploration rather than premature decisions. The simple checklist 'The Job I Would Like', provides a basis for small group discussion.

THE JOB I WOULD LIKE

What to do:

1 This form lists a number of things that are found in different jobs. It will be very helpful to you to know which are important to you. Your tutor will explain why.

2 Read each item and then tick the column which shows how important that job *quality is to you*: Very important; Fairly important or Not at all important.

	Very important	Fairly important	Not at all important
1 Lets me meet a lot of people			
2 Has a good pension			
3 Where I can be my own boss one day			
4 Gives me a chance of promotion – gets me somewhere			
5 Is near home			
6 Always offers new things to do			
7 Gives plenty of money straight away			
8 Where it is hard to get the sack			
9 Where I have to take a lot of responsibility			
10 Lets me use my hands			
11 Where somebody tells me just what to do			

12 Lets me work on my own at my own rate			
13 The same as my father/mother* does, or very like it			
14 Makes me think a lot			
15 The same every day			
16 Something skilled. Learning a trade or getting trained			
17 Where I have to talk to people a lot			
18 Be in a big firm			
19 Be useful to other people			
20 Be in a small firm			

*Delete the alternative you do not wish to use

The self-help groups discuss:

a The significance of the items they ranked as very important.
b The advantages of large and small firms. Which did they prefer and why?
c Is it really possible to avoid routine and boring tasks in any job? If not, what is the best way of coping?

21 Comparing standpoints about occupations:
It is useful to look at a job from different perspectives. Outsiders may see the work very differently from those who do it; subordinates see a middle management position very differently from superiors.

a The small groups are presented with a short, taped example in which two people are heard, giving their idea of a long-distance lorry driver's job. His wife and his employer describe it very differently; then the man himself gives his version, which is strikingly at variance with the other two.

b Groups select *one* of the following (or choose any other occupation) and develop sketches of the job.

  i A teacher's job as seen by a pupil, a parent, the head teacher and the teacher himself or herself.
  ii A police sergeant's job as seen by his or her son or daughter, spouse, a teacher and the man next door.
  iii A senior nurse's job as seen by his or her spouse, the 'houseman' or registrar, a patient and an insurance agent.
  iv A chef's job as seen by a waiter or waitress, a customer, his or her spouse and a mechanic.

c Groups discuss:

  i What tensions were created by the different views of the job?
  ii Would it be helpful for people to know more about one another's jobs?
  iii Jobs they would like to have a greater understanding of.

22 Parents, visitors and decision-making:

The pastoral head can usefully invite visitors to talk about their work. They are asked, however, not to describe the job in the usual way, but to bring examples of the decisions they have to make and let the pupils discuss them. They then compare the way they think and behave in the decision-making situation with the pupils' reactions. Obvious examples are: the bank manager's decision to allow a loan; a nurse on night duty in a short-staffed hospital who meets an unexpected emergency; a factory worker's decision whether or not to give up a Saturday trip and do overtime.

The following points aid the success of the activity:

  i The visitors answer questions that the pupils have prepared after the decision-making activity.
  ii Women in industry and the professions are as well represented as males.

23 Qualities and occupations:

a Pupils may not have realised how important personality qualities are for job satisfaction. They may concentrate on qualifications and skills, underplaying personality factors.

b Pupils are presented with the following list of qualities:

Confidence	Punctuality	Accuracy
Poise	Imaginativeness	Cleanliness
Patience	Good looks	Dependability
Sense of humour	Honesty	Loyalty
Clear speaking voice	Calmness	Fitness
Politeness	Warmth	Strength
Neatness	Trust	Bravery

They are asked to add to them.

c They are asked to select *two* each of the job titles below and select what they consider to be the key personality qualities for that job.

Factory foreman	Nurse	Double-glazing
Barman or Barmaid	Bank clerk	salesman or
Motor mechanic	Secretary	saleswoman
Beautician	Welder	

d In the small groups they then present their lists, modifying them where necessary.

Each small group meets another and discusses the importance of personality qualities for job satisfaction.

24 Lifestyle sketches:

Each small group selects an occupation which they will investigate. They consult books, pamphlets and other available information, but they also have to interview at least one person currently working in that job. Each group prepares a presentation to the form: taped programme; mock interview or real life interview, answering questions on lifestyle, including promotion prospects, future developments in the industry or profession, security and pensions.

25 Identifying lifestyles:

a Groups discuss the occupations which involve the lifestyles set out below. They assess the compensations and the tensions associated with these occupations.

   i Has to entertain clients at home quite frequently. Will have to spend time away from the family on business.

Finds it necessary to keep up a certain standard of living, even if s/he cannot comfortably afford it.

ii Never stays in one place for long. Unlikely to have a settled home. Works irregular hours. Visits many foreign places.

iii Has financial security. Has sometimes to live away from home, often sharing sleeping accommodation with others, having little privacy. Has to accept authority almost unquestioningly.

iv Works regular hours, e.g. from 9 o'clock to 5 o'clock. Earns somewhat above an average wage, but can also look forward to a good pension on retirement. Does very much the same each day, although s/he expects regular promotion every five years or so.

v Works very long hours, and even when off duty is liable to be called out if needed. Therefore an evening out or other arrangements frequently have to be cancelled at short notice. Has to drive a lot, although the distances involved are not great. The ability to get on with people is important.

b Within the small groups, pupils write down elements of the life style attached to an occupation they would:
  – welcome
  – tolerate
  – reject firmly.

They then try to relate this to their future plans. The message that emerges is not merely that sometimes one will have to compromise, but that one must accept realistically that to get something one wants, means doing something one does not like.

26 Comparison of successful and unsuccessful workers:
Pupils are given advance warning of this activity. They are asked to select two occupations in which they are interested. Their task is to detect the qualities and skills leading to success or failure as a worker in the jobs they investigated. General discussion follows:

i They look for elements leading to success or failure in both the jobs, and those specific to one.

ii They ask what is modifiable and what cannot be changed.

iii It is helpful for them to take the standpoint of the unsuccessful person, exploring what he could and should do.

27 Stress:

a As part of reinforcing positive vocational identity the pastoral programme must look at stress and coping with it. Pupils are asked to identify sources of stress in local industries or occupations through talking to workers. They are encouraged to find out the stresses that are experienced by young unemployed people. (Tutors should beware making bland statements about unemployment in areas where this is rife. Pupils will question the credibility of what teachers say because they feel rightly or wrongly that the teacher has no experience of unemployment and is unlikely to undergo it.)

b i Pupils discuss the nature of the stresses they have discovered.
   ii They then ask how they would cope, while still maintaining belief in themselves. How would they, for instance, overcome a sense of devaluation, and maintain self-respect and responsible behaviour.
   iii Subsequent sessions could provide opportunities for analysing sources of stress at school. The links between depression and erosion of the skills of self-organisation should be discussed, e.g. the depressed person may find it difficult to organise himself to begin the day.

28 Dislikes and anxieties:
This activity encourages pupils to identify work-related situations which they would welcome or avoid. They will be asked to consider the reality of the difficulties in disliked activities; to look at how they came to dislike them; and to discuss what could be done to overcome the anxiety, if this seems advisable.

a The tutor begins writing work-related activities on the board, e.g.
answering the telephone; working at a lathe or drill; using a calculator; making a complaint; explaining what is being done to somebody else; writing a report . . .
The form contribute as many other ideas as they can, which the tutor writes on the board.

b Working singly, pupils allocate the activities to one of three groupings on a sheet of paper: I would be happy doing this; I would worry about doing this; I am unsure how I would feel about this.

c Pupils share ideas in their self-help groups about the significance of the activities they rate positively. Do they contribute to school achievement? Are they likely to be important in work success?

d The negatively assessed activities are then considered. Is it important to change attitudes towards some of them? How can skill and confidence be developed so that feelings of dislike and helplessness are overcome?

Pupils take a counselling role, giving support and listening so that a climate of acceptance allows honest appreciation of anxieties and dislikes to develop.

e The 'uncertain' category merits a separate session. The groups discuss what lies behind the uncertainty. Do they take it for granted? Do they need to do something about certain activities?

29 Stereotypes of masculinity and femininity:

a Four pupils are selected in advance to prepare basic arguments for a debate about the topic. A small group of sixth-form students, (who will later be a panel which answers questions) helps them clarify their ideas. The girls may well wish to challenge the devaluation of women's ability to take responsibility, innovate, act as good administrators or make good judgements. Boys may wish to underline the familial responsibilities of men, their greater dependence on work as part of their lifestyle. The sixth-form briefing panel should include a female scientist and a male taking arts subjects.

b The first session consists of:

    i Presentation of the arguments by the teams. (Strict time limits are adhered to.)

    ii Discussion of the issues within self-help groups – especially the problem of females accepting negative evaluations of themselves from males.

    iii Questioning of the four presenters by the form.

    iv Tutor's summary – *not* evaluation – of the debate.

(The traditional vote has not seemed useful, but tutors have to decide this for themselves!)

c The next session consists of questioning the sixth-form group.

The original presenters are allowed the first two questions. The tutor gives his impression of the attitudes and opinions, suggesting topics which could be dealt with in the future. His summing up should be restricted to five minutes at the most.

30 Other topics for which pupils can prepare materials are:

a Relationships within the family.
b Relationships with authority figures, including informal as well as formal ones.
c The caring community: who cares and why? What help is available locally and for whom? How can the individual at school make a contribution?

10 The Fifth Year

At first sight, fifth-year guidance seems clearcut: whether we approve or disapprove of them, examinations are at the forefront of the minds of pupils and teachers alike. GCSE will, when implemented, increase the importance of self-evaluation by the learner and highlight motivation and effective learning about learning as crucial issues. The imminence of entry to work, selecting a training course or entering the sixth form provide strong pointers to content and an obvious structure for the fifth-year programme. Yet caution is necessary: past experience of pastoral care may have led pupils to regard it with suspicion as unwanted benevolent paternalism or maternalism and infringement of privacy. If there has been unthinking infringement of expectations of the role of teacher and pupil, then the fifth-year pupil may be determined to defend himself or herself against activities he or she interprets as assaults on identity. Over-ambition is equally unhelpful: in practice, teacher and pupils see this final year as consisting of two working terms only. Therefore content has to be restricted.

Process can be developed, however. Formative assessment, problem-solving and peer counselling can be extended within the self-help groups. The ethos of the pastoral programme conveys expectations of maturity and responsibility. This is challenging: we cannot assume that those who properly claim to be treated as more adult, necessarily know how to be rationally accountable for their learning. Attitudinal and motivational problems often defeat the adolescent learner who retreats to unthinking regurgitation. Hence the sixth-form student's major technique of learning is memorisation. We have to move away from the teacher's view of learning to that of the pupils, without being discouraged when we find they believe we want reproduction of our notes or statements. They may be all too accurate in that belief! Equally important, we must not disrupt or intimidate them by making unrealistic demands. The miniature peer groups, and the support they provide, act as a safeguard against this. Pupils decide for themselves what they want, and how they will achieve it.

The programme opens with an initial unit which looks at style of learning and self-management. Another unit provides the opportunity for pupils to use the experiences of mock examinations constructively, and look at anxiety honestly. A unit on vocational development looks at interview skills, vocational decision-making and job-search skills. A summary programme of the ways of coping with the social and psychological adjustments of work adds another dimension. Pastoral heads may find it useful to refer to appropriate sections of *Guidance: 16–19*. Personal guidance must be treated cautiously; pupils should be involved in selecting the content and developing ideas. The principle is that of building on strengths, increasing confidence realistically, and using supports that are available. The theme is partnership: essentially, this needs tutors and classes who have been together for several years, and developed working relationships.

The style of the pastoral programme should change in the fifth year, reflecting the maturity of the students, the changes in the curriculum. Choice should be possible for the small groups who are encouraged to follow their interests and meet their perceived needs. A uniform programme automatically imposed on fifth-formers conflicts with the principles of active learning, pupil responsibility and the trends of curriculum development and examination reform. The pastoral programme should reflect these trends. Indeed, it may initiate further developments. To ignore the need for change in the structure and content of the programme is to invite pupils' rejection of it as patronising or trivial.

Understanding and developing the individual's learning style

The first unit of guidance has two major objectives:

1 Encouraging pupils to work out the ways in which they will make the most of their last year of compulsory schooling.
2 Increasing the effectiveness of the mutual support provided in the self-help groups.

The approach is one which meets the fifth-year pupils' demands for recognition of their maturity. It encourages a measure of self-direction in a supportive context of peer counselling. The tutor acts as a consultant for particular groups as needed, not by always giving direct answers, but by clarifying the issues.

[1] The first topic is style of learning. We accept individual rhythms of activity in the physical field: yet we ignore their existence in study behaviour. The basic question is:
'When is it best for me to do certain things, e.g. read and take in facts, write essays or revise?'

The tutor points out that some people can read and assimilate facts early in the evening, and write later; some find the reverse more productive. Others have discovered that revision is best done early in the morning. There is no right way. Pupils must define their own style of learning, be able to justify what they decide to do, and take responsibility for their success or failure.

The session can end with a general discussion provided that the tutor helps pupils clarify their ideas and reinforces their sense of responsibility.

[2] The next item for consideration is, 'When I am working on my own or revising, which is the best pattern for me?' The tutor warns that what is effective for one person is not necessarily so for another. Some people may need to work without interruption; some prefer a short 'warm-up' period in which they organise themselves, followed by a break; others have their own strategy. If there are sources of difficulty or frustration how do pupils cope with them? Are problems put on one side and dealt with last, or do they prefer to tackle them immediately?

Again, the tutor ends by encouraging the sharing of ideas in a form discussion.

[3] The context of revision and learning can be discussed. The tutor may open the group work by remarking that one can feel lonely when revising. For some it may be helpful to work alone; it may be better for others to go to a library where pupils are working but where silence is preserved; some may prefer the company of others in the self-help group. Is it true that a quiet room is the best place to learn for everyone?

[4] This session leads to self-observation. The groups undertake further evaluation of their attitudes to certain subjects. Do they predict failure or feel they will appear inadequate to their class-mates? The issue of negative comparison with others is raised.

After initial discussion, the members of the self-help group work out a plan for self-observation which looks not only at situations of difficulty, but at those where they experience a sense of control. (A simple diary is usually the method they adopt.)

In a later session they discuss their self-observation, looking at ways of building on strengths and reducing the effects of the problem situations.

The tutor initiates a form discussion in which he suggests that the influence of friends can be used to overcome feelings of helplessness or failure.

5 Attitudinal and motivational elements of learning should be discussed. A session on frustration is helpful. Small group discussion identifies the frustrations that pupils anticipate they will meet during the year. Ways of coping with them or reducing their negative impact are produced.

The tutor introduces a final discussion on the possibility that over-reliance on the approval of others may be the cause of some frustrations.

6 Pupils discuss their ideas about what leads to success in:
– examinations;
– interviews.
After discussion, groups formulate questions which are answered by the tutor.

7 Partners within the self-help group then assess their strengths and weaknesses as learners. They discuss the implications of teachers' comments on their written work, asking how they can use those comments. (Checklists and questionnaires, if deemed useful, can be found in *The Teacher and Pastoral Care* and *Teaching Study Skills*.) Partners then specify the improvements they will attempt in the next four weeks before they have another opportunity to assess their progress.

8 The self-help groups end this unit of guidance by discussing the reality of the conflict between school success and enjoyment of life outside school. In one effective session the tutor acted as devil's advocate – supporting the idea that the two are antagonistic while the form rebutted his arguments.

9 Pupils discuss the kind of person who might make the following responses *and* the situations which might elicit them.

   i 'I've never been any good at that sort of thing!'
   ii 'I try to control my feelings that I am going to do badly, but it's never much use!'
   iii 'The others always seem to blame me!'
   iv 'It's all a matter of luck what turns up in the exams.'

[10] The groups can usefully anticipate situations which produce anxiety, e.g.

   i Getting unexpectedly poor mock examination results.
   ii Finding that you are losing your grasp on a subject and getting poor marks.

The tutor can provide some starter ideas, but pupils tend to associate this approach with the methods used with younger children. In practice, their need seems to be that of testing out their ideas in debate with their peers.

Mock examinations and understanding anxiety

A unit which considers the experiences provided by mock examinations in more depth is recommended. Without it, pupils' feelings subside, but no learning has occurred, so that the same mistakes occur in the real examinations.

[11] Pupils become aware of deficiencies in their revision strategies yet do little, if anything, to correct them.

The pastoral head prepares a taped narrative about a pupil's revision strategies after mock examinations. (Two or three first-year sixth-form students can combine to produce the script.) The tape shows how the pupil decided where to focus most effort, relating this to career considerations; the reasons for effort in certain weak subjects; how to maximise strengths; improve methods of study; and use the Easter vacation. The tutor plays the tape: then disrupts expectations by saying, 'That is not necessarily the best way; listen again and criticise it. Think of better ways suited to you. Use any ideas that seem helpful.' The groups use the tape as a stimulus for constructing their own strategy.

In a follow-up session the tutor encourages the form to draw up a wall chart showing their plans for revision.

[12] The next topic is the pupil's activities the night before the first examination in the 'mocks'. There are indications that those who are fatalistic, believing that controls lie outside them, allow a bad first experience to shape their reactions negatively to subsequent examinations. Others may see initial poor results as a challenge, setting out to show what they can do. The tutor can open the discussion by saying, 'How did you prepare the night before the first examination? Did you stay up until 2 o'clock trying to learn everything off by heart? The only results may have been you felt more and more you were unable to remember anything, and you were in danger of tripping over the bags under your eyes as you tottered into the examination room. Is there a better way?'

Groups then share ideas. The tutor collects suggestions and writes them on the board.

[13] The next session looks at two other aspects that concern the fifth year. The tutor points out that after the examination people sometimes discover there were one or two questions they could have answered better than those they did. Did they become over-anxious? Did they fail to scan the paper? How can they prevent this happening in the real examinations? The group is also asked to consider how they are likely to misuse good advice given by their teachers. If you do the question that you can answer best first, is there a danger of spending too long on it?

[14] The next topics are dealing with the 'low' or point at which things seem to get out of control, usually about two-thirds of the way through a morning examination. Blood sugar levels are dropping – especially if you skipped breakfast – and the initial impetus is lost. (It is worse still if you are a girl, suffering from premenstrual tension or menstruating.) Groups discuss ways of guarding themselves against this low point very sensibly, often looking at other learning situations where the hold on control is precarious.

The final topic is post-examination behaviour. Did pupils indulge in an interminable post-mortem, or perhaps adopt the 'insurance policy' response of telling people they had done badly, just in case they had.

[15] Examination anxiety is a real phenomenon. It is unprofessional to ignore it and unhelpful to exaggerate it.

 a The tutor points out that anxiety is a signal of danger due to some threat. Small groups discuss the threat that examinations present, evaluating the reality of their perceptions: do they exaggerate or deny?

 b Next, the tutor mentions that anxiety can take many forms. A flip-chart cartoon shows someone looking very comfortable, feet up, with a transistor radio, and a soft drink. The speech bubble says 'I'll start tomorrow!' – but the cartoon also shows his inner worry. Procrastination is one response to anxiety. Pupils then look at other possibilities.

 c The discussion moves on to productive or evasive ways of coping. The tutor mentions examples of evasion, such as blaming others, anger, opting out and denying that there is any problem. More positive ways of coping are identified by the small groups.

 d The groups are then introduced to the ideas of 'one-step-at-a-time' and minimal change. The tutor sketches someone carrying a bucket of water which is slopping over: the equivalent of stress and anxiety. The obvious thing is to take some water out of the bucket; under pressure one looks for a first step in taking away anxiety. This then stimulates further change. The self-help group discuss how this principle can be implemented if members find themselves under stress.

 e I have found it very helpful for pupils to discuss the use and misuse of humour. It can be used sensibly to put examinations into perspective and give the individual the confidence to cope. Defensively used, it allows the person to deny the need to tackle the situation, or to pretend that it is unimportant.

[16] Self-management is needed to overcome the problem shown in the common statement, 'I mean to get started on my revision when I get home, but somehow I can't'. The week's diary approach can operate within a longer term plan for revision. Pupils train themselves – train is the operative word – to write down on a piece of paper thoughts which come into their minds, e.g. 'I don't know much about that', 'That's a weak spot' or 'I ought to do something about . . .' At the end of the revision session they scan the paper, consider the things they have written down and make decisions about what they will revise next day. They enter it in the diary, *stating precisely what they will revise*. It is unhelpful simply to write chemistry, history or mathematics. After several weeks the benefit

appears, but members of the self-help group will need to reinforce one another's use of the week's diary.

17 Methods of revision should be debated by the groups. One part of the endeavour is to shift them away from unthinking regurgitation. One method I have introduced as a starting point for experimentation with revision in the small groups is outlined below:

a Make a contract with somebody taking the same subject or subjects as you to revise together and support one another.
b When you revise, the first step after agreeing on the topic is to independently write down all you know, as key phrases or as a diagram. Then briefly compare your papers, noting differences. (This activates existing knowledge and alerts pupils to weak points.)
c Next, revise independently for 20 to 25 minutes. Then use the old adage: if you want to find out whether you know something, try teaching it to somebody else. One pupil does a 'teach-back'. He is processing what he has revised, but the recipient may be thinking even more deeply as he corrects, revises questions and looks at the exposition critically. His may be more imaginative processing.
d The cycle is then repeated, the recipient giving the 'teach-back'.
e Some pupils have also used tape-recorders for the 'teach-back', when revising at home. One group I worked with some years ago, brought their recorded 'teach-backs' into the group for evaluation: a healthy approach to criticism!

These approaches to self-assessment, processing what has been learned, and self-management, can be adapted to meet the needs of those not taking traditional examinations. Another useful tool is the keeping of a learning diary in which the pupil records successes, difficulties, problems and feelings. If it is to be useful, the tutor should make it clear that the diary is not for his information, but for the pupil's use within the self-help group.

Understanding social interaction

It is important to remember the need for negotiation with pupils, and involving them in the construction of materials. Some ideas are given below.

18 Responsible action:
A cheeky second-year boy attracted your attention on the school bus. He was so obnoxious that you started to put him down by making fun of him and pushing him around. Now he has begun to refuse to come to school. You are fairly certain that you went too far, and that you caused his truancy. He has, however, said nothing about you to his parents or the EWO. What is your responsibility?

Small groups discuss the implications of the situation. Discussion focuses on:

i the fifth-year pupil's responsibilities after such an event;
ii responsible ways of dealing with individuals similar to this second year pupil.

Discussion of responsibility may be deepened by introducing consideration of what the fifth-year pupil does when:

i he finds that his best friend is sometimes taking drugs in the evenings at discos, or at the weekend;
ii his best friend brings cannabis into school and tries to interest other pupils in it.

The self-help groups can prepare their own list of problem situations about responsibility to investigate. The tutor can be a consultant called in by a group. Groups should be encouraged to consult one another.

19 For some fifth-year pupils the prospect of leaving home is alluring. It seems to offer escape from situations causing tension at home. Small groups discuss:

i Assess the circumstances which might induce such feelings. Without referring to specific circumstances, they discuss ways of coping with family pressures.
ii What circumstances they consider to be sufficient grounds for a boy or girl to seriously consider leaving home after the fifth-year?
iii What legal and practical difficulties have to be taken into account?
iv What preparations should the young person make?

Evaluation takes three forms:

a A peer judge who is appointed within the group.

b Two groups meeting and submitting their ideas to critical scrutiny.

c The tutor – who takes the standpoint of the parent.

20 Social embarrassments can be discussed. The tutor suggests that it is not only the middle-aged and middle-class who are discomposed by turning up in inappropriate dress. Perhaps adolescents and young adults have equally strong reactions? The groups discuss:

i Whether differences between the sexes in liability to embarrassment in this matter are real or imagined?

ii The problems of interpreting words such as 'casual' or 'informal' when applied to dress.

iii How to cope with refusal of entry to a disco or restaurant, especially when the others in a group are admitted because their clothes are acceptable. Attention should be given to the feelings of those correctly dressed.

iv The circumstances and motives for deliberately wearing inappropriate clothing.

The tutor may usefully refer in his summary to interviews and employment. Other examples of social embarrassment can be elicited.

21 This can be followed by a series of discussions where the group explore their experiences of feeling 'the odd one out' or 'not feeling right'. The tutor opens the discussions by listing possibilities on the board, e.g.

i Feeling depressed when others are cheerful.

ii Losing control of oneself when strangers are present.

iii Lapses in personal appearance and hygiene.

iv Meeting boyfriend or girlfriend's family and finding they are very different from your own family.

v Being the only one in a group of friends who does not want to do something.

The groups add other examples. Each group decides which ones they will explore more thoroughly. In a subsequent session two small groups join together to share ideas.

22 Fifth-year pupils are usually aware that they are straightforward in some situations, shifty in others. Profiling and formative assessment require them to think more deeply about such matters. Small group discussion on such qualities as reliability is useful. The tutor begins by suggesting that judgement of oneself or others as reliable is not without problems.

 i   What does *reliable* mean when we apply the word to a person?
 ii Can somebody be reliable with some people, and in some situations, but not with other people or in different situations?
 iii Why can the same person be judged by different people as reliable and as unreliable?

Similar judgements such as honest, persistent and mature can be examined critically. The tutor may explain the new developments in assessment or introduce aspects of assessment that interest him or her.

23 Discussions could follow which help pupils examine their perceptions of their responsibilities at school, college or work. The tutor writes, 'It is nothing to do with me,' on the board. Pupils are asked to examine the occasions when they have used this excuse. What functions did it serve, and what were the justifications? They are asked to examine the use of the phrase by adults in situations of child abuse, pilfering at work and tax evasion.

24 A tape is played where people are heard making statements which indicate a tendency to immediate judgements and refusal to think further and consider the evidence, e.g. 'He's nothing but . . .', 'Her problem just is . . .', 'They're all alike . . .', 'All they need is . . .' The statements are interspersed by more tentative ones, e.g. 'I wonder if it is possible that . . .' The tape is brief. Pupils discuss the style of thought and the personality that lies behind the dismissive, perhaps condemnatory judgements. They are then asked to identify situations in which they have dismissed something as rubbish or instantly devalued it. What lay behind such opinions? Pupils usually proceed to relate this to their success in personal relationships and schoolwork.

The tutor then writes on the board statements which direct attention to the source of the message, 'Bob Geldof says . . .', 'Hitler said . . .', 'Reagan claims . . .' or 'The Prime Minister states . . .' Groups discuss whether they pay more attention to the source than the message. Are messages from certain sources given a more favourable reception, irrespective of the content of the message? Do certain sources possess greater credibility for them than others?

They then go on to discuss which sources have credibility for them in their daily living. Does success and independence require them to take a more questioning attitude towards such influences?

Vocational development

Pastoral heads should consult the relevant section earlier in this book, where ideas for group activity and discussion will be found. Activities especially suited to the self-help groups are set out below.

$\boxed{25}$ Interview techniques can be discussed in the self-help groups. Intelligence is no guarantee that individuals can understand the interview processes. Discussion and simple partner role play covers:

-   i Sensitivity to reading the cues sent by the interviewer. University admissions tutors and personnel officers are often irritated by the interviewee's apparent disregard of the signals they send. Judgements are then made about the ability of the candidate to get on with others. The pupils discuss the way they can maintain an image of vitality and initiative while responding to the interviewer.
-   ii The skill of asking questions which are relevant, and also create a positive impression, needs to be practised.

Rather than tutors providing limits, interview effectiveness is presented as a problem to be solved by pupils who must also practice the skills without tutor direction.

$\boxed{26}$ It is becoming more common for people to experience temporary unemployment or be self-employed. In self-help groups, pupils can assess the value of their leisure interests as a means of creating exchange relationships with society which maintain self-respect. Some hobbies or skills may have entrepreneurial possibilities. Others lead to helping roles where the helper feels valued and valuable.

27 Having a sense of anchorage is important. The self-help groups build links with the youth service, bringing in youth workers to talk to the form. Groups investigate how the youth service can help during unemployment or give support if difficulties of adjustment arise during the first job. The youth club can be a base for entrepreneurial and community service initiatives. It is not too early to activate co-operation and joint projects in the fifth-year. The problem set is how can the youth club provide positive anchorage in society when identity is under threat and self-respect diminished?

28 Parents and local industry can usefully help pupils by producing decision-making materials concerned with work and career progress. More fundamentally, self-help groups, where appropriate, should undertake problem solving projects around work adjustment and career development. From interviewing young people at work and looking at the work of past students in this field, I suggest the project should touch on problematical areas such as:

i   Establishing credibility within a working group.
ii   Maintaining ambition and personal integrity when joining a group where the norm is 'do as little as possible for as much as possible'.
iii   Coping with the pressures of dealing with the demands of the public when fellow workers who provide 'back-up' are disparaging or obstructive, e.g. the helpful waiter or waitress and the chef whose major delight is saying, 'Tell them it's off!'
iv   General conflict where older workers retain out of date frames of reference in such areas as worker-management relationships, production procedures and promotion.
v   Colleague relationships, especially where the job creates special dependencies or opportunities for friction, e.g. conflicts between a maintenance man who is not on bonus and production workers who are; the miner and his 'marrer' or regular workmate; two workers on a machine who have to go
v   to the cloakroom together because the firm will not brook unauthorised stoppages.
vi   Reactions to mistakes, especially where first level supervisors are poorly trained and behave arbitrarily.
vii   The image of the firm held by local people, including the

view of those who work there. Such myths and attitudes have a greater significance than many careers teachers suspect.

viii The dependence of the firm on other local industries' wellbeing or susceptibility to fluctuations in demand.

29 Another project will include the identification of possibilities and making first hand contacts with those displaying entrepreneurial skills. Enterprise zones and developments stimulated by other forms of grant should be studied. Balanced risk-taking implies the ability to identify snags and miscalculations and, most crucially, the factors which determine success. Assessment of the potential for development in leisure interests is worthwhile: pottery, stained-glass and cooking are examples of interests which have led to careers because people have been encouraged to engage in this type of guidance.

30 Another project for some self-help groups would be the in-depth investigation of gender stereotypes. This could involve assessment of the reality of the claims about equality of opportunity in entry to courses. Even more important would be examination of post-entry experiences. The enquiry could highlight many associated issues. Girls appear uninterested in computer games, but one young woman wrote to a local newspaper to point out that most computer games are both competitive and aggressive. She asks why there is nothing between the exaggerated positions of macho violence and female sex symbolism. A pastoral programme cannot ignore these things: evasion destroys its developmental value.

The implications

It was argued earlier that there is justification for allowing tutors to select topics. There is no reason why every form should be doing the same thing at the same time in a particular year. In the fifth year the demands for recognition of maturity, responsibility and for independence have to be met by the pastoral programme. The diverse directions and aims which have developed inevitably mean that the self-help groups pursue their own interests and select their topics. They can co-operate with other groups and share resources as necessary. The demands on tutors for planning and organisation make staff development imperative, but this is essential in any case if we are to get professional satisfaction. Rigid imposition of a uniform programme invites from pupils at best a tolerant acceptance and at worst confirms their belief that guidance and pastoral care are irrelevant.

A note on the sixth-form pastoral programme

Guidance: 16–19 explores this fully. The methods are an extension of those used in the fifth form. A summary programme is presented which provides material for a debate on the pastoral programme between tutors and their students.

1 *Presentation of self.* This would look at the effects of anxieties and self-doubts on the achievement of goals. It would include discussion in a counselling ethos – stressing self-direction and responsibility – of the changing values and behaviours which result from the increasing maturity of the student.

2 *Investigation of the approach to problem-solving* creating hypotheses and validation by evidence; examination of when and why the individual retreats to early closure on a problem, evading the task of analysis and evaluation. This can be linked to the individual's reactions to challenge and criticism, and to the rewards, intrinsic or extrinsic, which are meaningful. Some knowledge of attitudes, their functions, and relationship to group influences would be useful. This, like pupils' views of social reality, should be a product of insights gained from shared experience within small groups.

3 *The maintenance of identity* without either dominating others or being submissive in relationships is another focal issue. With examination of the judgements made of others and exploration of leadership and group interaction this forms a crucial area for small group investigation.

4 *Decision-making* can be pursued in depth in relation to vocational development. The expectations and comparisons which influence decision-making are often critically examined, and their hampering effect on achieving goals is comprehended.

5 *The need for authority* and the conditions under which authority should be rationally repudiated, excite concern. (Recently, I sat in

on a session where sixth-formers' debated with integrity the compulsory hospitalisation of an AIDS victim relating it to their fears about the erosion of personal liberty.)

6 *Coping with tension, threat and anxiety* looking at anxieties which arise in social situations; but also looking at those derived from inner conflict.

7 *Debating the thinking person's role in the community* examining the personal strengths which can be harnessed to contribute immediately to the school as a caring community; but also looking at life plans in the same terms.

Bibliography

Adams, J., Hayes, J. and Hopson, B. (1976) *Transition*, London: Martin Robertson.
Adorno, T. *et al* (1950) *The Authoritarian Personality*, New York: Harper.
Allport, G. (1961) 'Values and Our Youth', *Teachers College Record 63*, pp. 211–19
Armstrong, D., Bazalgette, J. and Reed, R. (1981) 'The Place of Values in the Transition to Working Life', *British Journal of Guidance and Counselling*, Vol. 9, No. 1, pp. 46–55.
Aston, P. and Dobson, G. (1972) 'Family Interaction and Social Adjustment', *Journal of Child Psychology and Psychiatry*, Vol. 13, pp. 77–89.
Atkinson, J. and Feather, N. (1966) *A Theory of Achievement Motivation*, New York: Wiley.
Ausubel, D. (1968) *Educational Psychology. A Cognitive View*, New York: Holt, Rinehart and Winston.

Babington Smith, B. and Farrell, B. (Eds.) (1979) *Training in Small Groups*, Oxford: Pergamon.
Baron, R., Byrne, D. and Griffitt, W. (1974) *Social Psychology*, Boston: Allyn and Bacon.
Berkowitz, L. (1980) *A Survey of Social Psychology*, New York: Holt, Rinehart and Winston.
Blocher, D. (1966) *Developmental Counseling*, New York: Ronald Press.
Bloom, B. (1956) (Ed.) *Taxonomy of Educational Objectives, Handbook 1. Cognitive Domain*, New York: McKay.
Bloom, B. (1968) *Learning for Mastery, Evaluation Comment, 1*, Los Angeles: University of California, Center for the Study of Evaluation of Instructional Programs.
Bloom, B., Hastings, J., Madaus, G. (1971) *Handbook on Formative and Summative Evaluation of Student Learning*, New York: McGraw-Hill.
Bloom, B. (1976) *Human Characteristics and School Learning*, New York: McGraw-Hill.
Bolam, R. and Medlock, P. (1985) *Active Tutorial Work: Training and Dissemination, an Evaluation*, Oxford: Blackwell.
Brophy, J. and Good, T. (1974) *Teacher–Student Relationships*, New York: Holt, Rinehart and Winston.
Bruner, J. (1966) *Toward a Theory of Instruction*, Cambridge, Massachusetts: Harvard University Press.
Bruner, J. and Anglin, J. (1973) *Beyond the Information Given*, London: Allen and Unwin.
Buros, O. (1978) *The Eighth Mental Measurements Yearbook, Vols. 1 and 2*, New Jersey: Gryphon Press.

Carkuff, R. and Anthony, W. (1979) *The Skills of Helping*, Amherst, Massachusetts: Human Resource Development Press.

Carter, M. (1966) *Into Work*, Harmondsworth: Penguin.

Cartwright, D. and Zander, A. (1968) (Eds.) *Groups Dynamics: Research and Theory*, (3rd Edition), New York: Harper and Row.

Clydebank Project (1984) Cited in *New Developments in Assessment: Profiling*, Brussels: IFAPLAN.

Clydebank Project (1984) *EEC Pilot Project, Clydebank on the Transition from School to Working Life*, Brussels: IFAPLAN.

Coleman, J. (1974) *Relationships in Adolescence*, London: Routledge and Kegan Paul.

Collins, B. and Raven, B. (1968) 'Group Structure: Attractions, Coalitions, Communication and Power', In Lindzey G. and Aronson, E. (Eds.) *The Handbook of Social Psychology, Vol. IV*, Reading, Massachusetts: Addison-Wesley.

Cronbach, L. (1966) *Essentials of Psychological Testing*, (2nd Edition), New York: Harper and Row.

Curle, A. (1972) *Mystics and Militants*, London: Tavistock.

De Charms, R. (1968) *Personal Causation*, New York: Academic Press.

Denscombe, M. (1980) 'Pupils Strategies and the Open Classroom', In Woods, P. (Ed.) *Pupil Strategies*, London: Croom Helm.

Deutsch, M. (1973) *The Resolution of Conflict*, New Haven: Yale University Press.

Dewey, J. (1910) *How We Think*, Boston: Heath.

Dweck, C. (1975) 'The Role of Expectations and Attributions in the Alleviation of Learned Helplessness, *Journal of Personality and Social Psychology, 31*, pp. 674–85.

Edwards, E. (1974) *A Study of Age Related Trends Towards School Among Secondary Pupils*, University College of Swansea, Unpublished DSC Dissertation.

Edwards, J. and Morris, H. (1981) *The Employment Problems of Young People in Lewisham*, Koln: IFAPLAN. (On behalf of the Commission of European Communities.)

Erikson, E. (1968) *Identity*, London: Faber.

Evans, N. (1983) *Curriculum Opportunity*, London: FEU, Department of Education and Science.

Fishbein, M. (1967) *Readings in Attitude Measurement*, New York: Wiley.

Friedrich, C. (1964) 'Authority', In Gould, J. and Kolb, W. (Eds.) *A Dictionary of the Social Sciences*, London: Tavistock.

FEU (1983) *Flexible Learning Opportunities*, London: Department of Education and Science.

FEU (1985) *Changing the Focus: Women and FE*, London: Department of Education and Science.

Gagné, R. (1977) *The Conditions of Learning*, (3rd Edition), New York: Holt, Rinehart and Winston.

Galloway, C. (1976) *Psychology for Learning and Teaching*, New York: McGraw-Hill.

Garber, J. and Seligman, M. (1980) (Eds.) *Human Helplessness*, New York: Academic Press.

Ginzberg, E., Ginsberg, S., Axelrad, S. and Herma, J. (1951) *Occupational Choice*, New York: Columbia University Press.

Ginzberg, E. (1971) *Career Guidance*, New York: McGraw-Hill.

Ginzberg, E. (1979) *Good Jobs, Bad Jobs, No Jobs*, Cambridge Massachusetts: Harvard University Press.

Ginzberg, M., Meyenn, R. and Miller, H. (1979) 'Teachers, the "Great Debate" and Education Cuts', *Westminster Studies in Education*, Vol. 2.

Glasser, W. (1969) *Schools without Failure*, New York: Harper and Row.

Glassey, W. and Weeks, E. (1950) *The Educational Development of Children*, London: University of London Press.

Hamblin, D. (1974) *The Teacher and Counselling*, Oxford: Blackwell.

Hamblin, D. (1978) *The Teacher and Pastoral Care*, Oxford: Blackwell.

Hamblin, D. (1981) (Ed.) *Problems and Practice of Pastoral Care*, Oxford: Blackwell.

Hamblin, D. (1981) *Teaching Study Skills*, Oxford: Blackwell.

Hamblin, D. (1983) *Guidance: 16–19*, Oxford: Blackwell.

Hamblin, D. (1984) *Pastoral Care: A Training Manual*, Oxford: Blackwell.

Hamblin, D. (1968) An Investigation into the Ideal and Actual Selves of Boys in Secondary Modern, Grammar and Comprehensive Schools, Unpublished, M.Sc. Research Report, Department of Social Psychology, LSE, University of London.

Hamblin, D. (1983) 'Life Skills in an Age of Growing Structural Unemployment', In Galton, M. and Moon, B. (Eds.) *Changing Schools: Changing Curriculum*, London: Harper and Row.

Handy, C. (1984) *The Future of Work*, Oxford: Blackwell.

Harding, J. (1983) *Switched Off: The Science Education of Girls*, London: Longman.

Hargreaves, A. (1979) 'Strategies, Decisions and Control: Interaction in a Middle School Classroom,' In Eggleston, J. (Ed.) *Teacher Decision-making in the Classroom*, London: Routledge and Kegan Paul.

Hargreaves, D. (1967) *Social Relations in a Secondary School*, London: Routledge and Kegan Paul.

Hargreaves, D., Hester, S. and Mellor, F. (1975) *Deviance in Classrooms*, London: Routledge and Kegan Paul.

Heathcote, G., Kempa, R. and Roberts, I. (1982) *Curriculum Styles and Strategies*, London: FEU, Department of Education and Science.

Herr, E. (1974) (Ed.) *Vocational Guidance and Human Development*, Boston: Houghton Mifflin.

Himmelweit, H. and Swift, B. (1969) 'A Model for the Understanding of the School as a Socialising Agency', In Mussen, P., Langer, J. and Covington, M. (Ed.) *Trends and Issues in Developmental Psychology*, New York: Holt, Rinehart and Winston.

Hopson, B. and Hayes, J. (1971) *Careers Guidance*, London: Heinemann.

Hopson, B. and Hopson, C. (1973) *Exercises in Career Development*, Cambridge: CRAC.

Hopson, B. and Scally, M. (1979) *Lifeskills Teaching Programmes, No. 1*, Leeds: Life Skills Associates.

Huxley, A. (1974) *The Devils of Loudon*, Harmondsworth: Penguin.

Jahoda, M. (1958) *Current Concepts of Positive Mental Health: A Report; Joint Commission on Mental Illness and Health: Monograph Series No. 1*, New York: Basic Books.

Jamieson, I. (1981) 'Some Preliminary Results from the Questionnaire on Pupil Attitudes Towards Industry and the Trade Unions', *Schools Council Industry Project Newsletter, No. 6.*

Jamieson, I. (1983) 'Miracles or Mirages? Some Elements of Pupil Work Experience', *British Journal of Guidance and Counselling*, Vol. II, No. 2, pp. 145–59.

Jenkins, R. (1983) 'Goals, Constraints and Occupational Choice: the First Twelve Months in the Belfast Labour Market, *British Journal of Guidance and Counselling*, Vol. 11, No. 2, pp. 184–96.

Jersild, A. (1969) *The Psychology of Adolescence*, (2nd Edition), New York: MacMillan.

Johnson, O. and Bommarito, J. (1971) *Tests and Measurements in Child Development*, Handbook, San Francisco: Jossey-Bass.

Johnson, R. (1984) *Occupational Training Families*, London: FEU, Department of Education and Science.

Josephs, A. and Smithers, P. (1975) 'Personality Characteristics of Syllabus-bound and Syllabus-free Sixth Formers', *British Journal of Educational Psychology*, Vol. 45, pp. 29–38.

Kandel, D. and Lesser, G. (1972) *Youth in Two Worlds*, San Francisco: Jossey-Bass.

Katz, D. and Kahn, R. (1966) *The Social Psychology of Organisations*, New York: Wiley.

Kelly, G. (1955) *The Psychology of Personal Constructs, Vols. 1 and 2*, New York: Norton.

Klein, D. (1960) 'Some Concepts Concerning the Mental Health of the Individual', *Journal of Consulting Psychology*, 24, pp. 288–93.

Kline, P. and Cooper, C. (1985) 'Rigid Personality and Rigid Thinking', *British Journal of Educational Psychology*, Vol. 55, 1, pp. 24–27.

Kohlberg, L. (1969) 'Stage and Sequence: The Cognitive–Developmental Approach to Socialisation', In Goslin, D. (Ed.) *Handbook of Socialization Theory and Research*, Chicago: Rand McNally.

Kohlberg, J. (1976) 'Moral Stages and Moralization: The Cognitive–Developmental Approach', In Lickona, T. (Ed.) *Moral Development and Behaviour*, New York: Holt, Rinehart and Winston.

Krathwohl, D., Bloom, B. and Masia, B. (1964) *Taxonomy of Educational Objectives, Handbook II: The Affective Domain*, New York: McKay.

Krumboltz, J. and Thoresen, C. (1969) *Behavioral Counseling*, New York: Holt, Rinehart and Winston.

Kubie, L. (1958) *Neurotic Distortion of the Creative Process*, Lawrence, Kansas: University of Kansas Press.

Large, P. (1980) *The Micro Revolution*, London: Fontana.
Laycock, S. and Munro, B. (1972) *Educational Psychology*, London: Pitman.
Lazarus, R. (1966) *Psychological Stress and the Coping Process*, New York: McGraw-Hill.
Likert, R. (1961) *New Patterns of Management* New York: McGraw-Hill.
Lindley, L. (1976) *An Investigation of the Perceptions of the Links Between Home and School held by Teachers, Parents and Pupils in a Comprehensive School*, Unpublished DSC Dissertation, University College of Swansea.
Lipset, S. (1960) *Political Man*, New York: Doubleday.
Livesley, W. and Bromley, D. (1973) *Personal Perception in Childhood and Adolescence*, London: Wiley.
Lorac, C. and Weiss, M. (1981) *Communication and Social Skills*, Exeter: Wheaton.

Marland, M. (1980) 'The Pastoral Curriculum' In Best, R., Jarvis, C. and Ribbins, P. (Eds.) *Perspectives on Pastoral Care*, London: Heinemann.
Marland, M. (1983) (Ed.) *Sex Differentiation and Schooling*, London: Heinemann.
Marton, F., Hounsell, D. and Entwistle, N. (1984) (Eds.) *The Experience of Learning*, Edinburgh: Scottish Academic Press.
MacIver, R. (1950) *The Ramparts We Guard*, New York: MacMillan.
McLeish, J., Matheson, W. and Park, J. (1973) *The Psychology of the Learning Group*, London: Hutchison.
McPhail, P. (1982) *Social and Moral Education*, Oxford: Blackwell.
McQuail, D. (1975) *Communication*, London: Longman.
Measor, L. and Woods, P (1984) *Changing Schools*, Milton Keynes: Open University Press.
Ments, van M. (1983) *The Effective Use of Role Play*, London: Kogan Page.
Milgram, S. (1974) *Obedience to Authority*, London: Tavistock.
Miller, N. (1952) 'Comments on Theoretical Models Illustrated by the Development of a Theory of Conflict Behavior', *Journal of Personality*, 20, pp. 82–100.
Miller, N. (1964) 'Some Implications of Modern Behavior Theory for Personality Change and Development', In Worchel, P. and Byrene, D. (Eds.) *Personality Change*, New York: Wiley.
Morrison, A. and McIntyre, D. (1969) *Teachers and Teaching*, Harmondsworth: Penguin.
Morton-Williams, R. and Finch, S. (1968) *Enquiry 1, Schools Council*, London: HMSO.
Mueller, R. (1974) *Principles of Classroom Learning and Perception*, London: Allen and Unwin.
Musgrove, F. (1971) *Patterns of Power and Authority in English Education*, London: Methuen.

Musgrove, F. (1974) *Ecstasy and Holiness*, London: Methuen.

Natale, S. (1972) *An Experiment in Empathy*, Slough: NFER.
Nelson-Jones, R. (1982) *The Theory and Practice of Counselling Psychology*, London: Holt, Rinehart and Winston.
Nelson-Jones, R. (1983) *Practical Counselling Skills*, London: Holt, Rinehart and Winston.
Nuttall, D. and Goldstein, H. (1984) 'Profiles and Graded Tests: the Technical Issues', In *Profiles in Action*, FEU, Department of Education and Science.

Oliver, R. and Butcher, H. (1968) 'Teachers' Attitudes to Education', *British Journal of Educational Psychology*, Vol. 38, pp. 38–44.

Pidgeon, D. (1970) *Expectations and Pupil Performance*, Slough: NFER.
Parsons, T. and Bales, R. (1956) *Family: Socialisation and Interaction Process*, London: Routledge and Kegan Paul.
Phares, E. (1976) *Locus of Control in Personality*, Morristown, New Jersey: General Learning Press.
Phillips, B. (1978) *School Stress and Anxiety*, New York: Human Sciences Press.
Pool, I. and Schramm, W. (1973) (Eds.) *Handbook of Communication*, Chicago: Rand McNally.
Postman, N. and Weingartner, C. (1971) *Teaching as a Subversive Activity*, Harmondsworth: Penguin.

Raths, L. *et al* (1966) *Teaching for Thinking*, Columbus, Ohio: Merrill.
Raths, L. *et al* (1967) *Values and Teaching*, Columbus, Ohio: Merrill.
Reid, M., Barnett, B. and Rosenberg, H. (1974) *A Matter of Choice*, Slough: NFER.
Reynolds, D. (1976) 'The Delinquent School', In Hammersley, M. *et al The Process of Schooling*, London: Routledge and Kegan Paul.
Reynolds, D., Jones, D., St. Leger, S. and Murgatroyd, S. (1980) 'School Factors and Truancy', In Hersov, L. and Berg, I. (Eds.) *Out of School*, Chichester: Wiley.
Richardson, S., Goodman, N., Hastorf, A. and Dornbusch, S. (1961) 'Cultural Uniformity in Reaction to Physical Disabilities', *American Sociological Review*, 26, pp. 241–47.
Riesman, D. (1951) *The Lonely Crowd*, New Haven: Yale University Press.
Roberts, K. (1984) *School Leavers and Their Prospects*, Milton Keynes: Open University.
Rosenthal, R. and Jacobson, L. (1968) *Pygmalion in the Classroom*, New York: Holt, Rinehart and Winston.
Rosser, C. and Harris, C. (1965) *The Family and Social Change*, London: Routledge and Kegan Paul.
Rotter, J., Chance, J. and Phares, E. (1972) *Applications of a Social Learning Theory of Personality*, New York: Holt, Rinehart and Winston.

Rubenowitz, S. (1963) *Emotional Flexibility as a Comprehensive Dimension of Mind*, Stockholm: Almquist and Wiksell.

Rutter, M., Graham, P., Chadwick, O. and Yule, W. (1976) 'Adolescent Turmoil, Fact or Fiction', *Journal of Child Psychology and Psychiatry*, Vol. 17, pp. 35–56.

Rutter, M., Maughan, B., Mortimore, P. and Ouston, J. (1979) *Fifteen Thousand Hours*, London: Open Books.

Schools Council Careers Education and Guidance Project, (1978) *Work One, Work Two and Work Three*, London: Longman.

Scriven, M. (1967) *The Methodology of Evaluation: AERA Monograph Series on Curriculum Evaluation, No. 1*, Chicago: Rand McNally.

Shaw, M. (1971) *Group Dynamics*, New York: McGraw-Hill.

Sherif, M. (1966) *Group Conflict and Co-operation*, London: Routledge and Kegan Paul.

Social Europe (1985) *Supplement on Education, Vocational Training and Youth Policy*, Luxembourg: Directorate General for Employment, Social Affairs and Education.

Spielberger, C. and Sarason, S. (Eds.) (1976) *Stress and Anxiety*, Washington: Hemisphere.

Stanton, G. (1984) 'A Profile of Personal Qualities, In *Profiles in Action*, FEU, Department of Education and Science.

Starishevsky, R. and Matlin, N. (1968) 'A Model for the Translation of Self Concepts into Vocational Terms', In Hopson, B. and Hayes, J. *The Theory and Practice of Vocational Guidance*, Oxford: Pergamon.

Stonier, T. (1983) *The Wealth of Information*, London: Methuen.

Super, D. (1953) 'A Theory of Vocational Development', *American Psychologist, 8*, pp. 185–90.

Super, D. (1957) *The Psychology of Careers*, New York: Harper.

Thomas, J. (1974) (Ed.) *Behavior Modification Procedure: A Sourcebook*, Chicago: Aldine.

Toffler, A. (1980) *The Third Wave*, London: Pan.

Traxler, A. and North, R. (1966) *Techniques of Guidance*, (3rd Edition), New York: Harper and Row.

Truax, C. and Carkhuff, R. (1967) *Toward Effective Counseling and Psychotherapy*, Boston: Houghton Mifflin.

Turner, R. (1961) 'Modes of Social Ascent Through Education: Sponsored and Contest Mobility', In Halsey, A., Floud, J. and Anderson, C. *Education, Economy and Society*, Glencoe, Illinois: Free Press.

Turner, R. (1964) *The Social Context of Ambition*, San Francisco: Chandler.

Tyler, L. (1969) *The Work of the Counselor*, New York: Appleton, Century, Crofts.

Vorrath, H. and Brendtro, L. (1974) *Positive Peer Culture*, Chicago: Aldine.

Watkins, C. (1981) 'Adolescents and Activities', In Hamblin, D. (Ed.) *Problems and Practice of Pastoral Care*, Oxford: Blackwell.

Watts, A. (1980) *Work Experience Programmes. The Views of British Youth*, Paris: Organisation for Economic Co-operation and Development.

Watts, A. (1983) *Education, Unemployment and the Future of Work*, Milton Keynes: Open University Press.

Watson, D. and Tharp, R. (1972) *Self-Directed Behaviour: Self-Modification for Personal Adjustment*, Monterey, California: Brooks-Cole.

Weber, M. (1947) *Theory of Social and Economic Organisation*, (Trans. Henderson, A. and Parsons, T.), New York: Oxford University Press.

Weiner, B. *et al* (1971) 'Perceiving the Causes of Success and Failure', In Jones, E. *et al Attribution: Perceiving the causes of Behavior*, Morristown, New Jersey: General Learning Press.

Weiner, B. (1972) *Theories of Motivation*, Chicago: Markham Publishing Company.

Welford, A. (1968) *Fundamentals of Skill*, London: Methuen.

Williams, K. (1973) *The School Counsellor*, London: Methuen.

Willis, P. (1977) *Learning to Labour*, Farnborough: Saxon House.

Wills, D. (1971) *Spare the Child*, Harmondsworth: Penguin.

Wilson, A. (1967) 'Educational Consequences of Segregation in a Californian Community', In U.S. Commission on Civil Rights, *Racial Isolation in the Public Schools*, Washington: United States Government Printing Office.

Wilson, B. (1962) 'The Teacher's Role – a Sociological Analysis', *British Journal of Sociology*, Vol. 13, No. 1, pp. 15–32.

Withers, M. (1976) *An Experimental Study in the Development of Peer Counselling Skills*, Unpublished DSC Dissertation, University College of Swansea.

Young, T. (1972) *New Sources of Self*, New York: Pergamon.

Index

Accountability 9–10
Achievement motivation 44–46
Activity:
    nature and purpose 116–118
    pupil and task related 21–22
Adams, J. 7–8
Adaptation to physical environment 21
Adorno, T. 55
Allport, G. 22
Anomy 5,98
Anxiety 29, 92
Armstrong, D. 62
Aston, P. and Dobson, G. 145
Atkinson, J. and Feather, N. 43, 44
Attitude:
    reversal 6
    to learning 92
Ausubel, D. 34, 35, 36
Authority:
    of expert 58–59
    relation to power 51

Babington-Smith, B. and Farrell, B. 54
Backward-looking guidance 65
Baron, R. 114
Berkowitz, L. 114
Berger, B. 47
Blame-pinning 55–56
Blocher, D. 106
Bloom, B. 22, 33
Bolam, R. and Medlock, P. 14, 25, 31
Brophy, J. and Good, T. 44
Bruner, J. 33, 34
Buros, O. 98

Careers education 65, 67
Carkhuff, R. and Anthony, W. 108
Carter, M. 74
Cartwright, D. and Zander, A. 115
Chance: pupils' beliefs in 45–47
Clydebank Project 86, 97–98
Coleman, J. 104
Collins, B. and Raven, B. 8
Comparability assessment 98
Comparisons 52
Competition 52
Conflict 71
Content clarification 17
Counselling:
    and formative assessment 88-89
    gender-based reactions 111
    peer 103, 104–115

CPVE 31, 63, 75, 78–79, 102, 115
Criterion-referenced assessment 97
Cronbach, L. 96
Curle, A. 2

Dalton Plan 37
De Charms, R. 28
Decision-making; retarded or impaired 36
Denscombe, M. 12
Deutsch, M. 114
Development of pastoral programme 24–25
Dewey, J. 34
Disjunctions 30
Dionysian Man 47
Dweck, C. 4

Edwards, J. 142
Edwards, J. and Morris, H. 79
Erikson, E. 143
Evaluation:
    of activities 25–27
    self 31
Evans, N. 105

Family interaction 79–80
Feelings:
    importance 28–30
    tutors 227–228
FEU 48, 80, 96, 105
Fifth-year activities: 210–224
    relevant considerations 210–211
    self-help groups 221–223
    understanding learning anxieties and
        revision 214–217
    understanding learning style 211–214
    understanding social interaction 217–221
    vocational development 221–223
First-year activities: 116–141
    induction phase 120
    learning about learning 130–137
    personal and social development 137–141
    problem-solving 137–140
Fishbein, M. 92
Formative assessment 86–96
Fourth-year activities: 186–209
    aspects of developmental guidance
        186–187
    key facets of self 186
    self-management and learning 187–193
    social and personal development 193–201
    vocational development 201–209
Friedrich, C. 58

Gagne, R. 36
Galloway, C. 36
Galton, M. and Moon, B. 79
Garber, J. and Seligman, M. 44
Gender:
  attitudes and beliefs based on 42
  stereotypes and equality of
    opportunity 47–51
Gestalt 2
Ginzberg, E. 62, 64, 66
Ginzberg, M. 228
Glandon, N. 39
Glasser, W. 93
Glassey, W. and Weeks, E. 96
Group counselling: 84
  and formative assessment 92–95
Group dynamics, discussion of 53–54

Handy, C. 59, 62, 63, 64
Harding, J. 49
Hargreaves, A. 60
Hargreaves, D. 6, 7, 39
Hayes, J. and Hopson, B. 68
Heathcote, G. 31, 89, 105
Herr, E. 68
Himmelweit, H. and Swift, B. 1
Hopson, B. and Scally, M. 73
Huxley, A. 47

Identity: 27
  belonging 2–3
  crisis 143
  self-awareness 3–4, 72–74
IFAPLAN 87, 97
Impact of school on individual 6–7
Individuality, threats to 53
Internal or external control 4

Jahoda, M. 22
Jamieson, I. 83
Jenkins, R. 74–76
Jersild, A. 146
Job satisfaction 1
Johnson, O. and Bommarito, J. 98
Johnson, R. 87
Joking 145–146
Josephs, A. and Smithers, P. 94

Kandel, D. and Lesser, G. 104
Katz, D. and Kahn, R. 16
Kelly, G. 2, 19, 41, 44, 61, 68
Klein, D. 22
Kline, P. and Cooper, C. 51
Kohlberg, J. 58, 59
Kramer, J. 48, 79
Krathwohl, D. 22
Krumboltz, J. and Thoresen, C. 87
Kubie, L. 28

Large, P. 3
Laycock, S. and Munro, B. 36
Lazarus, R. 92
Learning, experiential 21–22, 32–34

Legitimacy of pastoral care 8–11
Likert, R. 85
Lindley, L. 104
Lipset, S. 8
Livesley, W. and Bromley, D. 146
Lorac, C. and Weiss, M. 78

MacIver, R. 5
Mansell, J. 105
Marland, M. 11, 19, 42, 48
Marton, F. 41
McLeish, J. 54
McPhail, P. 23
Measor, L. and Woods, P. 6, 45
Membership of school 6
Ments, van M. 37, 39, 40
Methods 14–19, 31–40
Milgram, S. 53, 59
Miller, N. 71
Modules 40–41
Morrison, A. and McIntyre, D. 6
Morton-Williams, R. and Finch, S. 5
Mueller, R. 36
Musgrove, F. 47, 58

Natale, S. 36,
Negotiation: 11–13, 37, 68
  of relationships 59–60
Nelson-Jones, R. 87
Norm-referenced assessment 97–98
Nuttall, D. and Goldstein, H. 96, 97, 98

Obesity 146
Objectives:
  debate of 76
  work experience of 83
O'Connor 43
Oliver, R. and Butcher, H. 6
Organisations, federal or dispersed 64

Parents 12–13
Parsons, T. and Bales, R. 79
Pastoral programme content 40–41
Peer groups 101–104
Perceptions of women's work roles 50–51
Phares, E. 44
Phillips, D. 133
Pidgeon, D. 44
Postman, N. and Weingarten, C. 57
Predictions 146
Preliminary evaluative year 15–17
Problem-solving skills 34–37
Profiles 95–99
Pupils:
  contributions to pastoral programme
    13–18
  in helping roles 36
  involvement of 12–13

Raths, L. 34
Reid, M. 104, 166
Responsibility of individual 61–62
Rewards 11

Reynolds, D. 60
Richardson, S. 146
Riesman, D. 66
Roberts, K. 62, 63, 64, 95
Role:
    conflict of teacher 56–57
    of teacher 5
    -play 37–40
Rosenthal, R. and Jacobson, L. 44
Rosser, C. and Harris, C. 79
Rotter, J. 44
Rubenowitz, S. 46
Rutter, M. 1, 102

Schools Council Careers Education and
    Guidance Project 72
Second year: 142–165
    activities 147–165
    decision-making 154–160
    dissociation from school 142
    impact of family on learning 143–146
    irritability 143
    learning 144, 146
    learning about learning 160–165
    personal and social development 147–160
    trust within tutor group 143

Self:
    as a learner 41–47
    -management in a social context 51–54
    -observation 89–90
Shaw, M. 115
Sherif, M. 115
Sixth form, outline programme 224–225
Skills: 19–24
    of constructive coping 18–19
    ownership, training for 87
Social Europe 48, 82
Social roles, adjustment in 66–67
Spielberger, C. and Sarason, S. 92
Staff development 109–110, 114
Stanton, G. 98
Stanworth, M. 42
Starishevsky, R. and Matlin, N. 72
Stereotypes, occupational 77
Stonier, T. 3
Summative assessment 96
Super, D. 62

Times Educational Supplement 50

Third year: 166–185
    activities 168–185
    background factors 166–167
    decision-making 174–181
    learning and subject choice 168–174
    social skills and stress 181–185
    truancy and absence 180–181
Thomas, J. 87
Threat 92
Time 21
Toffler, A. 3
Transfer of training 100
Traxler, A. and North, B. 96
Truax, C. and Carkhuff, R. 108
Trust 114–115
Turner, R. 75, 76
TVEI: 31, 60, 63, 80, 115
    Insight One, Insight Two 31, 106
Tyler, L. 62

Unemployment 62, 78–80

Values 2, 22–23, 65, 76
Vocational development: 65–78
    activities 72–74
    key areas 68–69
    pessimism of disadvantaged 74–75
    retarded and impaired 69–71
Vocational topics:
    coverage 77
    questions about 78
Vorrath, H. and Brendtro, L. 93

Walkins, C. 38
Watson, D. and Tharp, R. 89
Watts, A. 2, 62, 63, 82, 83
Weber, M. 8
Weiner, B. 44
Welford, A. 19
Williams, K. 106
Willis, P. 74
Wills, D. 109
Wilson, A. 75
Wilson, B. 56
Withers, M. 106
Work:
    experience 82–86
    adjustment 80–81
Young, T. 3
YTS 69, 75